Alfreda,

The Lord will fulfill His purpose for me; your love, O Lord, endures forever
Psalm 138:8

Rose Linda Castellano
12-07

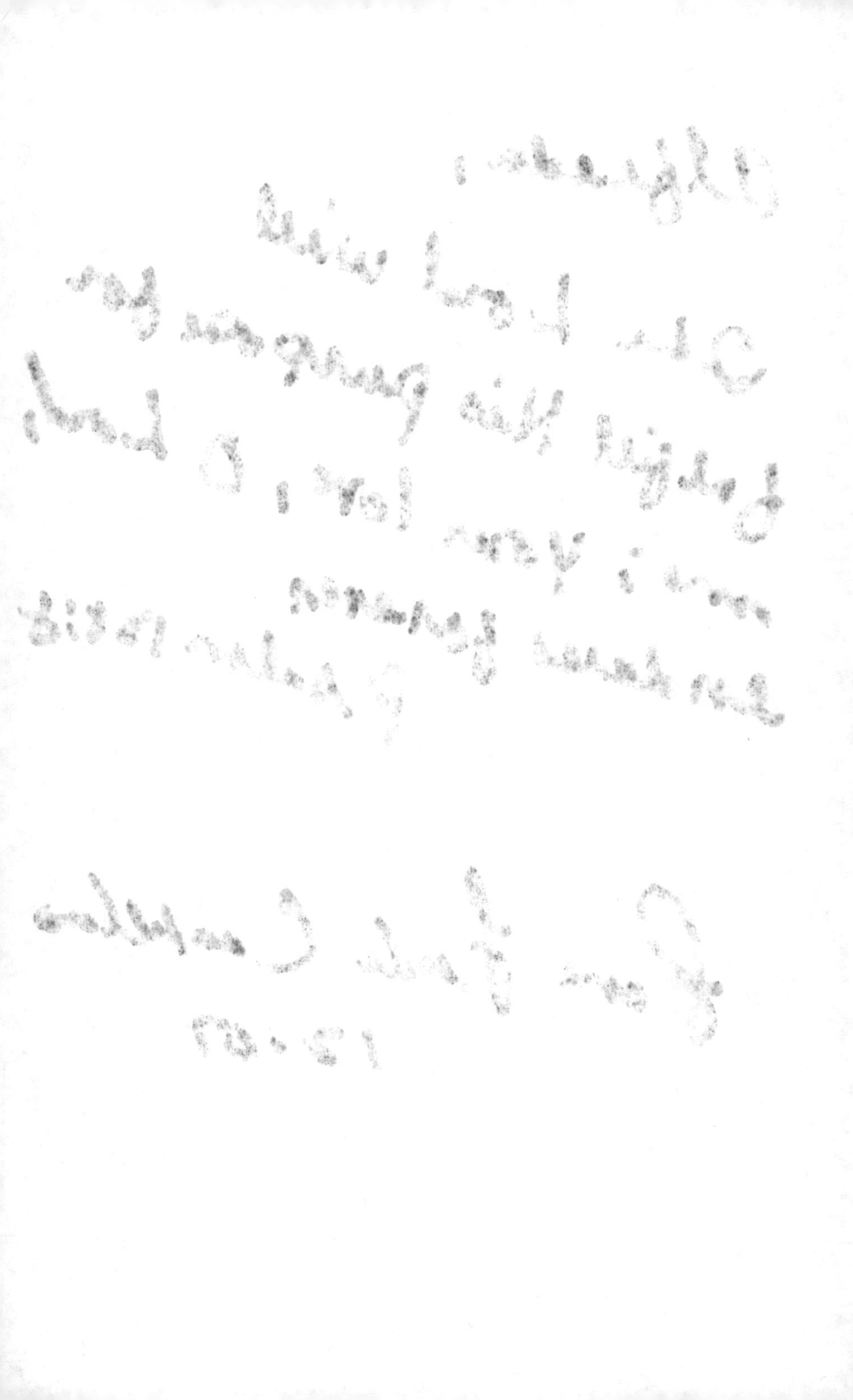

Jesus & Me

Linda L. Castellano

ISBN 0-7414-4280-9

Cover design by David Castellano

Book edited & proofed by David Castellano, Ta-Tanisha Hall, and Maryse Theodule

Published by:

1094 New DeHaven Street, Suite 100
West Conshohocken, PA 19428-2713
Info@buybooksontheweb.com
www.buybooksontheweb.com
Toll-free (877) BUY BOOK
Local Phone (610) 941-9999
Fax (610) 941-9959

Printed in the United States of America

Printed on Recycled Paper

Published November 2007

Copyright Permissions

This book is dedicated to my loving *savior*,
Jesus Christ.

Acknowledgements

With special thanks:

To my husband, David who I believe God created just for me. Thanks for being my constant support and rock. Thank you for understanding the importance of this project and being ever so patient throughout this experience. Thank you for single handedly taking care of the family, preparing meals and cleaning the house, while I was occupied working on this project. Thank you for every meal and beverage you brought to me while I worked at the computer. Thank you for allowing and encouraging me to tell our stories in the truth and love of them. Thank you for editing the book and every moment you spent aiding, comforting and encouraging me through this journey. I love you more than words can express. Your love for me makes me glow. Never stop loving me the way you do.

To my children, Joey, David and Kaylin, who were such good and patient children while I was busy writing this book.

To my mother, Frankie Wilson, who raised me to be the woman I am today. Mom, I thank you for your constant support, protection, imparted wisdom, guidance, patience, perseverance, friendship and belief in me. Thank you for sharing the truth of your heart even when it hurt. Thank you for bringing me back, when I sometimes have gotten lost in the process. I hope that I make you proud even in the nakedness of this book. Mama, know that it is all for HIS glory. I love you so much.

To my only sister, Yvonne Wilson, for encouraging me to keep up the God work. Thank you for your ability to share the truth of your thoughts and heart, no matter what. I love you.

To my aunt, Juanita Douglas, thank you for being so exceptionally encouraging and complimentary.

To my cousin, Ta-Tanisha Hall, (affectionately known as Ta-Ta) thank you for editing the book, for being my confidante and biggest cheerleader. I love you with a sisterly love.

To Joseph Washington, thank you for blessing me with my first-born son and for loving me enough to ultimately let me go.

To my girl friends: Oleatha Alexander, Patricia Bunkley, Tia Burgess, Susan Hampton, Tiffany Harston, Valerie Hill, Etrenda Jones, Janet Mattocks, Karen Miller, Tamekie Moore, Nikki Murray, and Maryse Theodule. Thanks to each of you for being the best friends a girl could have and allowing God to use you to be a blessing to me. Each of you has blessed me in your own unique way, that only you could have provided and that is why God placed you so perfectly in my life. Through your encouragement, understanding, prayer, listening, reasoning, supporting, believing, arguing, repeating, correcting and loving me through this process, I thank you. Each of you is irreplaceable. Know that your expressed words and ongoing belief in God's need to write this book through me helped me gather the strength to complete this project. Know that I love each of you and you all have been a value added to my life.

Thanks to every person that I met in my lifetime and especially to those I met during this specific journey and the creation of this book. Thank you for encouraging me in anyway to complete this assignment. Thank you for your expressed excitement about the release of this book.

If this book blesses you, please share your thoughts with me at Linda@Jesus-and-me.com

Contents

Preface

I have been mandated by God and encouraged by many to compile my life experiences. Some of these stories include very personal details of my life. They are factual stories that reflect my walk with God. Some stories are funny, some are serious, some are detailed and lengthy, and some are short and sweet, but all are special, and each carry a specific message relative to my journey. My hope is to impart the wisdom that I have learned through these experiences to help enlighten you on your journey.

My stories are similar to the stories, examples, and miracles of the bible. They are my true-life stories that express God's care for me. These stories demonstrate some practical application of God's Word and the consequential repercussions that follow when I did not adhere to His instructions. For your convenience, I have also included the supporting applicable scriptures. The only real difference between the stories in the bible and mine are the times in which they were written. My events occurred in the twenty-first century. This mere fact alone may help you better relate to the timelessness of God's Word and that He is the same yesterday, today, and forever more. **(See Hebrews 13:8).** My purpose will be served if even one of these shared experiences enable you to trust and depend only on Jesus.

> **And they have defeated him by the blood of the Lamb and by their testimony. And they did not love their lives so much that they were afraid to die. Revelation 12:11 (NLT)**

1. Read and Apply

The bible is God's written expressed will for mankind. The words in the bible are infallible truths.

> **Every word of God proves true. He is a shield to all who come to Him for protection. Proverbs 30:5(NLT)**
>
> **God forbid: yea, *let God be true, but every man a liar*; as it is written, that thou mightest be justified in thy sayings, and mightest overcome when thou art judged. Romans 3:4(KJV)**
>
> **For they bring life to those who find them, and healing to their whole body. Proverbs 4:22(NLT)**
>
> **These things happened to them as examples for us. They were written down to warn us who live at the end of the age. I Corinthians 10:11(NLT)**
>
> **All Scripture is inspired by God and is useful to teach us what is true and to make us realize what is wrong in our lives. It corrects us when we are wrong and teaches us to do what is right. II Timothy 3:16(NLT)**

The word of God (The Bible) is the guide for human life. It is the truth and everything outside of it is a lie. If you are not sold on this fact, this book may not be suitable for you.

Since it is the guide for human life, it is also the only source that I site. It is this foundation that I substantiate, prove, and support all my views. This book is about my experiences based on these truths. It is about biblical principles I have learned, the choices I have made, consequences I have suffered, and victories I have won. It is not about embellishing or changing the parts that make me appear bad, deceitful, or stupid. As you read, you will find that I have been, at one time or another, all of the above.

Truth or Mask

Telling the absolute truth can be challenging to most people. That is why people lie, stretch the truth, and embellish. This is all done in an effort to save face and to create the desired image of how they want to be perceived by the world. Telling the truth would reveal how incredibly selfish and sometimes ugly their motives, intentions, and actions really are. It would expose who they really are and eradicate the established image they tirelessly have worked to create.

People create masks to cover up their sins, bad choices, and embarrassing moments all because of how they want to be perceived. People, including church folks, are guilty of this. This cover up does not help edify the body of Christ. The body of Christ is composed of Christians (Christ Followers). The Christian body is a family. The blood of Christ unifies us. We should support, share, help, love, confess, forgive, and correct one another in love.

> **Just as each of us has one body with many members, and these members do not all have the same function, so in Christ we who are many form one body, and each member belongs to all the others. Romans12: 4-5(NIV)**

If everyone is wearing perfected masks and hiding behind a false image of perfection, then they are ineffective at building up the body of Christ. These masks actually have a repelling quality for most unbelievers. I have heard unbelievers say, "I'll come to church after I get myself together." or, "I don't know if I can stay saved because of this or that." This is said in response to how some Christians are perceived. Many unbelievers feel as if they cannot give their life to Christ until they somehow perfect themselves. THIS IS A LIE!!! This is a deceptive tactic of the enemy. It is an effective tool used by the devil to keep unbelievers from giving their lives to Christ. It is Christ who cleanses the sinner.

Those responses are directly related to how the patrons of the church are perceived. The perception is either, that church folks or Christians have made all the right choices and decisions since they met Jesus, or they are fakes. The truth is this: Christians fall down and get up daily. How can we help one another if we are all pretending to be perfected? Christian's testimonies are priceless. They are encouraging and absolutely necessary components for building up the body of Christ. They give people hope and a point of reference. I'm not suggesting that you start airing your dirty laundry, but if opportunity presents itself, tell the truth of your experience through your testimony in order to build up and edify the body of Christ.

> **The faithful love of the Lord never ends! His mercies never cease. Great is His faithfulness; His mercies begin afresh each morning. Lamentations 3:22-23(NLT)**

> **Let us then approach the throne of grace with confidence, so that we may receive mercy and find grace to help us in our time of need. Hebrews 4:16(NIV)**

The beauty is in the getting up, and maybe even helping someone else not to fall. This is accomplished through your testimony. **James 5:16** says, **"Confess your sins to each other and pray for each other so that you may be healed."(NLT)** The truth of a shared, personal experience has the potential to encourage, guide, and protect others. The truth is liberating and continuing in truth can set people free.

> **Jesus said to the people who believed in him, "You are truly my disciples if you remain faithful to my teachings. And you will know the truth, and the truth will set you free. John 8:31-32 (NLT)**

Satan is a liar! **John 8:44** reads, **"For you are the children of your father the devil, and you love to do the evil things he does. He was a murderer from the beginning. He has always hated the truth, because there is no truth in him. *When he lies, it is consistent with his character; for he is a liar and the father of lies*."(NLT)** Satan strongly encourages everyone to lie and feels justified in doing so. It is easy for Satan to get people to lie because no one wants to share their dirty laundry anyway. Lies are heavy and they are hard to keep up with. Once our enemy gets us to lie, cover up, or sin, he uses the same lies and sin to hold us captive. After awhile, telling the truth seems nearly impossible, but God's Word tells us that everything done in the dark will come to the light and God will judge.

> **So don't make judgments about anyone ahead of time before the Lord returns. For he will bring our darkest secrets to light and will reveal our private motives. Then God will give to each one whatever praise is due. I Corinthians 4:5 (NLT)**

When someone lies, they do it to save face to preserve their image. Self-preservation used in this way is a basic human response, but it is not a characteristic of Christ and simply has no place in the body of Christ. Let's give that some thought. Self-preservation, in and of itself, is based on selfishness. As it states in **Matthew 16:25, "For whosoever will save His life shall lose it: and whosoever will lose His life for my sake shall find it."(KJV)** Self-preservation only has the potential to preserve one. However, the truth has the power to set others free as well. Being transformed into the image of Christ is a daily process. Even Christians, who are in committed relationships with God, still make bad choices. Christians are not perfect, yet they are striving for perfection. I strongly believe that Christians should be more transparent and truthful in sharing their experiences, whether good or bad, ups or downs. In doing this, they would expose the tricks and maneuvers of our enemy, and help to equip other Christians for spiritual warfare. Doing this would make every Christian more useful for the kingdom and help others avoid the same pitfalls.

The Word Requires Your Participation

I have learned that when I do what the bible instructs me to do, I have what the bible says I will have. God is not challenged by His words, His people are. The challenge is that the Word requires your participation. Typically, something specific has to be done to receive the desired result, and the result is contingent on your action. Let's use baking a cake as an example. I am not a good cook, but I can follow instructions. Typically, if I follow the instructions or directions I will have the desired result.

When Isaiah is speaking to God, he said,

You will guard him and keep him in perfect and constant peace whose mind [both its inclination and its character] is stayed on You, because he commits himself to You, leans on You, and hopes confidently in You. Isaiah 26:3(AMP)

Now, lets think about that for a minute and decipher this scripture. The scripture begins with an instruction. It is telling you to do something. It implies that in order to receive the desired results, you have to do something. The something that must be done is to keep your mind on Him. That is what's required of you. Keeping our mind focused on

Jesus is work and it may sound easy, but really, it takes concentrated effort.

How is this done? Nobody has taught me how to do this. I was not raised to keep my mind on Jesus. It is not taught in school and not even in many churches. It is not a natural action. What we are taught and raised to do is worry, compete, and compare our selves to others. We are not raised to keep our eyes on Jesus. We are raised to keep our eyes on the people across the street, circumstances, and situations.

The whole idea of keeping our eyes on Jesus is totally against our human nature. It takes conscious effort. You will not keep your mind on Jesus by accident. It only happens with purposed, determined, and concentrated effort. The key here is learning to trust God. The reason He instructs us to keep our mind on Him is to build our confidence in His ability, and not our own. Our essential action is to keep our minds on Him. Only after this is accomplished will it create the desired result: of peace.

Word System/World System

There are only two systems: The Word System and the World System. There are many reasons why people don't apply the Word System.

1. The word system is derived from the Word of God, the bible. Some people do not read their bibles; therefore, they do not know the Word. If they are Christians and they do not attend a bible based church to learn the Word, or have personal study time, getting to know the Word is pretty hard to do. It is like learning algebra without a book or a class. It is not likely to happen and therefore, they do not have access to the powerful information and knowledge that is in the Word. One cannot do what one does not know, but once you know better you are supposed to do better.

2. Some hear the Word, but to them the Word sounds too complicated, or like a fairytale that it is never applied or acted on.

3. Some people understand the Word, but recognize immediately that some action is required on their part and they make a conscious choice not to do it. They lack faith or discipline to actually apply it.

4. Some people are under false impressions and have been misled by others to believe words that are not represented in the bible. For instance, they are expecting peace to come some other way outside of keeping their minds on Jesus. Even though they have heard the Word. They will say, "I prayed about it, and yet I'm constantly worried." and then they'll even ask the question, "Why can't I get any peace?" The Word never stated that prayer would grant one peace. It stated that keeping ones mind on Jesus would grant peace. Not repeating the problem in a repetitious manner, but by remembering and meditating on the promises of God and His experienced goodness.

So when you study, read, and ponder the Word, ask yourself, "What does the Word require of me? What instructions are given to me?" In doing this you will quickly recognize your part; learn to do your part; and make the Word work for you.

Let's review another scripture using the scenario that your boss is hateful, mean, and mistreating you. The bible tells you what you are supposed to do concerning this. It says to pray for those who despitefully use you. In **Matthew 5:44**, Christ tells us, **"But I say unto you, love your enemies, bless them that curse you, do good to them that hate you, and pray for them which despitefully use you, and persecute you."(KJV)**

Under the circumstances, prayer would be the last thing one might think to do. You might think to do some other choice things, but prayer would not be one. Praying for someone in this scenario would be completely unnatural. However, that is the instruction that God gave for this situation.

So, just do it!!! Pray for those who use you and watch God work! God does not lie. He will take care of it, and as most biblical instructions, it is an obedience, trust and faith thing. He didn't tell you to pray for them so that they can harm or hurt you. He told you to pray for them to expedite your miracle and blessing! In following His instructions you get the desired result. In the natural, I don't understand how this works, but I have witnessed in the natural that it does work.

Thinking of it that way really simplifies it for me. It has helped me to apply the Word and therefore, obtain the desired result. Study and read from the perspective, "What should I be doing?"

2. It's Not Personal, It's Spiritual

There are times when I forget that I am at war. I forget this whole thing is spiritual. I would get so caught up in everything regarding my husband, my kids, my job, my bills, my church, and my relationships because this is what I can actually see. This becomes "the real". This is what I can see, feel, and understand. But, the actual "real", the spiritual part is easily forgotten and ignored. I believe one of the enemy's primary goals is to keep us completely occupied with only what we can see, feel, and understand therefore, we are of no effect or ineffective in the spiritual realm. We are so involved and engaged in what we call reality that we are rarely cognizant of the spiritual reality and the power that is available to us. Therefore, we are no threat to Satan and his kingdom.

Satan desires to keep us away from the spiritual realm because he is aware that it is where the real work is activated. The spiritual realm is where the infinite possibilities reside, and can be accessed through Christ. This is where the impossible becomes possible and where real miracles happen. The bible states that the fervent effectual prayers of the righteous accomplish much. In the book of **James 5:16**, we get specific instructions. **"Confess your faults one to another, and pray one for another, that ye may be healed. The effectual fervent prayer of a righteous man avails much."(KJV)** So, we are to pray. That is the bottom line! In prayer, we hear from God and God hears from us. While we pray, we learn more of Him and He enjoys spending time with us. Prayer, spending time with God, reading His Word, or praising Him creates a personal relationship. This is essential to our growth.

The only way one learns of a person's character is by spending time with them. It works the same with God. Over time, you will gain a sense of who He is. Your weapons of warfare are spiritual and can only be activated in the spiritual realm by applying the Word of God to your life. In **II Corinthians 10:4,** it states, **"The weapons of our warfare are not carnal (fleshy), but mighty through God (Spiritual) to the pulling down of strong holds."(KJV)**

So, now do you see why our enemy, the devil, wants to keep us busy and occupied? This is done so we will not recognize or remember the spiritual realm. The spiritual realm is the only way we can defeat the devil in our lives today. Once this is truly understood, it creates a different type of need. We must meet, talk, and walk with Jesus daily to get clarity, direction, and guidance.

In the spiritual realm, you also become aware that He (Jesus) is all you need. Acknowledge Him as your only source and recognize that there is no help from any other source. Once that is fully appreciated, you stop looking at other areas for assistance. It is then, and only then, can you really rest in His ability to take care of you. Our enemy, Satan, is totally focused on doing one job. Satan's job is to keep us preoccupied and so distracted and caught up in "reality", that there is no, or very little time for anything else. ***Could you imagine the outcome of your decision making process and use of time, if you were just as focused on remembering that your reality today is not all there is, and that there are powers working that you cannot see, that are just as real?***

3. Your Thought Life

Everything begins with a thought. Before I actually began to write this book, it started as a thought. If the thought had not occurred, then I would not have written this book. Every thought is not from God. There are three forces talking to you at any given time.

God – Typically is stating His Word, or instructing you to do something.

Self – Typically is thinking about needs, wants, and goals.

Satan – Typically leans toward unhealthy comparisons, envy, anger, jealousy, selfishness, strife, and discontentment.

I understand that my voice is not the only voice speaking. Satan's first level of attack is in the mind. The battle is going on in your head, **DAILY**! Satan's goal is to infiltrate your mind. If he can get you to think it, he can get you to do it. This is why the Word says in **II Corinthians 10:5**, **"Casting down imaginations and every high thing that exalts itself against the knowledge of God and bringing into captivity every thought to the obedience of Christ."(KJV)** Your first level of defense is to compare the thought, to the Word of God. It wouldn't hurt to ask yourself, "Who is talking?" Take a moment to think it through. Line it up with the Word of God. If it does not line up, then it should cause you to pause. **You have options! You do not have to accept or believe every thought.** Your options are:

*Accept the thought and act on it.

*Dismiss the thought.

*Rebuke the thought.

Take notice to the power that God placed in you to recognize that you are making conscious decisions that will affect this moment, future growth, and your tomorrows.

4. Praise Is What You Do

Once, when I was in a very difficult situation, I asked my mother, "What am I suppose to do until things get better?" She replied, "To think on the good." I asked her if that was in the bible and she replied yes. She then led me to **Philippians 4:8, "And now, dear brothers and sisters, one final thing. Fix your thoughts on what is true, and honorable, and right, and pure, and lovely, and admirable. Think about things that are excellent and worthy of praise."(NLT)** I remember being amazed at God and how His Word covers everything helpful to guiding and developing His people.

Since then, I have tried to remember to focus on the good. The way I do this is when faced with negative information or obstacles, my standard remark is, "Well the goodness is…"or "At least this…" The goal is to locate, pull out, and extract whatever you can to offset the enemy's attack. Praise God for the mundane, the forgotten, and the seemingly unnecessary. By doing this exercise, somehow God transformed the rest of my thoughts into sincere praise. This will also allow you to remember that God is in control and that He is watching over you. You will begin to develop an attitude of gratitude. We have a tendency to forget how blessed we are. We unconsciously begin to take things for granted and focus on the negative.

During prayer one morning, I was thanking God for everything I could think about until I ran out things to thank Him for. I said, "God, I know there's more." I was quiet for a few moments. He reminded me of other things that I could thank Him for. I never got around to actually making any prayer request that day because I had so much to thank Him for.

The next time you are facing a mess, a difficult situation, trial or test, do not focus on the issue or the problem. Try to praise God for the obvious things, and while your praising Him, the peace will come and direction will soon follow.

Satan is a master distracter. If he can keep you busy worrying and talking about your problem, he is content. We do not want the devil to be happy about our behavior. We want to wreck him, like he tries to wreck and annoy us. So, remember to look for the good in every situation. If you cannot find good in it, thank God for other obvious blessings. There is actually so much to thank Him for. You will be surprised, after you make an actual effort, at how easy it is to praise Him.

The good outweighs the bad, however, it does not appear to be that way until you count your blessings. It is a human tendency to focus on the negative. It takes discipline to do otherwise. Consider the one bad thing that happened, or even a series of bad things that occurred, and weigh them against the good things God has done for you. You will soon recognize that He is Good. Since we are wrapped up in the flesh, it will take purposed effort to do this. Focusing on the positive will not happen automatically. It must be vehemently practiced to become apart of who you are.

I am sure that if you give this significant thought, you will agree that God has been good to you. This is the choice you have to make in order for you to fully realize and value His continual provisions.

5. The Word

The power of the Word is so significant. In **Proverbs 4:20-23**, it reads, **"My child, pay attention to what I say. Listen carefully to my words. Don't lose sight of them. Let them penetrate deep into your heart, for they bring life to those who find them, and healing to their whole body. Guard your heart above all else, for it determines the course of your life."(NLT)**

The written and spoken words of God are powerful. When Jesus was in the wilderness being tempted of the devil for forty days and nights, He responded to Satan with the Word. Each time Jesus responded "It is written…" The words of God are the only effective weapons against our enemy, the devil. Read carefully **(See Matthew 4:1-11)** how Jesus used the Word on the enemy and won the victory.

Satan said, **"If you are the Son of God command these stones to be made bread."**

Jesus replied with the Word, and said, **"<u>It is written</u> man shall not live by bread alone but by every word that proceeds out of the mouth of God."(KJV)** Jesus referenced the Word of God, where it is written in **Deuteronomy 8:3, "…man doth not live by bread only, but by every word that proceedeth out of the mouth of the LORD doth man live."(KJV)**

Satan said, **"If you are the Son of God cast yourself down: for it is written, He shall give His angels charge concerning you: and in their hands they shall bear you up, least at anytime thou dash your foot against a stone."**

Jesus replied with the Word, **"<u>It is written</u> thou shall not tempt the Lord thy God, and him only shall thy serve."(KJV)** Again, Jesus referenced the Word of God, where it is written in **Deuteronomy 6:16, "Ye shall not tempt the LORD your God…"(KJV)**

Satan said, **"All these things I will give you if you fall down and worship me."**

Jesus replied with the Word, **"Get thee behind me Satan: for <u>it is written</u>, Thou shall worship the Lord thy God and him only shall thy serve."(KJV)** Notice each and every time Jesus responds with only the Word. This response from Jesus came from **Deuteronomy 6:13, "Thou shalt fear the LORD thy God, and serve him, and shalt swear by his name."(KJV)**

If you are a born again believer, living a God centered life you have the power within you through Christ (who lives in you) to put the enemy under your feet. You have the power to speak life to death through the authority of God in you. I am not talking about the power of positive thinking, law of attraction or magic. The power that I am referring to is the activated power of God's word spoken by faith through your mouth. God is not Santa Claus; He is not interested in fulfilling your every whim and desire. He is interested in your spiritual development and you prospering in alignment with how your soul is prospering.

> **Beloved, I wish above all things that thou mayest prosper and be in health, even as thy soul prospereth. 3 John 2(KJV)**

God is sovereign he knows your needs before you have them and He is aware of your motives and the thoughts and intents of your heart. God answering your prayers or your spoken word is not brought into manifestation by the works of your speaking alone. Your spoken word works in concert with your faith in His ability to bring it to past as you live in alignment to His will. It is all about Him.

Our job is to learn to be just as effective as Jesus. Jesus demonstrated perfectly how we are to warfare. Let's imitate Jesus. We cannot use words we do not know. So, first things first, get to know the Word of God and begin to use it. Every word you say has an effect. Words can hurt, heal, destroy, build up, win the war, or lose the war. Our enemy is not affected by your opinion, debate, or knowledge concerning any book or earthly understanding. He will even toy with you, just to waste more time. If you want to win the battles and the war, you must get God's Word pressed down into your heart. You must extract it daily. Be aware that the spirit world and warfare is real, more real than the nose on your face.

Since the Powers of life and death are in the tongue we should choose carefully the words we let pass through our lips. *Once you are aware of the power of spoken words, you should be speaking life continuously.* As it is written in **Proverbs 18:21, "*Death and life are in the power of the tongue*: and they that love it shall eat the fruit thereof"(KJV)**

The word instructs us in **Romans 4:17** to, **"...call those things that be not as though they were."(KJV)** *For example, God said, by His stripes you were healed.* ***(See I Peter 2:24)*** *Speak it! Say, "By God's stripes I am healed!" In doing this, you are calling those things that are not as though they were. "I am healed. I believe I am healed!" You may not feel healed, but since healing is not about a feeling, it needs to be ignored. God's spoken word combined with your faith is powerful. This combination creates the manifestation of your healing.*

What you say is what you believe. You can fully believe a lie, which will become more real than the truth, and then it will hurt you. **Matthew 15:18** says, **"But the words you speak come from the heart that's what defiles you."(NLT)**

You can only speak out of the abundance (overflow) of your heart. *When you speak, your heart is on display. The*

Word tells us in **Matthew 12:34, "...out of the abundance of the heart the mouth speaks."(KJV)**

Have you ever heard someone say, "I knew that was going to happen to me?" Well, they spoke it through their faith into existence. It did not have to come out that way, but they repeatedly spoke the negative outcome and believed in their heart that it would be the outcome, and then they wondered why they received the negative outcome. You get what you say. So watch your mouth! Matthew knew these spiritual principles and shared them with us in **Matthew 12:37, "For by your words you will be justified and acquitted, and by your words you will be condemned and sentenced."(AMP)**

> **If thou have done foolishly in praising yourself or if you have thought evil, lay your hand over your mouth. Proverbs 30:32 (KJV)**

I laughed when I read this scripture because basically, God is giving instructions on what to do after having prideful or bad thoughts. He covers everything!! Simple enough instructions: cover your mouth! Why you might ask? Because the words that come out your mouth are powerful! God doesn't want you to accidentally hurt yourself. Every word begins with a thought and spoken words are powerful. It was a lie when they told you as a child that words don't hurt, they can. They can also help, bless and build.

If you get this principle down you are wise. <u>Most people don't.</u> They speak every thought, and sometimes they use excuses and say, "This is just who I am." However, the truth of the matter is; it is not who they are. People who use this as their excuse simply lack understanding and discipline. **Proverbs 17:28** states, **"Even a fool is thought wise if he keeps silent, and discerning if he holds his tongue."(NIV)**

Once again, it is all about words. He did not say it is all about action. He said it was about His Word. The Word has to be in your heart and mouth to be able to accomplish His will. You will have what you say. For instance: If you say, "I am broke." You will be broke. Instead of speaking the fact that you are broke, try speaking God's Word concerning your situation. Say, "God is going to supply all my needs according to His riches in glory." **(See Philippians 4:19)** The power that we have in our tongue is also referenced in **Deuteronomy 30:14, "But the word is very nigh unto thee, in thy mouth, and in thy heart, that thou mayest do it."(KJV)**

Guarding your heart basically means not allowing anything contrary to God and His goodness into your heart. Your heart is precious and it is the repository for good and evil. If you allow evil to continually penetrate your heart, it will affect your life. You can only speak and magnify what lives inside of your heart. Your heart is accessed through your mouth, your ears, and your eyes. So, be careful to meticulously guard what you allow to gain access into your heart, and make an effort not to harm yourself with the words that come out of your own mouth.

> **Guard your heart above all else, for it determines the course of your life. Proverbs 4:23 (NLT)**

Watch what you say. Your words are powerful. Once I understood the power of the spoken word in the Bible, I was amazed. This world was created by a spoken word. God spoke this world into existence. He did not create the world with His hands; He created the world with His mouth. Do not forget that your words are powerful. If you match your spoken words to His written word you will have great success. If you speak every thought contrary to His Word, then you will get that as well.

If you have accepted Christ as your savior you can be certain that God's plans for your life are good. **(See**

Jeremiah 29:11). It is His will for His children to be well. It is clear this is the will of the Lord according to the words written in the bible. He clearly stated that by His stripes we were healed **(See 1 Peter 2:24).** Christ came so that we might have life and have it more abundantly. It is the devil that is seeking to destroy you **(See John 10:10)**. God wants you to prosper as your soul prospers **(See 3 John 2)**. I am not saying that Christians are exempt from suffering or trouble because we are not, not in any way. I am saying that it is not God's will or His best for you to suffer. He allows it, but it is not His perfect will. It is His allowable will. Since God is all knowing and sovereign He can even use suffering for His glory and our benefit. We do not always receive God's best because we live in a fallen world, we make bad choices and there is a devil here on this earth seeking whom he can destroy **(See I Peter 5:8)**. The Devil is constantly trying and tempting God's children. Do you remember Job? He was an upright man, but he constantly worried about his children. Worrying is the opposite of trusting or faith. In my opinion, I believe this was the devil's point of entrance into Job's life.

It is the devil's job to touch and offend what is most dear to you and he takes his job quite seriously. He is hoping that in doing so, he will cause you to fall. However, the miracle and beauty of God is that God uses the trouble and adversity to draw you closer to Him This trouble also builds up your character, tenacity, and faith in God. God is not infirming you. He is not the one making you sick. He does not benefit from you being sick. It is the enemy, via the power of **<u>your</u>** thoughts, **<u>your</u>** life-choices, and **<u>your</u>** words working against you, not God. It is the enemy who comes to steal, kill and destroy. God is trying to get you to believe that He is able to make you well. He already paid the price, of 39 stripes for you to be well **(See I Peter 2:24)**. Why would Christ pay the price for you to be well and then afflict you?

Think back for a moment to Adam and Eve. God gave instructions to them not to eat of the tree in the midst of the garden. That was God's perfect will for them. Adam and

Eve disobeyed. They had a choice, just like we have choices. God did not place barbed wires or angels around the tree to keep them from disobedience. Adam and Eve were responsible for being obedient to God's instructions. The devil was in the world with them. The bible does not mention if God told them about Satan, but what is clear is that God told them that they were IN AUTHORITY OVER ALL THE EARTH, and WHAT NOT TO DO. Adam and Eve were responsible for their obedience. That was it. There was no mystery about God's will; they could not plead ignorance because God made His perfect will plain to them.

When the serpent approached Eve, she had already received her instructions. The bible does not state Adam's location at the time, but it implies that he was near to Eve. When Eve reached for the fruit, God did not slap Eve's hand to protect her from herself and her bad decision because God gave Eve free will to make her own choice. God will not violate His own will, He gave her the authority and ability to choose.

Eve chose to disobey God's word and ate the fruit. She approached Adam, and then Adam chose to eat the fruit. God's perfect will was for them not to eat the fruit, but His perfect will was not obeyed. They both decided that their will and desire was a better choice than God's will. God gave Adam and Eve the option to choose, they chose to disobey, and they paid the price. They could have remained in paradise, but because of their choice they were evicted, and by default of their choice their power and authority was given to the devil. There are consequences or rewards associated with choices. If you follow through with the will that God laid out for you in the Word, you can depend on receiving God's best. If you decide to lean toward your own will, you will receive the consequences of your choice, which is not God's best, but the result of your choice.

Now we get into God's allowable will. Satan cannot do anything to you unless God allows it. Satan does not have free reign over your life. (Remember Job) It is true that we are living in a fallen world, but there are boundaries and limitations that the devil cannot cross. God's word says that He will not allow you to be tempted or tested above that which you are able to bear. **(See I Corinthians 10:13)** God gave them the power to choose their path. God did not make them robots. He gave them the power to choose for themselves. He gave Adam, Eve, you and I free will to choose our paths.

Now let's bring this into alignment with our lives today. It is really the same as it was for Adam and Eve. God's written word is the bible, which is His perfect, will for your life. You have the power to choose to get to know God's will by reading the bible and applying it to your life. We do not always make right choices, and the results of those choices fall into the category of God's allowable will. God allows you to receive less than His best due to your bad choices. This concept is very hard for some to receive because people do not want to be held accountable for their choices, actions, spoken words, faith, and consequences. Some people would rather prefer to believe that their outcome or reality had nothing to do with their choices so they can easily say it must have been God's will.

Now let's bring this into correlation with faith. God never healed anybody that did not believe that He was able to do it. He always asked what would you have me do? (What can I do for you?) To the woman with the issue of blood who pressed up behind Jesus and touched Him, He replied, "**Your faith** has made you whole." He did not say I made you whole. It was important for her to <u>believe in His ability to be made whole through Him.</u> To the blind man He said, "According to your faith be it unto you." Are you following me? **Your faith in His ability is the key**!

You might say, I prayed and believed, but "this" or "that" still happened. That may be your truth. I will not debate or question your experience. God's word say's that

He would not leave you **(See Hebrews 13:5)** or allow you to be overtaken. **(See Jude 1:24)** You must remember that we are living in a fallen world and just because something bad is allowed does not mean that it was God's perfect will. It could have been the result of a bad choice. It is not God's will for murders to happen, but they do, even to innocent little babies and children. Earth is not heaven. We have an active enemy among us, and bad things do happen, even to Christians. **(See Ecclesiastes 9:11)** God does allow these things to happen, but He is able to turn them around for His glory, honor, and your good if you stand on His word.

> **Whosoever keeps his mouth and His tongue keeps His soul from trouble. Proverbs 21:23(KJV)**

6. The Honor In Being Offered Up

No one thinks of being tested or chastened as a pleasant experience. As it describes in **Hebrews 12:11, "No discipline is enjoyable while it is happening- it's painful! But afterward there will be a peaceful harvest of right living for those who are trained in this way."(NLT)**

I believe it would be a true statement to say most shudder at the mere thought of being tested. Usually, it is a painful exercise and it makes you tired. Weighing out all your options and constantly considering everything is exhausting to say the least. It raises the level of consciousness to the spiritual and if you are not accustomed to operating in this realm it can be exhausting.

My initial response to being tested was typically, "Oh no, more drama! It was always accompanied with a great sense of dread, irritation, and a twinge of fear. I would say, "Lord, aren't there any other Christians that needs developing?" I felt as though I barely passed the last test, and the one before that I failed completely. So the whole idea of being tested made my stomach knot. Over time, I learned that there is honor in the test. We have the confidence that we can overcome any test that we face because it is written in **I Corinthians 10:13, "No test or temptation that comes your way is beyond the course of what others have had to face. All you need to remember is that God will never let you down; He'll never let you be pushed past your limit; He'll always be there to help you come through it."(MSG)**

> **Dear brothers and sisters, when troubles come your way, consider it an opportunity for great joy. For you know that when your faith is tested, your endurance has a chance to grow. So let it grow, for**

when your endurance is fully developed, you will be perfect and complete, needing nothing. James 1:2-4 (NLT)

God promised not to allow testing above that which you can stand. The first thing you need to know is, the mere fact that you are being tested, means that you are able to bear it, or God would not have allowed you to be in that situation. *If you are in it, you can win it!* The second thing you need to know is, He offered you up as He did Job. God said, "Have you considered my servant *(Put your name here)?"* God knows what you are capable of because He created you, and He has been working on and developing you to prepare you for this new test.

Paul says in **II Corinthians 12:9-10, "Each time he said, 'My grace is all you need. My power works best in weakness.' So now I am glad to boast about my weaknesses, so that the power of Christ can work through me. That's why I take pleasure in my weaknesses, and in the insults, hardships, persecutions, and troubles that I suffer for Christ. For when I am weak, then I am strong."(NLT)** Therefore, we should actually boast in our weaknesses so that God's power will work through us. Therefore, we really should take pleasure in necessities, reproaches, persecution, and distress for Christ's sake: For when we are weak, then we are strong, because at that time God is working in us.

After the test, then comes the testimony. No test, no testimony. *Without a test, you have no personal point of reference of what God in you can accomplish, and without personal experiences how can you encourage others?* Testing serves many purposes and it displays your growth. Some test will be repeated several times until you pass. This motivates me to pass the first time around. I really, really don't want to retake any test. I want to learn and apply what is required for me to pass the test the first time. I am painfully aware of when I am retaking a test it deeply pains me. It is true that you have to go through it until you get through it successfully. So be cognizant of your position, apply what you know, and continually focus on God's Word.

In conclusion, you can accomplish anything through Christ. If you try to rely on your own power, know that you will not get very far. Just resisting the devil on your own strength and ability will not help you. **James 4:7** tells us, **"Submit yourselves therefore to God. Resist the devil, and he will flee from you."(KJV)** *Please realize that you cannot successfully resist the devil without submitting yourself to God first.* This is the critical first step in winning the battle. Submitting yourself to God shows your dependency on Him. What you don't realize is that in doing this, it allows God to fight for you in the spiritual realm.

7. Recognize Your Position

It is important to recognize when you are being tested. Usually they come without warning. For example, you are just going along on your merry way and something happens like this.

You go into the jewelry store to replace the backs of your earrings. Usually you are with your girlfriends, but this day you are alone for whatever reason. The jeweler looks at your earrings and makes a couple of weird gestures and you ask, “What’s the problem?”

“These stones are of a low quality. Where did you purchase them?”

“They were a gift from my husband.”

“Oh!”

The jeweler goes to the back of the store and began to make the requested repair. During that time you are busy looking at all the beautiful sparkling diamonds. The jeweler emerges from the back of the store and says,

“Pick out whatever you want in the case. It’s yours if you go on one lunch with me: just a lunch, not a dinner, not anything else, just a lunch. You can have anything in the showcase!”

Now before I go any further there are a few things you need to take notice of.

A trap has been set! I call it a ***‘Tricky Trap’.*** The fact that you are alone and you typically go to lunch with friends opens up the opportunity for the enemy to try you. The test is will you be able demonstrate Christ-like values and character when no one is watching?

The criticizing of your jewelry is ***the hook***.

The temptation of looking in the showcase is ***the bait***.

The indecent proposal, offering anything in the case for a supposed innocent lunch, is ***the kill***.

Know that there is nothing innocent about the offer, or the lunch. There are no free lunches! **The devil had a trap set**. I call them tricky traps. Tricky traps are very easy to fall into because they typically cater to our fleshy desires and wants. They are flattering and can easily lure you into dangerous territory.

Initially, I was flattered by the offer. Wow! What a compliment. I laughed and smiled. He continued to talk.

Satan begins to talk as well, he says, "What's a lunch? Nobody will even have to know. Then you can have those two-carat earrings. None of your friends have two-carats earrings. You can tell your husband that they are cubic zirconia's and he would never know the difference. This is a no-brainer. Don't pass up this opportunity. This is a once in a lifetime offer."

This is when it is key to recognize your position. Stop and ask yourself, "Who is talking?" Once you identify that it is the enemy, know that it is Satan speaking to your mind. Recognize that you are either being tested, or tempted. At this point, you should be aware that you have to make a decision to either pass, or fail. The right thing to do is crystal clear, but if feels stupid to pass up on such an easy offer. The jeweler and Satan are still speaking. You have given it enough thought and decided to pass the test. You decline the offer, pay the jeweler, and thank him for his service. You're walking toward the door and the jeweler shouts,

"Why not? What could be the harm in having lunch with an old man?"

"Because I'm married, and I don't go to lunch with other men." Because you really know that it would be more than lunch. Lunch is just bait to get you hooked.

"So what, I am married too."

"I'm a Christian."

He laughs and says, "Come back when you get over that."

You exit the store feeling victorious and recognize that God is pleased. You just victoriously stomped on the devil's head. You did not fall for the devil's rope-a-dope of lies and God smiles when He thinks of you. You passed the test. Victory is so sweet! However, I must warn you that past victories do not measure your current state, or even future successes. Due to pride, most defeats in the bible occur immediately after a victory. Do not get cocky, or a big head. The enemy uses pride on a daily basis to defeat God's people. Applying God's word is a daily effort. To be consistently triumphant, you must only rely on, and apply the written word of God.

> **Behold, I send you forth as sheep in the midst of wolves: be ye therefore wise as serpents, and harmless as doves. Matthew 10:16 (KJV)**

> **To keep Satan from getting the advantage over us; for we are not ignorant of his wiles and intentions. II Corinthians 2:11 (AMP)**

8. Evil Is Contagious

Evil communication ruins good manners. (**See I Corinthians 15:33)** I use to wonder why my good behavior would not rub-off on others, but my bad behavior would. I do not understand it, but if the bible says it, then I believe it.

Sanctification is a process of discipline. It does not happen automatically. It is a transformation process, accomplished by the renewing of your mind with God's word. After giving this subject some considerable thought, I understand that we are born into sin, and therefore, we are sinful by nature. Wrapped in this shell of sin called flesh, we are also living in a sinful world. **Romans 12:2** says, **"Don't copy the behavior and customs of this world, but let God transform you into a new person by changing the way you think. Then you will learn to know God's will for you, which is good and pleasing and perfect."(NLT)**

Constantly being around sinful people has the potential to lower a Christian's values and standards (if you are not properly armored up). (For example, if a warrior is not properly armored up while going into battle, the outcome could be fatal because the warrior is exposed to the weapons of the enemy.) The constant exposure to sin makes it easier to sin. Over time, the idea (of indulging in sin, eventually turns into the act of sinning itself) and then the act of sinning become more acceptable as you are immersed in it. As human beings, we often imitate the people we are around. Have you ever had a friend that you began to speak like; imitate gestures like, and eventually, emulated altogether without you realizing it? You never would have known if someone hadn't brought this fact to your attention. This is exactly how sin rubs off on you, a little bit at a time.

On the other hand, your demonstrated goodness also has the potential to cause people to praise God. **Matthew**

5:16 tells us to, **"Let your light so shine before men, that they may see your good works, and glorify your Father which is in heaven."(KJV)**

Christians are the lights and ambassadors of Christ to a lost world. **Ephesians 6:20, "I am in chains now, still preaching this message as *God's ambassador*. So pray that I will keep on speaking boldly for him, as I should."(NLT)** Christians should not isolate themselves from unbelievers. We are God's light in a dark world. God in us should be attracting unbelievers to want to know the God we serve. If you are not attracting the unbelievers, then you are either repelling them, or blending in so much with the world that you are not identified as a Christian at all. Take a minute and evaluate yourself to determine if you are attracting, repelling, or blending in with unbelievers. The goal of course is to attract. Not by preaching to people, but by living a life that glorifies God. People watch what you do; they do not listen to what you say. I heard a Minister once say, "Your actions should line up with your beliefs." This is a powerful statement of truth. You would not steal if you believe stealing is wrong.

Christians have standards and values that are outlined in the Bible. It is recognizable when a Christian is living a life that resembles Christ's standards. It is also recognizable when they are not. Your life is a ministry, an epistle, and a living testimony. You are either positively affecting the people within your realm of influence for God's Kingdom or, you are negatively affecting them. Every Christian should be striving to imitate Christ and to impact God's kingdom in a positive way.

Christians should pray for God's will regarding the unbelievers. Jesus spoke in **Acts 26:18,"To open their eyes, and to turn them from darkness to light, and from the power of Satan unto God, that they may receive forgiveness of sin, and inheritance among them which are sanctified by faith in Christ. (KJV)**

Christians are transformed by the word of God and in the process of time their minds are renewed. The old world system and way of thinking must be removed and the new renewed way of thinking must be introduced.

> **Since you have heard about Jesus and have learned the truth that comes from him, throw off your old sinful nature and your former way of life, which is corrupted by lust and deception. Instead, let the Spirit renew your thoughts and attitudes. Put on your new nature, created to be like God truly righteous and holy. Ephesians 4:21-24(NLT)**
>
> **Abstain from all appearance of evil. I Thessalonians 5:22(KJV)**
>
> **Do not let any unwholesome talk come out of your mouths, but only what is helpful for building others up according to their needs, that it may benefit those who listen. Ephesians 4:29(NIV)**
>
> **For we are God's workmanship, created in Christ Jesus to do good works, which God prepared in advance for us to do. Ephesians 2:10 (NIV)**
>
> **But now is the time to get rid of anger, rage, malicious behavior, slander, and dirty language. Don't lie to each other, for you have stripped off your old sinful nature and all its wicked deeds. Put on your new nature, and be renewed as you learn to know your Creator and become like him. Colossians 3: 8-10(NLT)**
>
> **And the Lord's servant must not quarrel; instead, he must be kind to everyone, able to teach, not resentful. Those who oppose him he must gently instruct, in the hope that God will grant them repentance leading them to a knowledge of the**

truth, and that they will come to their senses and escape from the trap of the devil, who has taken them captive to do his will. II Timothy 2:24-26(NIV)

Then the way you live will always honor and please the Lord, and your lives will produce every kind of good fruit. All the while, you will grow as you learn to know God better and better. We also pray that you will be strengthened with all His glorious power so you will have all the endurance and patience you need. May you be filled with joy, always thanking the Father. He has enabled you to share in the inheritance that belongs to His people, who live in the light. Colossians 1:10-12(NLT)

Let your conversation be gracious and attractive so that you will have the right response for everyone. Colossians 4:6(NLT)

Christians need to keep in mind that a lost world is watching their behavior. If you are a Christian, please remember, you are a representative of Christ!

9. Sowing and Reaping

There is a biblical law called seedtime and harvest, and sowing and reaping. **Galatians 6:7** says, **"Be not deceived; God is not mocked: for whatsoever a man soweth, that shall he also reap."(KJV)** Basically, that means whatever you do, comes right back at you. This principle and law works on everyone. It does not matter if you believe it or not. It applies to everyone, not only Christians. It even applies to you, even if you are unaware that it exists.

One morning, I dropped my son off at the baby sitter's house. My son and a little girl went into the kitchen to have breakfast. The little girl started crying and we all rushed to see what was wrong with her. Her face was wet with juice. The sitter asked her what happened and she said that my son threw his juice in her face. Well, the first thing you need to know about my son David, is that he is a very gentle, loving, little boy. This behavior was totally out of his character. He had never demonstrated that type of behavior. I was having a very hard time understanding his behavior, but I was under pressure to get an answer. The mother of the child was staring me in my face. I asked him what happened. He was so overwhelmed with the event that he could not respond quickly enough for me. I was totally outdone. Under pressure and about to miss my train, I asked him again. He was attempting to explain, but was stuttering. I could not take it anymore. I popped him in his mouth and said, "Don't ever do that again!"

I apologized to the mother of the little girl and the babysitter, and I left as fast as I could to catch the train. I was so disturbed by the morning events. I could not wait to get to work to call the sitter to see if she had found out exactly what happened. In route to work, I took a short cut through the Sears Tower and out of nowhere, I got hit in the mouth really hard. My fur wrap fell off my head and I just stood there.

A person had asked the man in front of me for directions, the man in front of me threw back his hand to point, out the direction the person needed to go, then Bam! I was struck smack dab in my mouth! I was so into my thoughts that I did not notice that the man in front of me had stopped, and that I had practically walked right into his hand. I was stunned, because of course, it was unexpected and it hurt. To add insult to injury, it was in the middle of a really busy place. Everyone stopped to see what was going to happen. Somebody yelled, "That white man hit that black lady in the mouth!" At this point tears were rolling down my face and the man who hit me in the mouth is repeatedly apologizing. I picked up my wrap, kept walking, and never looked back.

Somewhere between that point and work, it hit me. I was reaping what I had done to my son. When I got to work, I called the sitter. She was very irritated. She began to explain that the leg of the chair, in which my son was sitting, had broken. This is how the juice got thrown into the little girl's face. She also explained that he did not know how to explain it and that I should slow down and listen. She told me to hear him out next time and to take a later train. She also asked me why I had hit him and stated that she had never seen me treat him like that before.

It was true. I had never done anything like that before. There was never a need because he was such a sweet kid. That was a mistake. Don't get me wrong, I believe in discipline, but not done in that way. The awesomeness of the story is how swift I reaped my actions, even though I was not completely aware that I had done anything wrong. The hit I received was just as painful and surprising as the one I had delivered to my son. I shared the story with the sitter and she was so happy to hear it. I could not wait to tell my son I was sorry.

In this lesson, I learned that sowing and reaping is real and it applies to everyone. It is a foundational biblical principle.

> **If you set a trap for others, you will get caught in it yourself. If you roll a boulder down on others, it will crush you instead Proverbs 26:27(NLT)**

10. Secret Praise

Christians need to be careful not to give the devil secret praise. You are probably wondering what I am talking about. Secret praise is when you talk about everything the enemy is doing, or has done, over and above what God has done. Have you ever been with a person who claims to be Christian, but all they talk about is bad news, what is wrong in their life, and the world? To think of anything good is their challenge, and when they are asked, why they are harping on the negative, they get angry.

I refer to this behavior as secret praise. I call it that, because it is even a secret from the person who is actually doing it. They are not fully aware that they are praising the devil. They believe that they are just sharing information. The problem is that this sharing is not balanced with any good news, praise, or recognition of what God has done or is currently doing. This dialogue lacks any mention of the promises of God. It is a continual reflection of what the enemy is doing, or has done to them. God's Word tells us what to focus on.

> **Finally, brethren, whatsoever things are true, whatsoever things are honest, whatsoever things are just, whatsoever things are pure, whatsoever things are lovely, whatsoever things are of good report; if there be any virtue, and if there be any praise, think on these things. Philippians 4:8 (KJV)**

It does take concentrated effort to look for the good, and God in things. It is a part of being transformed into His image. If you find yourself focusing on the negative, pull your mind in and really think about how good God is. Put things in their right perspective, and make the effort to recall just how wonderful God has been in the past. Take a moment to reflect on the promises that He has made, in His Word, concerning your future, and you being a conqueror.

> **And we know that all things work together for the good for those who love the God, to them who are called according to his purpose. Romans 8:28 (KJV)**

> **No, in all these things we are more than conquerors through him who loved us. Romans 8:37(NIV)**

If you find yourself consistently focusing on the bad, which is, in effect, being negative, know that this behavior is unbecoming for a Christian and a bad representation of Christ in you. Christians are being watched by sinners and are mandated to reflect Christ's goodness. We are not to talk about "on purpose" or, "by accident" what Satan is doing, or has done to us. God does not get any glory in that activity. We need to be sure to keep our minds focused on the good that God has already done and the promises He made to us in His Word and believe Him.

I am as human as anyone else and I know it is challenging not to complain and vent the issues of the day. It takes discipline to abstain from speaking negatively. It would be easier to reframe from speaking every negative thought if we were trained early in life to control this impulse. Most Christians do not learn or understand the power of words until much later in life, but this is why the bible instructs us to teach our children of His word and His way when they are young. **"Impress them on your children. Talk about them when you sit at home and when you walk along the road, when you lie down and when you get up." Deuteronomy 6:7(NIV)**

Christians are ambassadors for Christ. We need to praise and worship God, extract and repeat the good that God has done, and purposefully remind others of God's goodness and faithfulness. **II Corinthians 5:20** provides a model of how we, as Christians, are to be; ***"We are therefore Christ's ambassadors*, as though God were making his appeal through us. We implore you on Christ's behalf: Be reconciled to God"(NIV)**

The Enemy wants the world to believe that he is stronger and more effective than God. Think about this, when you turn on the news all you hear is bad news. Rarely, is there a story about something good. Satan uses all available resources to sell the idea that he is stronger than God and that he is doing significant damage to God's kingdom. As Christians, we need to challenge ourselves to be mindful of what we are saying and whom we are talking about.

No more secret praise and testimonies about what the devil has, or is doing in your life. Good and bad things happen to all people. It is a part of life. However, God has given instructions regarding how you are to behave, so apply what you know.

> **If you are wise and understand God's ways, *prove it by living an honorable life,* doing good works with the humility that comes from wisdom. James 3:13 (NLT)**
>
> **If you have done foolishly in exalting yourself, *or if you have thought evil,* lay your hand upon your mouth. Proverbs 30:32 (AMP)**
>
> **We can make a large horse go wherever we want by means of a small bit in its mouth. And a small rudder makes a huge ship turn wherever the pilot chooses to go, even though the winds are strong. In the same way, the tongue is a small thing that**

makes grand speeches. But a tiny spark can set a great forest on fire. And the tongue is a flame of fire. ***It is a whole world of wickedness, corrupting your entire body. It can set your whole life on fire, for it is set on fire by hell itself.*** **James 3:3-6 (NLT)**

As Christians, we must exercise self-control over our mouths and discipline ourselves not to speak every thought. Every thought does not have to be shared. Every thought is not beneficial for the building up of the body of Christ or God's kingdom. I recognize when we are facing difficult situations, God's kingdom is the last thing on our minds, and at that point, it is all about us. We are not fully cognizant of the damage we are doing to the kingdom, but we should be. Ignorance is no excuse. The Word of God is clearly stated and when we know better we should do better. "**My people are destroyed for lack of knowledge…" Hosea 4:6(KJV)**

Pity parties are the platforms for praising the devil for his torment, and I bet he loves every minute of it. *You cannot effectively complain and praise God in the same breath.* **James 3:10** says, **"And so blessing and cursing come pouring out of the same mouth. Surely, my brothers and sisters, this is not right!"(NLT)**

Once you begin to practice self-control over your mouth, it will bless you and those around you. If faced with a situation where someone is giving the devil secret praise, gently remind the person of God's goodness. We all fall short from time to time, and need to be reminded of God's faithfulness and goodness. Let your mouth and actions bless those around you.

11. First Time Hearing From God

I remember having a conversation with my mother many years ago. She was telling me about something the Lord had instructed her to do. I asked her, "How did you know that it was God and not your own thoughts?"

"You just know." She went on to say, "God talks to you too."

"He never talks to me."

She said that He does, but that I was too occupied to hear His voice. Many years later, I was on my way to the train station after a long day at work. I passed a homeless lady and her little girl begging for change. Seeing this disturbed me. The poor kid being raised on the streets and the woman looked so sad. I gave her some change and kept going. I don't recall at what point, but I heard a quiet, small voice in my mind saying to give the woman a large amount of money.

> **And after the earthquake a fire; but the LORD was not in the fire: and after the fire a *still small voice* I Kings 19:12 (KJV)**

I remember pondering for several minutes thinking to myself, "I don't have money like that to give to anyone." The thought kept repeating in my mind. It irritated me because it was not something I wanted to do. I cannot remember how long it took me to finally say okay, but I eventually did. When payday came, I went to the bank to get the money and while standing in line, I clearly heard in my mind exactly what denomination of money to get and to seal it in an envelope to give to the homeless lady.

At this point, I was frantic to get it over with. After work, I rushed to the train station to be obedient to God's instruction and give her the money, but she was not there. I was deeply troubled. I did not understand why God would instruct me to go out of my way to bless the lady, all the while knowing she would not be there. This went on for almost two weeks. I was walking around with a sealed wad of cash, of several hundred dollars, in my purse to give to a total stranger, who seemed to have just vanished.

Well, it got worse. During this time, my own money was running out and my car was almost out of gas. I had not shared my situation with anyone. I went to visit my mom's house one night after work. She asked me how my money was looking. I was a bit surprised that she asked, because I was typically okay. I said,

"I finally heard from God."

"What did He say?"

I told her the whole story and she asked to see the envelope. I took the wrinkly, worn envelope out of my purse and gave it to her. She held it for a moment in her hand and then said,

"No matter what, do not open this. Follow His instructions."

"This really feels crazy! I think you are the only person who would understand this."

She stood up and went upstairs. When she returned, she gave me money. I think it was $20. I almost started crying because I was so broke, *but I had not shared that with her*. She held both of my hands and said,

"Linda, do not open that envelope for any reason. If you need any money come see me."

I left her house feeling weird, happy, and overwhelmed. Later that night, we talked on the phone and I asked her,

"How are you so sure that this is God talking to me?"

"Only God would ask you to do something so wonderfully unselfish, and giving. The devil does not ask you to do anything like that."

During this time, I was attending night school after work. I tried to find that lady for a few more days, but still nothing. I was spent! My head throbbed from thinking about it. One day, I went totally out of my way, in the rain, before class, to see if she was there. She was nowhere to be found. That was almost the proverbial straw that broke the camel's back! I was so frustrated! I was walking in the cold rain, fussing and complaining to God. I truly don't recall how many more days I carried the envelope in my purse, but I forgot about the money entirely.

Finally, one day I saw her and the little girl. I ran over to her looking absolutely crazy. I hugged her and started rambling about what God had told me to do. She was looking at me so strangely. I pulled out the now dirty, wrinkled envelope, put it in her hand, and hugged her tightly. I have never been so happy to give somebody something in all my life. She was still looking at me really weird. She said,

"Thank you."

"God bless you, I gotta go or I'm going to miss my train."

I never saw her again. Apparently, the need was met and she was allowed to escape a terrible situation or, I entertained an angel unaware. Either way, God's will was done. Through this first hand experience, I learned that God speaks to people, even in this day and age. And he still gives very specific instructions.

> **Don't forget to show hospitality to strangers, for some who have done this have entertained angels without realizing it! Hebrews 13:2 (NLT)**

In everything I did, I showed you that by this kind of hard work we must help the weak, remembering the words the Lord Jesus himself said: 'It is more blessed to give than to receive.' Acts 20:35 (NIV)

When you hear God's voice, you will know it. His Word says in **John 10:27, "My sheep hear my voice, and I know them, and they follow me**:"**(KJV)** Keep in mind that God does not violate His own word, so whatever He asks of you, it will line up with His written word in the Bible.

12. Bread of Deceit

During prayer and meditation on my commute to work, I read the scripture **Proverbs 20:17,** which reads, **"Bread of deceit is sweet to a man; but afterward his mouth shall be filled with gravel."(KJV)** I remember thinking, "Praise God! That scripture does not apply to me. I'm not looking to deceive anyone." A few seconds, later, God said, "Yes you are."

"Huh?" I was actually insulted and said, "No I'm not!! Who?"

God replied, "Peoples Gas."

When He replied Peoples Gas, I was outdone. I forgot that God knows the intent of our hearts. I was considering not paying the final bill to Peoples Gas at the house I was selling because there was a different gas supplier for the new house.

Normally, this would not be something I would have considered doing, but the situation surrounding the final bill was difficult for me to accept. My final bill was $1,400! It was totally unexpected, because I was on a budget and paid my monthly bill on time. I called them and asked how could this be, and they told me the meter had not been read in two years. I was so disturbed! Moreover, I did not have $1,400 to pay to them.

What they did not know was that I was selling the house with the big bill and moving into a new house in couple of months. The key thing here to remember is that I shared this thought with no living soul, so for God to "bust me out" like this was unnerving to say the least. So, there I was looking crazy and saying, "You're right, I'm busted." So I tell God, "You know I do not have this money, if you send me the money I'll pay it."

A week later, I got a call at work telling me that my parked car had been hit. I thought, what else can happen? I took a few minutes to remind myself of God's Word. **Romans 8:28** says, **"And we know that all things work together for good to them that love God, to them who are the called according to his purpose."(KJV).** A few days later, I got a call from the insurance company asking questions about the car. They made an appointment to evaluate the damage. I did not want them to see the car because it had been in a previous accident and I knew the car was not worth much. If the car had no previous damages I could get a decent amount, but with prior damage I knew I really should not get anything.

Earlier that week, I moved the car into the garage just to get the extra raggedy car from in front of my house. During that time, the storage bins I ordered for moving were delivered to my home for us to start packing for the move. My intent was to move the car so that the insurance agent would not ever see the car, but because the storage bins blocked the way I could not move the car. The insurance man called my job and said he went by and looked at the car. He laughed. I laughed too. The whole entire thing was really funny. He asked,

"Does the car work?"

"Yes, it's just ugly."

"You know that car is not worth anything?"

"Yeah."

A few weeks past and a check came in the mail to my brother's house, which is where we were living during the interim period, until we moved into our house. I almost tore the envelope in half because it look so much like junk mail, but something told me to open it. I ripped the envelope open expecting some type of junk mail? It took my mind a few minutes to comprehend the information. It was a check from the insurance company for $1,400. I stared at the check in sheer disbelief! The Lord whispered, "Peoples Gas." I had to take a seat after that. Once again, I was outdone.

Almost in tears, I shared this information with my husband. I would have felt better about it if the check was a little bit over the amount that I owed Peoples gas, but the exact amount left me so irritated. I could not buy lunch or gas! There was nothing left for me!

So, I went directly to Peoples Gas the next day and paid them. I was so angry I could hardly stand it! I felt faint! It was a hard victory, but I did not feel victorious. I felt annoyed! This was a situation where I acted UGLY because I was selfish. I was not satisfied with the needed amount being supplied because I wanted more. My flesh could not stand doing the right thing without any gratification for it. Being obedient is hard on the flesh. My flesh wanted to be appeased. I think I would have been satisfied with even five dollars over the amount, for lunch or something.

Don't forget, I was a Christian, in relationship with God, and I loved the Lord, but as you can see, I was far from perfect. Instead of being grateful for God supplying my needs, I was irritated. This irritation stemmed from my selfishness (my flesh). I did not see the good in God supplying the need right away. I paid the bill out of sheer obedience. God was working out His righteousness in me.

What I learned from this experience is that God knows your heart. His word in **Hebrews 4:12** says, **"For the word of God is living and active. Sharper than any double-edged sword, it penetrates even to dividing soul and spirit, joints and marrow;** ***it judges the thoughts and attitudes of the heart."*****(NIV)** There are no secrets from Him, and if you ask Him to do something to enable you to accomplish His will that is what He will do. Once God does His part then you will have to "**man up**" and do your part, just as I did. God is righteous and He is going to work out His righteousness in each of us. Christians should not steal, or lie, or defraud anyone at any time.

13. Spoke Into Existence

One time my husband and I moved into my parent's house to help pay their bills. My dad's employer had gone bankrupt and they could no longer afford to pay their own expenses. Living there was very hard for both my husband and I, mainly because my grandmother also lived there. She could be incredibly mean and a busy body, but she was the matriarch of the house and she ruled with an iron fist. We lived with them for about one year. One night, my husband came home from work and said he couldn't take it anymore! We had to move. I told him that we did not have any money, because we were paying my parent's bills. He repeated himself, "We have to move." I was hurt and very concerned about what was going to happen to my parent's home if we left them. That night, when we got into the bed, I began to ask my husband questions. I asked him, "Where would you want to live?"

"Someplace close to Joey's school."

"How many bedrooms?"

"Two bedrooms and a den."

"Hardwood floors or carpet?"

"Carpet, with a dining room, a nice sized kitchen, in a two-flat brownstone with a fireplace."

We fell asleep talking about it. The next day he called me at work. He was very excited. He had gotten a $1,000 bonus check! In David's mind this meant we could move! I did not think it was enough for us to move, but I suggested that we save it for our move.

The following day, work was extremely difficult for me. My manager was stomping on my very last nerve. One of my co-workers was talking on the phone, and she put her call on hold. She asked a question, but I did not hear her. I was so distracted by what was going on with my manager. Another employee repeated the question, "Linda aren't you looking for an apartment?" My first response was no, and then I remembered my conversation with my husband and replied, "Yes."

I had an opportunity to speak to the owner. I asked her a few questions and we scheduled to meet. Unbelievably, the apartment had everything my husband had mentioned, including the small den and it being a two flat brown stone building. It was perfect. She informed us the rent was $500 a month with one month's security deposit. I could hardly believe it. We had exactly $1,000, we told her we wanted it and completed the necessary paper work and transaction.

We had three existing obstacles to face, my parent's financial situation, a moving truck and help to move. Well, I don't recall the details of my parent's, money situation, but all of a sudden they were okay. My brother Ricky was the only person who was available to help us move. I had only one, nearly exhausted, credit card. David and I went to the nearest U-haul rental store with my brother in tow. Amazingly, my brother knew the man working at the front desk. Apparently, they must have been good friends, because he let us use the truck for free. I could not believe it! We were in shock. We could not believe how quickly things turned around. The part of this story that demonstrated God's love for us the most was the fact that He sent the money before we knew about the apartment.

He took the edge off. God did not allow us to stress, or to even know about the apartment before we had the money to get it. God loved us in a special way and we got exactly what we asked for. When my husband and I were talking that night about what our new apartment would have in it, I had not considered it prayer. I was really just trying to calm my husband down, because he was so upset. We were talking, about our desired apartment, but really; we were speaking it into existence through our faith in God's ability to supply our need. As it reads in (**See Romans 4:17**) this was a demonstration of the power of God's Word activated in our mouths.

> **No, the message is very close at hand; it is on your lips and in your heart so that you can obey it. Deuteronomy 30:14(NLT)**

14. God Works Through People, Even Little Children

After many years of distractions, problems, sickness, death, issues and fears, situations arose that prompted me to continue my pursuit of a collegiate degree. I initially rejected the idea, because I was relatively successful without a degree. God had taken such great care of me, that I no longer saw the need to continue my education. I was doing better than most people that had degrees. However, God sent this woman May to deliver his message. May was in her last year of college at a major university. Sometimes, she would ask me to help her with her homework. I thought her asking for my help was strange, since I had dropped out of college and all. However, I helped her as best I could each time she asked.

During a conversation one day I told her, I did not have a college degree, only a General Education Diploma (GED). She appeared to be surprised by that information and she asked me why I had not pursued a collegiate degree. The question annoyed me, because my reasons why, were very personal. I eventually confided in her the many obstacles I faced and my fear that prohibited me from continuing my education. She replied,

"That was then. What is your excuse now? Imagine how much further God could bless you with a degree."

She kept telling me how smart I was and that my not pursuing a degree was just laziness. May was born and raised in Haiti, and her perspective and concepts on education were very different than mine. She felt that most Americans did not take advantage of the educational opportunities that were available to them. She had no understanding for my lack of interest and enthusiasm for higher education. She stated that she felt led by God to encourage me to go back to school.

Her questions plagued me, because they forced me to ask myself questions that I really did not want to face. What was I really scared of? The truth was… that I had been out of school for so long…and only had a GED to begin with...Truths, nonetheless, EXCUSES. School exposed how very little I knew, even on the foundational level. In every other arena of my life I was considered smart. But in school, I "felt" stupid, and I felt others could see that as well. May's questions prompted a forgotten dream of finally graduating from someplace. The only graduation I ever had was 8th grade. At that time in my life, I was filled with promise. I was a very bright student and everyone expected me to become something special.

No one expected me to become a dropout and a teenage mother. I had been accepted into a reputable high school, and my parents were very proud of me. Once I became pregnant, I continued my education at a high school for pregnant, teen-aged girls. However, I was forced to drop out after my son was born, to care for him. I received my General Education Diploma in August 1986. Eight years later in 1994 I started my collegiate Journey, I decided to go back to school. Incredibly, I was accepted into a major university and struggled like you would not believe to keep my head above water.

The years of missed schooling were evident. I could no longer take the abuse of the professor's instruction, and lack of understanding or concern for my inability to keep up. Eventually, I transferred to another major university. I was doing really well at the university when suddenly, my father got sick with cancer in 1995. I stopped attending school 1996 when it was apparent that my help was needed. My mother, my sister and I loved my dad. We expressed our love by doing what families do. We transported him to and from the hospital; cared for him, cleaned and made him feel comfortable until he made his transition.

The day after he passed, I found out I was pregnant with my second son, David. Who was born in the fall of 97 about a year later I got pregnant with my daughter Kaylin and had her in 1999. My daughter was 4 years old when I had the conversation with May.

Now there I was, realizing what I was facing, if I decided to go back to school. Going back to school seven years later from when I initially started felt ridiculous. Rolling this idea over in my mind was exhausting and it made me address my deepest fear. Which was, that everybody would discover how really stupid I was. This was a terrible struggle for me.

I had so many layers of insecurity and of course there was the issue of money. After several discussions with God, I finally began the process of getting into school.

Dreadfully, I took care of all the necessary paperwork, transferring grades, completing applications, and registration. During the registration process, I was informed that my credits were not accepted, because I had been out of school for too long. I was so disappointed! I did not have many to begin with, but I had previously earned them, and I wanted the credit for my work. Plus, that meant more school for me. Yuk!!!!

When I got into the car with my family, my husband asked what was wrong?

"Nothing."

"I am not moving this car until you tell me."

I was trying so hard not to cry, but the tears came anyway. My two small children were sitting in the backseat. I began to explain why I was so upset. I told him that all my credits did not transfer. It was like I was starting over from scratch.

My 6-year-old son said,

"Mommy, you have to start over from kindergarten?"

"No."

"From first grade?" He questioned.

"No."

"You *still* get to go to college?" My son asked earnestly.

"Yes."

"That's not so bad!" He exclaimed.

We all laughed so hard and I recognized God used my son to help me see that things were not as bad as I was making them out to be. In **Matthew 21:16, Jesus said, "..Yea; have ye never read, Out of the mouth of babes and sucklings thou hast perfected praise?"(KJV)**

We were able to enjoy the rest of the day. Later, I found out that the school decided to accept half of my credits. I also found out that I'm not stupid at all. As a matter of fact, I am still very bright and have been on the Honors Society for the last two months. I love how God moves through people even my own children.

Do not forget about your adversary. The devil is focused on your destruction. He does not like you at all and will try to tear you down and attempt to make you believe lies about yourself. Remind yourself that you are more than a conqueror.

> **Nay, in all these things we are more than conquerors through him that loved us. Romans 8:37(KJV)**

15. Drove Out By Mice: First House

One day, while living in the apartment we believed God for, I saw a little mouse. That same mouse was everywhere I looked. I called my mother to tell her about my mouse predicament. "What makes you think it's only one mouse?" she asked. I was thoroughly perturbed and disgusted by the mere thought. She said, "When you see a mouse, you can bet your bottom dollar there are others." My husband and I went to the store right away and purchased sticky pads to catch the critters. We placed the mice traps all over the apartment.

The next day, all of the sticky pads we had put down had mice on them. I could not believe how many mice we caught. I called the landlord and told her about the situation. In a nonchalant tone, she said, "Mice get in." What a big help she was! I told her that was unacceptable and she needed to call an exterminator. Over the next several weeks, some mice had died in the walls. It was downright awful! The rotten, putrid smell was sickening, and the stench of flea bitten decay just lingered in the air. We could not escape it! I kept calling the landlord complaining, but she refused to be proactive in the matter.

I was praying to God to get rid of the mice, but He did not. My prayer went something like this:

Lord God, I know you control everything in the earth, and there is nothing too hard for you. I know you are aware of my problem and you see these mice in the place you blessed my husband and I with. Lord, please remove these mice from here.

After my praying to God, it seemed as though the menacing mice got bolder! The mice would be waiting in the bathroom, in between my husband's legs as he ran bath water. The mice would also sit on the stove, waiting for us to come home. These mice were very bold and would not flinch. They would threateningly stare us down. I knew Chicago rats had a reputation, but the mice too? They would boldly scratch on the wood and walls so loudly it would keep us awake. I was petrified! I was disappointed that God would not take the pestilence away and I knew He had the power to do so.

In June, when the landlord left the lease for us to sign, we sanely refused. Nevertheless, in September, I decided to go ahead and sign it, because winter was coming. I needed to feel secure about my living arrangement…mice and all. At that juncture, the landlord decided that she did not want to extend us the lease. She said I was "petty". I was peeved to say the least.

Suddenly, it seemed my situation went from bad to worse. We were still living in the mouse-infested apartment, without the security of a lease, and with the knowledge of a Chicago winter steadily approaching. In addition, the landlord who just told me I was "petty", had made me feel as though she might evict us at any time. I was so upset!

I went to my mother's house to vent. On my way there I could not believe my eyes. The house I prayed for when I was 17 yrs. old was on the market for sale. I parked in front of the house and cried. I don't know how long I was there, but I cried until I was tired.

If there was one thing I knew for sure, it was that I did not understand God. Why would this house be on sale now when I did not have any money to buy it? Why now? I prayed for this house years ago. I asked God to let me be able to buy the house when I grew up, and I asked Him not to let the owners die in the house. Now there I was sitting in my car, on a cold, rainy September night, and there was a "For Sale "sign on the house that I prayed for years ago. This situation was much too much. I went to my mother's house and vented all my troubles.

"You can get that house." My mother said emphatically.

"How?" I asked, "I have no money!"

"Both you and your husband have good jobs. You can purchase the house." She encouragingly said. "Call the realtor tomorrow and check the house out. If you want it you can have it."

I shared the information with my husband and he said, "Let's take a look, it wouldn't hurt to take a look." The realtor met us and showed us the house, as best he could under the circumstances. It was dusk and the electricity was off, so we had to look very quick. Everything looked outdated and old, but I still wanted the house. It was a decent size house. It had a large family room and it would be *my own* property. If we got the house, it would mean no more apartments with mice and crummy landlords!

When we were leaving, the realtor asked if we were interested in purchasing the house.

"YES!" I said quicker than lightning.

My husband almost threw his neck out looking back at me, because we had no money.

The realtor asked when we would be able to put down the earnest money.

"Tomorrow." I said just as quickly. "How much?"

"One thousand dollars." The realtor informed us.

My husband could not take it anymore. He asked to speak to me in private.

"What are you doing?! When did you start lying like this?"

"I don't know, it came out of my mouth before I knew it."

"I am going to tell him the truth." He fervently stated.

"Please don't embarrass me." I pleaded. "I will call

him tomorrow and cancel the deal."

After this ordeal, we went directly to my mother's house. David and I told her about the house and what had transpired. My mother walked into her bedroom and came out with a check for one thousand dollars! We could not believe it!

I asked my mother how she had gotten so much money. She said things had gotten much better. She reminded us of when we had been a blessing to her, by taking care of her for the year we had lived with her. We rejoiced every step of the way!

My husband was really amazed at how things were working out. After we put down the earnest money, somebody called me and asked what colors I wanted the rooms painted, and what color carpet I wanted. The questions took me by surprise, because I thought we were buying the house in the initial condition it was presented. Then my grandmother started calling me daily, to keep me abreast of what the contractors were fixing on *my* house. The day before closing they called us for a final walk through.

We had not walked through the house since that dark day in September. It was two months later and we could not believe what we were seeing. It was beautiful! At the entrance, the foyer was painted a sparkly white. The living room was painted butter yellow, and trimmed in antique white. They had installed light beige carpet throughout the living room and dining room. It looked so huge, larger than I remembered. Every room was painted and trimmed with new carpet and light fixtures. It was absolutely beautiful!!! On top of that, we were able to get our deposit back from the landlord, because we never signed the lease.

When I look back, I see God so very clear. While in a perceived negative experience, we cannot always see or readily embrace that God is working things out for our good Afterward, we can quite often see how God was moving on our behalf. I believe it went something like this in the spirit realm. Prior to the house being put on the market, the owner went to live with her daughter. God had to get my attention. He allowed the mice to come into our apartment so we *would not* sign the lease. If the mice had not came when they did, we could have signed the lease and would not have been desperately trying to buy the house. If we had signed the lease, I really believe the landlord would have sued us for breech of contract and we definitely would not have received our $500 deposit back.

Scripture **Romans 8:28** comes to mind, **"All things work together for the good to them that love God, to them who are called according to his purpose."(KJV)** All those events, independent of each other, were pretty painful, but together they all worked out for good. In every instance, when I did not know what to do, God sent somebody with information. He is a very present help in a time of need.

> **God is our refuge and strength, always ready to help in times of trouble. Psalm 46:1(NLT)**

16. Second House

The day before closing on our second house, Yolanda, a friend and a woman of faith called me. She said that we were going to receive money back at the closing. I wanted so badly to tell her that she had a bad connection, because according to my calculations this was impossible. We had put down less than 1% of the purchase price. Knowing this, her words sounded like a lie.

The same day the bank called to tell us how much to bring to the closing. I made a notation of the amount and the numbers seemed too small. At closing, we did indeed receive a check, just like the Yolanda said. After the closing my husband and I went to Red Lobster to celebrate.

Once I remembered what Yolanda said, I immediately called to tell her she was correct. I almost couldn't eat my dinner, because of God's prophetic word.

This experience taught me that I would not always be in "the-know". Sometimes, it's strictly blind faith. What I can do and should do is to confidently put my trust in God and know that He will always work things out for my good.

The day after I wrote this chapter, I saw Yolanda and told her I had written a chapter about the time when the Lord used her to let me know I would receive money back at my closing. She shared with me how my initial reaction hurt her and made her feel embarrassed, because she recognized that I did not believe her. She told me how she felt when she told me what God had revealed to her, that people don't receive and don't believe, and how that sometimes weighed on her. I told her although I did not believe her, she was right. I never shared my thoughts about the situation until it was over. I might have thought she was confused prior to it playing out, but I loved her and did not want to say anything bad about her to anyone. If her words had not come true I was not going to mention it.

Some people feel like Yolanda is much too deep. I believe that she is in tune with the spirit and obedient to speaking what God says to her and she flows in her gifting as God intends.

> **Now these are the gifts Christ gave to the church: the apostles, the prophets, the evangelists, and the pastors and teachers. Ephesians 4:11(NLT)**

17. My Strength is Small

If you fail under pressure, your strength is too small. Proverbs 24:10(NLT)

The first time I was made aware of this scripture was from Yolanda. I was in a situation that had me on a continuous cycle of aggravation. It was the people closest to me, causing me harm. During this time, I would see Yolanda daily, because she was my daycare provider. She was aware of my trouble and often shared the word of God with me, which sustained me during these times. I often looked to her for advice.

There was one particular situation so ugly I wanted to just crawl up in a ball and disappear. The same situation was cyclical and kept rearing its ugly head. Each and every time it presented itself, my reaction was the same. During one of these many episodes, I was telling Yolanda what was happening.

She told me, "If you faint in the day of adversity your strength is small."

I could not believe what she was saying that to me, when I needed her to support me. Yes, I was having a pity party, but she would not allow me to take her for the ride. I had experienced so many negative situations that a "victim mentality" was creeping up on me. I needed a shoulder to cry on and instead she gave me a scripture. I asked her where the scripture was located and she responded, Proverbs 24:10. I read the scripture several times in disbelief. I was astonished at the existence of this scripture and the fact that I had never read it. The totally amazing part is God knew I did not know that scripture and He dispatched Yolanda to share that information with me when I needed it most.

After giving it some thought, I was grateful that He loved me like that. I was also grateful that God gifted her to speak His word with authority and love the way that she did. Yolanda did not buckle under the pressure of delivering this message to me. I could be pretty rough when I wanted to, but she truly was a soldier in delivering His word, which has aided me tremendously over the years.

This scripture keeps me in check more than I can explain. Once you know better you should do better! The last thing I wanted to embody was an unfruitful Christian. Everyone who knows me knows that if they are giving me advice I'm going to ask, "Is that your opinion or the word of God, and if it is the word of God tell me where I can read it."

It was not my intent to be annoying, but I realized that many times people say what they think you want to hear or give their own personal opinions. Though appreciated, this does not help me at all. They are giving me their opinion when I simply need the Word. I need to know what and where the Word is for the particular situation, for that moment and for future references, because you don't know what you don't know and knowledge is power.

18. Trip to Washington

My oldest son had no recollection of his father. He was two or three years old when they last saw each other. At about fifteen years of age my son expressed an interest in seeing him. I tried several times to locate him, but was unsuccessful. Once I finally located him, I made arrangements to visit. I bought two coach tickets to Washington DC.

I was pleased that I could provide this closure for my son. Knowing his father was vital to him. He was looking forward to finally seeing his father. I had given him pictures years before, but they had gotten misplaced. I only had one fuzzy picture left of his father. It was taken the summer his father left for the Army.

A few weeks before our big trip, my mother called and asked,

" Are you wearing your fur coat to Washington?"

"I don't know mama. I really had not thought about it. Why?"

"What do you mean you have not thought about it? I would wear it just for him to see that I came out just fine without him!"

"This trip is not about me. It's about my son. I don't want to do anything that may be perceived as otherwise."

"Your success is evident, no matter what!"

"Thanks mom, I really appreciate the compliment, but wearing the fur coat is an extravagant gesture, and I don't want to distract from the real purpose of the trip."

"Linda, people wear fur coats all the time. It's going to be cold in Washington. You know it's winter there too?

Fur coats are to be worn in the winter, and what's the purpose of having a fur coat if you're not gonna wear it?"

"Mom, I still don't think it's a good idea, but I'll think about it."

"What's there to think about? Whatever! You're wearing the coat!"

"Okay mom, I'll talk to you later."

She would not let it go, and she rode me about wearing that fur coat until the day I left. She was determined that I would wear it. I could not fully understand her reasoning for wanting this so badly. I chalked it up to pride. I was having some anxiety about the trip. I had a deep sense that my son would never see his father. Of course that thought troubled me and left me with a sense of foreboding. I could not imagine traveling for the purpose of them to meet and they not meet. The sense of apprehension remained.

My son's father called me the day before we were to leave, and I even had an opportunity to speak to his wife. She seemed like a nice lady. This made me feel so much better. Maybe it was all going to work out after all. My son was so nervous. This trip carried a lot of first time opportunities for him. It was our first trip alone, his first plane ride, and the first time he would see his father. I was trying very hard to hide my nervousness so that he would feel secure. My mother called right before we left the house to make sure I had my fur coat on. I said, "Mom, I'm gonna wear it only, because it's so important to you." She replied, "Good! The entire time I was thinking this is nuts and I did not really understand, but I wore it anyway.

My husband David drove us to the airport. I was so nervous. This was a first for me too. I had never traveled without David. He was my security blanket. I could always depend on him to figure it out, or read the map, or whatever. This was going to be a different experience, because for the first time, I would be traveling without my him When we got to the airport, my husband prayed a long prayer and kissed us goodbye. He had the strangest look on his face and it concerned me for a minute, but I shook it off. I had to focus on the task at hand, which was taking my son to see his father.

When we were boarding the plane, we walked through the first class section where all the large, leather seats are located, to the coach section of the plane where our seats were located. My son asked,

"What's that section up there?"

"That's first class, and first class is expensive. The people who can afford those seats are treated special. These seats are called coach which are more affordable."

"Have you ever sat up there before?"

"No, even the coach seats cost too much."

"Ma, one day, you and I are going to fly first class."

"Boy, do you have any idea how much those seats cost? I'm barely able to pay for these."

While the words were yet coming out my mouth, I remembered God's Word. It says, "Call those things that be not as thou they were." God reminded me of the power of believing and speaking His promises into existence. I told Joey to forget what I said, that he was right, and that I was wrong. I agreed with him that we would ride first class one day. I told him that what he said was biblical and what I said was worldly. I also explained that I was challenged in the area of applying God's word to everything. He smiled and said, "Ma, that's okay, nobodies perfect." I replied, but we're supposed to be busy trying, he laughed.

Once we landed in Washington, I had the eeriest feeling I've ever had. My hairs were standing up on the back of my neck and I could not explain why. I later found out that my son was experiencing the same thing. His dad was supposed to meet us at the airport, but he was not there. I called his house, but there was no answer. I was trying to think logical like they must be stuck in traffic or something, but my gut was telling me something different. We waited for a while, and then my son said, "Can we just go to the hotel?" I said "Sure".

When we arrived at the hotel I immediately checked with the front desk to see if anyone came by, or left a message for me. The answer was no. At that point I was getting irritated because I still had not received a call from my son's father. My son was looking crazy and stressed out, and I had nothing to offer. I called his house again. His wife answered the phone. This time she was very mean. She was being very curt, and I could barely understand what she was saying, because of her thick accent. I replied, please just let him know that we are here. He called me hours later. He had a terrible attitude and I could not understand why.

A couple of days before we actually got to Washington DC, he was receptive to our visit, but now he was acting like he was too busy to see us. I was so angry, but I had to keep a cool head for my son. The original plan was for his father to come by the hotel, but during our call he informed me that he would not be able to stop by. He said he only had about 15 to 20 minutes to meet with us. He gave me the address and the time we were supposed to meet him. Oh how I wanted to curse him out. There we were visiting him and he was stating that he was too busy to take an hour break to see the son he has never known. I replied, "Okay, we'll see ya then." My son and I tried to keep busy that night. We booked some tours, since it was clear to us that he would not be spending much time with his father.

The next day we woke up early and went to see the sights. We went to every famous place in Washington DC, including the White House. While we were at the White House, my son had a conflict with this officer/guard who was flirting with me. It was the third time that day that someone had flirted with me in front of my son. It happened earlier in the mall, and once at another place that we were at. My son claimed this guy was looking at my butt, and that made him crazy. I said, "What difference does it make. He can't even see it because I have on this big ole coat." My son replied, "It's the principle of the thing ma!"

I tried to calm the situation down by intervening on my son's behalf. The officer was ready to hand cuff my son at that point because of my son's bold disrespect to an officer of the law. The last thing I needed was for either of us to be thrown in jail. I apologized for my son's behavior, and the officer replied, "You need to talk to him ma'am. He needs to calm that attitude down. Someone will seriously hurt him without a second thought." I was outdone by the level of annoyance the officer displayed, he was suppose to be professional, and a keeper of peace, yet, he was acting just as out of control as my teen-aged son. Couldn't the officer tell that my son was just a kid? I did not understand why the officer was responding so terribly? The whole thing wore me out.

After a long day of keeping ourselves occupied, it was time to meet his dad. We hailed a cab and gave him the address of where we needed to go. He was a Jamaican man, about 55 years old. He looked in the rearview mirror and said, "You need to work on forgiveness. Forgiveness is good." I don't remember everything else he said, but as he was talking, he reminded me of my deceased father. The second I was getting ready to share that thought with my son My son reached across the seat and touched my arm and said, "He looks like granddaddy." I told the cab driver that he strongly resembled my deceased father. He smiled, and kept looking back at us in the rear view mirror. He pulled over and said, "This is it." I paid him the fare, but before he drove off he said, "Don't forget that forgiveness is always good." I said, "Okay."

I did not know what he was talking about, because I did not have any unresolved forgiveness. Not even with my son's dad. It was what it was, and I did not harbor any ill will or anger toward him. At that moment, the only emotion I felt was excitement. They were finally going to meet. After the cab left, we looked around for his father. He was not there. I looked at the address again to be sure we were at the right place. We asked some people walking by if we were at the right address. They said no. Well, to our surprise, the cab driver took us to the other side of town. He took us to the Pentagon.

I was so angry! Why would the cab driver do such a thing? It was not a free ride. I paid for that ride, and he purposefully sent us off. I then realized that I left one of my leather gloves in his cab. That about took me over the edge. I was about to start crying when I remembered that I had to be strong for my son. So, we found the subway and asked for directions to get our desired destination. The directions were complicated to me, but I was willing to try. The clerk suggested that we take a cab instead. I called my son's father to let him know we were still coming, but he did not answer. I was praying that he did not leave. I would hate for the entire trip to be a waste. My son informed me that there was a cab across the overpass, behind a shed. I said,

"What?"

"I saw it when we were driving to this place. It's right across the way."

Well, that meant we had to cross a busy, three-lane overpass on foot, and slide down the side of a snowy, iced embankment. I was not interested. We waited and waited for a cab, then my son forced the issue and then off we went, across the overpass and down the embankment. There I was, slipping and sliding down an icy embankment in my fur coat and cute boots. My feet were starting to hurt and I was trying so hard not to cry. Once we reached the bottom of the embankment, fear gripped my heart and a hundred questions flooded my mind all at once. I thought, what if this supposed cab driver was a serial killer? What was he doing parked behind this shed? Who would park here? Wonder if he's with a prostitute?

I wanted to go back so badly. I looked back at the embankment, sizing it up to see if I could climb it in the boots I had on. I came to the conclusion that was not an option. I told my son to stay put because I did not want to scare the driver. I was walking toward the cab saying hello, are you for hire? We need a ride. An old, white man turned his head toward me and said, "Well, I was resting, but yeah, I'll give you a ride." I informed the driver that my son was with me and then I waved for my son to come over.

Once we got into the cab, he adjusted his rear view mirror the same way the other driver did and I thought to myself that was peculiar. I quickly began to explain how we wound up in that precarious situation. I gave him the address. The same as I did the other cab driver and he asked, "Do you have a gun on you?" It took my brain a moment longer than usual to process the question, because it was such a strange question to be asked. Was it possible that he thought we were trying to rob him? I replied, "No, why would you think that? Do I look like the type of person that would rob you?" He said, "No, but you need a gun if you want me to take you to this address."

"What? Are you for real?"

"Very."

"I usually don't take fares to this location, but I'll take you. You have to be ready to jump out quickly. You're not from around here are you?"

"No, we're from Chicago."

My son sat silently during this entire dialogue. The cab driver asked, "Who are you going see?"

"My ex-husband, his father."

"Well, if I were you, I would not go. You have on that nice fur coat and would be a sitting duck, but it's your dime either way."

Instantly, I thought if somebody tried to do anything to me my son would die trying to protect me. I did not realize that tears were all over my face, and I could not stop them. It was like an overflowing river. The cab driver turned off the meter and said, "Take your time, it's your choice. Where are you staying?"

"The Hilton."

"That's a nice hotel, if he was really interested in seeing you he would meet you there. Why would he send you to this place?"

My son made a strange noise and said, "Take us to the hotel." I was hurt down to the bone. I did not understand why he would agree to see us and not see us. My gut was right from the beginning. I wanted to find his dad and set him on fire. I was as mad as they come. When we got back to the hotel, I went directly to the bathroom and cried my eyes out. My son said he needed to go for a walk, and I understood that he needed to grieve alone.

I planned to order room service, wait for my son to fall asleep, and then take a cab to his father's house. I was so angry that I was planning to hurt him in some way. At least break a window or something. I wanted so badly to get him back. I called the front desk to check if I had any messages. There were no messages. I checked my cell phone for messages and there were none.

Once my son got back to the room, we both tried to act normal, but we were both deeply wounded. Our wounds were too fresh, and we both needed to mend them in our own personal ways. We called room service and I let my son order whatever his heart desired. It was the best tasting, room service food we ever had. We ate, and then lay across our beds. I tried to stay awake, but I felt drugged and could not keep my eyes open. My son said that he thought I fell into a coma or something. He said he never seen me sleep that hard before.

The phone awakened us. It was the front desk informing us that our tour was leaving shortly. We jumped up, got dressed, and off we went. We had a totally awesome day. The Lord made sure that we were totally occupied so that we could not focus on our pain. We went to see all the sights, saw the play "Shear Madness", and then went to dinner at an upscale restaurant that was highly recommended by the hotel. We were so exhausted when we got back to the hotel that we fell straight to sleep.

Our flight left early the next morning, and wouldn't you know it, we woke up late again. We were throwing clothes into suitcases and rushing to catch our plane. Once there, while we were waiting to board the plane, I noticed a lady looking at us, but I did not think much of it. We showed our plane tickets and boarded the plane. The same lady that was staring at us was on the plane. She was a stewardess. Now she was smiling at us. She said, "Don't get too comfortable because you're going to fly first class today." I could not believe what I was hearing. My son looked at me like I was totally gullible. We found our seats and I kept my coat on. My son said, "Ma, you might as well take your coat off. That lady was not for real."

While the words were still in his mouth, she said, "Excuse me Sir, and Ma'am, please follow me to first class." I smiled and stood up. I had to give my son a bit of a nudge to follow her. I thought he was in shock. My son actually spoke this into existence through his words and faith during our flight to there. Neither of us expected such a quick response. First class was awesome! The size and comfort of the seats, the food and the drinks, and those lovely warm, hand towels made it the best plane experience I ever had.

When my son went to the restroom, I asked the stewardess why she decided to place us in first class. She said, “Whenever I have extra seats in first class I try to bless somebody with them. I asked God whom should I bless today, and he pointed you all out to me. I shared that my son had spoken these words of faith on the flight there. I also told her what happened to us in Washington DC, about his dad not showing up. She was so overwhelmed by the story that she began to cry. I asked her to please be discreet because I did not want my son to feel any further discomfort.

One of my son’s favorite rappers also happened to be in first class, and we were able to take a few pictures with him once we got off the plane. God made everything so wonderful and had taken the sting out of that huge disappointment. I saw God’s grace and the special care He was providing us through His people. Once we got home, the strangest thing happened. My husband had to run an errand and decided to take the kids with him. That rarely ever happens. I’m never alone. Well, that was a first. I went upstairs to rest. Once I got still, God started speaking. He made it clear that our lives had been spared. That was the second cab driver’s sentiment, but that was too hard for me to wrap my brain around at the time. He told me that I needed to forgive him and continue to move on. I then remembered the first cab driver and his message of forgiveness. Then it dawned on me that his father had not even called to ask why we hadn’t shown up.

When I got back to Chicago, I found out that everyone had been praying for our safe return because they felt that we were in danger. When I returned to work, I opened my emails and saw that a Christian co-worker had sent me an email the day I left to go to Washington. She intended for me to receive the blessing before I left. Her email was basically bidding me farewell and good time, but her real message was a word from God that said, “No weapon formed against you shall prosper!” This totally blew me away because before I left, I did not sense that I would be in any danger. I just felt like we would never get a chance to see his father. God did not want me to be aware of any pending danger because He wanted me to do this for my son. If I had a premonition about any potential danger, I would never have gone. God wanted me to do what was best for my son. I did, but he also wanted me to know that he had provided protection.

> **For he will rescue you from every trap and protect you from deadly disease. Psalm 91:3(NLT)**

From this experience I know God as a protector. I never found out exactly what was waiting for me at that destination in Washington DC, and I could live the rest of my life without knowing. I was so happy to be safe and back at home. I followed God's instructions and forgave my son's father for everything that happened along with everything that did not happen. We did not hear from his dad again until five years later, and only because of God's expressed love for me, was I able to welcome him when he surfaced.

19. Unconditional Example

In the summer of 2005 my husband and I went to breakfast at a near by restaurant. We were quickly seated and began to review the menu. My attention was drawn to this noisy little girl sitting with her parent's cattycorner from us. I immediately noticed that she was handicap. She had Down's syndrome.

I was amazed at how the mother cared for the little girl. She continually calmed her by stroking her hair, and holding her hands to comfort her. I've never seen so much love displayed before my eyes. My husband followed my gaze to the family, and then he wanted to move.

My husband stated he wanted to enjoy a quiet, normal breakfast without our children. Plus, he took notice of the affect this scene was having on me. He asked me why I was about to cry. I explained that I could actually *see* her love. I told him that I did not want to move because that would be rude. I would behave myself and not cry, but focus on enjoying our time together.

The little girl got louder and louder until her food arrived. Her mom positioned the food so that she could feed her daughter without the threat of her daughter knocking the food over. She moved her own food as far over as she possibly could. Her husband began to eat his breakfast while the mother fed her daughter. I was thinking in my heart why doesn't the dad help. The mother could not even get a bite of her own food. As quick as I had the thought the father took over the feeding responsibility. The mother was enjoying her food now and everyone was content. I realized what I thought about the dad was pre-judgment and that I was incorrect. This day stuck with me I thought about it myriad times and it always moves me to tears. It has had the same effect each time I've thought of it.

The Lord used this experience to show me how to love my firstborn son. He told me to love my son Joey like he had Down's syndrome. I was annoyed by this command because Joey did not have Down's syndrome. I thought I was doing a good job loving him already. The Holy Spirit reminded me of the little girl in the restaurant who had Down's syndrome. Needless to say the very mention of this little girl in the restaurant fully got my attention. I listened and pondered. God's conviction reminded me of the mother demonstrating unconditional love and she was not embarrassed about the condition of her child. She loved her just as she was without any pause or hesitation. She loved her daughter despite herself. She loved her without any conditional provisions. She just loved her.

The mother gave her daughter what she needed. She gave her love and care. She loved her without resentment of her illness, without obligation to feed her, and without a conditional disclaimer or requirement. She just loved her and anyone looking at her could see it… feel it.... get physically lost in its aura.

God allowed me to see this love demonstrated months prior to this little chat. He gave me a point of reference to aid me. I never knew that I had a problem in this area. I always gave my very best to my firstborn. Anybody watching would see a mother doing just that, but God saw so much more. God saw that *my* best was not what Joey needed at all. He saw that Joey needed unconditional, unadulterated love. There are lots of different types of love. The recipient of the love feels the clause that is attached to the love.

Like, I'll love you if you do this or that (Conditional love)

I love you because I'm expected to (Obligatory love)

I love you because you a reflection of me (Reflective love)

I'm going to give you a little history. I was 15 yrs. old when I gave birth to Joey, *but* he was not a mistake. His father and I decided to have a baby for two reasons.

The first reason was because his father wanted to have a child of his own. He had been adopted and badly wanted to genetically belong to someone. He wanted a family. I loved him and I wanted to help him become fulfilled.

Secondly, we thought, if I were pregnant, it would force my parents to allow us to get married. We thought we knew what we were doing. Finally, after months of trying, I got pregnant. Pregnancy was blissful, despite what people were saying about me. My man and I were having our love child.

After the birth of our son things began to change quickly. We needed to take care of this baby. I was stressed to the max. In addition, my mother and grandmother were driving me crazy. His father could not keep a job and I strongly recommended he find stable work by any means necessary. Per my suggestion, he joined the Army. It appeared that we had an opportunity to have a real family. What we didn't bank on was the Army stationing him in Germany. My parents were opposed to me going to Germany and I did not go. Long story short, we soon were bitter and divorced. I was alone raising my son in my mother's house.

Accepting this reality was very difficult and I fell into a very dark place for a while. I could not believe this was my reality. All of my dreams died a slow and painful death. God via my mother's love helped to resurrect me from this obscure abyss. The abyss was not a part of my plan. Raising a son alone was unchartered territory. I did not know what I was doing by any stretch of the imagination, but at some point I was determined not to be a complete failure. I wanted to prove to the world that I was a still a success despite my situation. I decided I would be the best single mom I could possibly be.

All was going well until Joey was in second grade when he asked me, "Where is my daddy?" He said all his friends had daddies. I told him that he had a dad too, but he lived far away. Keep in mind, before this conversation I was already internally bruised by just being in the situation. This was not supposed to be my life. In my mind, life had dealt me a bad hand and I was very hurt, but I was still moving forward. I'm sure my son felt my hurt, because hurting people, hurt people. I was internally angry, frustrated, stunned, and lonely. I loved my son the best I could with all those feelings living inside of me.

After I told my son about his father, I saw my son's heart turn dark along with his behavior. I've always regretted telling him the truth because it had the worst affect on him. I wished I had been more creative and said something like God is your father, maybe that would have made it better. I never had a peaceful moment after that conversation. He was constantly in trouble in school. We changed schools often because they would eventually put him out. My frustration grew because he was a reflection of me. The single black mother who was doing her absolute best and it was not good enough. Nothing I did was ever good enough.

I needed to raise a good son to show the world that I was not a failure. Yet, he was making me fail.

I sent him to the best private schools my money could afford. I would ride the bus for hours to get him were he needed to be. I would convince school directors to allow me to enroll my son into their schools and after a few weeks I would plead with them to allow him to stay. All of the hard work I put into trying to "raise him right" and still we were failures.

All the while, I knew he was difficult to raise because he had an emptiness in his heart that could only be filled by his father's acknowledgment and love. There is a song that speaks to this pain so pointedly. *These are the words:*

> *There is a hole in my heart that won't heal; there is a rage and a pain. Even now I still feel, even though*

I'm a man I don't quite understand, but that is what happens when you don't have a father.

When I first heard this melody I cried. Someone else had lived this kind of experience and wrote lyrics about it. That song encapsulated my son's pain. I tried my best to fill his void and make it better, but I could not fix it. This has troubled my son more than words can express. I made efforts for him to meet his father, but it did not work out. It was clear to us that his father did not want to see him.

The additional rejection my son experienced from the failed meeting in Washington hurt my son worst than anything. His darkness turned hard, which exhausted me to no end. I never stopped trying to help him, but it was seemingly all in vain. Then one day, the Lord told me to love Joey, just as though he had Down's syndrome. After a moment of confusion, I recalled the morning my husband and I went to breakfast together and saw that little girl. I remembered the love and patience the mother showed her little girl who had Down's syndrome it made me realize that this is how God must love us.

As humans, we are all handicapped because of our flesh. When we are born, we are born into sin. As human beings, we have a proclivity to sin. Sin, is what separates us from God. God has enough love to be patient, and allow us to go through whatever phase (rebelliousness, disobedience, pride, etc…) we are going through. God doesn't become frustrated and cast us away. His mercies are renewed every morning for us. **(See Lamentations 3:22-23)** God loves us despite ourselves and through any condition we may be in, even if we do not love ourselves, God loves us unconditionally. God loved us even unto His death.

But God commendeth his love toward us, in that, while we were yet sinners, Christ died for us. Romans 5:8 (KJV)

After this profound word from the God, I changed my behavior and love technique toward my son. The parent of a child that has Down's syndrome might have very limited expectations. The Lord instructed me to relieve Joey from my expectations. This perplexed me, because I felt everyone needed objectives and purpose to their life. According to how I figured expectations helped to foster growth.

The Lord used many Christians to drive home exactly what He wanted me to do and how to do it. For lack of a better word, I became a puppet, but really it was just obedience. At this point of my life, I understood that I just needed to follow God's direction.

You might not expect a child with Down's syndrome to go to college, or remember every instruction you give them. So, I had to let go of a lot of stuff. Amazingly, this release was liberating for the both of us. I told Joey he was free of every expectation, and I repented for everything I had ever done to make him feel like a disappointment, small, stupid, lazy, no good, slothful, aimless, in the way and shiftless. ***I told him from that day forward that I was just going to love him as he was, because he was my son***.

I explained to Joey, that my love was not going to be contingent on his actions. I was simply going to love him. I told him he was liberated and that I wanted him to set his own expectations. I began to slowly see him change. He tried me from time to time to see if I was serious, but I remained steady in my demonstration of love. I did not condone wrong behavior, but I did not judge. I loved him regardless of his behavior. I loved him despite the obvious imperfections. ***In doing this, I learned how God loves me and this exercise was priceless.*** Real, true love is freeing, and it makes things grow. It encourages… it nurtures… it makes one strong. It is the one absolute, necessary, essential, vital ingredient for everything.

> **Love is patient, love is kind. It does not envy, it does not boast, it is not proud. It is not rude, it is not self-seeking, it is not easily angered, it keeps no record of wrongs. Love does not delight in evil but rejoices with the truth. It always protects, always trusts, always hopes, always perseveres. I Corinthians 13:4-7(NIV)**

I also have learned that what I have to offer is not always what is needed. Furthermore, just because I give what I have doesn't mean that it will benefit the recipient. It was just the best I had to offer. My best does not always equal what is needed. I could give you lunch money, but if what you needed was somebody to have lunch with, what I offered would not have been good enough. Do you see the difference?

20. Vacation Cruise/Unbelievable Outcome

Many months before my son, his girlfriend and newborn baby moved in with us, I'd booked a family vacation to the Caribbean to witness a good friend get married. The cruise was to the Cayman Islands and Jamaica. We were all so excited. This was the first cruise for my children and I was so glad that we could afford to have this experience with them. Now that we had live-in guests, it turned my excitement for the upcoming cruise to fear and worry. I was very uncomfortable leaving my son and his family in our house alone for a week. During that time of their lives they both good judgment. They were very immature and required lots of instruction and guidance.

Finally, it was vacation time. You would think that I would have been excited right? I was completely and utterly stressed out. I took them shopping for food and gave them money in the unlikely event they had an emergency. I took all these precautionary measures to make sure their needs were met. I talked extensively to both of them about my expectations. They both appeared to understand and tried to assure me that they could be trusted to take care of the house and to use good judgment. They encouraged me to relax, have a good time and enjoy my long deserved vacation.

I created a list of things I needed to accomplish before leaving for the cruise. One of them was to either put my fur coat in storage or in the trunk of my car. It was insured, but I just wanted to take away any potential temptation, risk or exposure due to any company my son might of had while I was away. I was so stressed out because I had so many things to do to get me in a peaceful state of mind. Of course, the one thing that was the most important to me was the thing I forgot to do, which was to put away my fur coat. And wouldn't you know it, I didn't remember this until we were in the limo on our way to the airport.

From that moment on, the entire trip was terrible. On the way to the airport, my son called me on my cell phone to tell me my home phone was disconnected. I forgot to post the payment on-line, which resulted in its disconnection. I was so annoyed because the payment was for such a small amount that I did not think the phone company would disconnect the phone. Of course, I immediately had to call the phone company and make the payment. The thought of my son with my newborn grandbaby without a working phone was more than I could bear! Several other small, annoying things happened before we got on the plane. I could not wait to get this trip over with and return home. I was a mess before the vacation even started. I never achieved peace of mind and I allowed the enemy to steal all of my joy.

My friend's wedding was very beautiful. However, I was not impressed with the cruise ship or any of its amenities. I was doing my very best to act as if everything was okay, but my friends saw right through me. On the last night of the cruise, I was on a natural high. I was so excited about returning home the next day. This was the best day of the entire vacation. I'd already packed our suitcases and sat them in the hall. We were getting dressed for dinner when the captain notified us over the ship's intercom of Hurricane Katrina, which touched down in Miami were we where suppose to dock. He said we could possibly be at sea for an additional couple of days.

At that point I almost lost my mind. My husband did his best to comfort me by making the best out of a bad situation, but I could tell he was stressed out too. The additional days at sea were filled with fear and seasickness. I'd tried several times to reach my son by phone, which was futile because of the type of cell phone we had and the severe weather interference. Later that night, we heard that only certain types of phones were getting calls through.

Finally, we found someone with that type of phone and asked if we could use it to call our family. We were allowed to borrow the phone. However, in order to get a decent signal we had to go out on deck where it was extremely windy, and raining cats and dogs. I managed to reach my mother who sounded surprisingly jovial. She kept saying, “Everything was going to be alright.” She also assured me that everything at my house was all right. I did not believe her. I was a mess. I stayed in my room and smoked cigarettes every chance I got. I began to feel extra sick and guilty of smoking at the same time. I thought the whole cruise was being affected by my disobedience. This thought terrified me.

You need to know that I do not smoke. I think I picked up the first cigarette the first day of the cruise. The smoking was directly related to my stress over what might be happening in my house, the cruise itself, and Hurricane Katrina. The fact that they kept showing the film “The Titanic” was making me go crazy. Things continued to digress which ultimately lead me to repentance. My smoking changed into praying. I tried very hard to stay away from everyone. When we finally docked in Miami I wanted to kiss the ground. I was so relieved and elated! More drama occurred from the airport to my house, but it’s not worth mentioning in detail. Just know that this vacation was no cakewalk. Nothing about the entire experience was easy or enjoyable. When we finally pulled up in front of my house everything seemed normal. My son David went to knock on the door and fell in the house. The door was not locked just pushed up and nobody was home.

My son and his girlfriend had left the house and left the door unlocked. Why? Why would they do that? I was livid! My kids entered the house first while my husband and I were getting the luggage. When I entered the house two things hit me at once. The smell, and my daughter voice asking, “Why would they do this to our house?” It took a moment for my eyes to adjust, but once they did I was out done. It was a pigsty! What made this even worse for me was the fact that I made sure to call my son from Miami in order to let him know what time we would be home. They had ample time to get the house in order before we got there.

The more I looked around my house the angrier I got. I was fuming and about to spin out of control when my husband grabbed me by both shoulders and said, "Linda, mental retardation." I said, "What?" He said, "You know, mental retardation, love him like Jesus!" He was using the wrong words, but at that point I understood what he was trying to get me to remember. He was trying to get me to recall what God told me about my son and my ability to love him unconditionally.

Recall the mother and her little girl with Down's syndrome from chapter 19. Needless to say, once I remembered God's instructions, I was able to calm down. I thanked God for my husband that day for remembering what God said to help me get back on track. I was so far off my square it was ridiculous. The damage to the house was insignificant, superficial but annoying. Things like garbage on the floor, in the living room, dining room, family room, bedrooms, and the kitchen, basically, every room. The dirty dishes in the sink smelled awful! To top everything off, they had the nerve to sleep in my bed!

There were two reasons why this was supposed to be the proverbial straw that broke the camel's back. The first reason is because my bedroom is my personal space. I purposefully left it a mess to discourage any temptation they might have to sleep in my bed. I even bragged to some of my friends on the boat at what I had done. But what I did not consider was the type of people they were. My mess, what I considered dirty, was clean to them. It did not cause them to pause or halt in any way from jumping up in my bed. My plan to protect my space was foiled, and my space had been violated! The second reason was the only thing I could think about, and wanted to do from the supposed last day of the cruise was crawl up in my bed and get a goodnight's sleep. I shared this with anyone and everyone within earshot of me, from the moment we docked in Miami until the limo picked us up from the airport. So, after finally arriving home and not being able to get right into the bed was the worst-case scenario for me. It took Godly intervention, via my husband to get and keep me on my square.

After they chilled in my room all week they made half an effort to wash the sheets. However, they did not complete the task. The sheets were still in the washing machine when we arrived home. My son and his girlfriend arrived about 20 minutes later acting like everything was okay. I calmly asked them to fix my house. My husband put fresh sheets on the bed and put me in it. The next day I talked to both of them about what had occurred and instructed them to do better. I wanted so badly to put them out and rid myself of this burden, but it was not time yet. They had been living in our house for six months and were destroying our property and spirits at an enormous rate. I managed to endure them until God released me from this extraordinary weight.

One night that week, my husband and I went to dinner. I don't even think it was a week after we returned home from vacation. Before we left, David was connecting the video camera to the computer to transfer the footage of our vacation to DVD. He said he would finish up after we came back from dinner. We went straight to bed when we got home. The next day, David went to finish the video, but the video camera was gone. My husband searched around the whole house thinking that perhaps he just put it away or hid it out of habit before we left.

We dreaded asking my son and his girlfriend about the video camera. When we asked, they both pleaded innocent, but I was very suspicious because to my knowledge, they were the only people in the house. Video cameras just don't walk away unless carried by human feet. We lost all the footage of the worst vacation ever along with the new video camera we bought specifically for the trip. The video camera we bought on credit was not even a month old. The fact that I still had to pay for something we no longer had was additionally frustrating.

My husband's feelings were hurt because he knew that our son was aware that the video camera was special to him. This was the second time a video camera had been stolen from my husband. The first one was stolen while our house was on the market for sale. During the open house someone stole the first camera. I'd told my husband a million times to put away anything valuable to him, since the house would be open to the public. Of course, he never listened and someone eventually stole the little handheld video camera. David was hurt and embarrassed for not listening, and I was fighting the worst case of 'I told you so!' in America.

When David realized the second video camera was missing searched through the house, the car and the garage looking for it. This got on my last nerve, because I knew our son had taken it. David was hoping that by habit he hid it somewhere in the house. Two months after my son and family moved in, I began to distrust my son. I started hiding my small valuables, which was a very exhausting exercise. Many times I would forget the last place I hid something, which was very frustrating. I did not know that David was doing the same thing. The tripped out part about this was that neither of us shared this little secret with each other until after the video camera went missing. I didn't want to admit to David that I thought our son would steal from us and David didn't want me to know that he felt that way as well.

One morning, David woke me up at 3 a.m. He had found some receipts of things our son had stolen from us and sold to a resale shop. I already knew in my heart he was guilty, but this was actual confirmation. David was disturbed by the reality of the truth that our son would steal from us. David woke him up to confront him. Our son, being the kind of person he was at the time, only copped to the items on the receipts. These were the missing CD's and DVD movies my husband owned. My husband began noticing that some movies were missing, but he thought he had misplaced them. Our son never admitted to stealing the video camera. David told him he had a week to return his video camera or else.

I changed my husband's statement by saying, "If the video camera is not returned in two days, you and your family have to leave." I was not going to live like this anymore! Our son smirked and said, "I might as well leave now, because I don't know where the camera is. I didn't take it." I wanted to punch him square in his lying lips, but of course I did not. I responded, "That's completely up to you. You got two days to get it back or pack your bags!"

Two days passed and the video camera did not surface. We never saw that video camera again. This resulted in the eviction of our son and his family. On the day of their evection I was incredibly upset. They, on the other hand, both acted like arrogant, prideful zombies. I was torn and hurt, because I did not know where they would end up. They could possibly end up homeless. However, in the back of my mind, I was certain that one of her family members would take them in before things got drastic. I also had to miss work that day, so they could use my cell phone to contact her family. Which was another outrageous, unnecessary irritant. When we returned home from vacation, none of the phones in the house worked. Somehow, after speaking with my son from Miami, both phones were mysteriously broken. So, in order for them to have access to a phone (so they could figure out their next move) I had to miss a day of work.

While they were calling around for a place to stay, I went upstairs to try to unwind. When I went back downstairs to check on their progress they were gone. I looked out the door and didn't see them. I assumed her aunt had come to pick them up. They didn't even say goodbye. Lucky for them I had already said goodbye to my grandbaby. It still broke my heart to know those knuckleheads were alone taking care of my grandbaby. This was tuff-love if I ever heard of it. I wanted to go rescue my grandbaby from those crazy zombies, but I wasn't allowed to. I tried to get on with my day thinking that they were okay. But low and behold, around midnight the doorbell rang. It was the police. My heart was racing. What could have happened?

The police officer said that my son, his girlfriend and their baby were at the police station because they didn't have any place to go. He also told me that they had been walking around all day and were tired and hungry. Basically, this police officer came to see what type of person would put out their own son, a diabetic and infant child into the streets. I shared my story with him. After which he fully understood. He asked me if I could let them stay the night and give them one more day to find someplace to go because the shelters were all full and closed for the night. I asked my husband if he was comfortable with the idea. He said okay, so they stayed the night. I'll never forget the look on their faces when they came back in the house. My son looked proud, like he knew I would let him back in. His girlfriend looked tired and embarrassed, and my grandbaby looked tired and sad. This scene was too much for me. I told his girlfriend to get something to eat and I told my son, "I see you! You have one day and back to homelessness for you." I went to bed.

The police officer left a list of shelter numbers for them to call, which was a great relief for me. I had not even thought of shelters because I've never been in this type of situation and God knew that. God used the police officer to get this yoke off of me. He was a blessing in disguise. I knew in my heart that my marriage was going to suffer if they stayed and it was going to end badly for everyone. David's heart changed the day he found the receipts in Joey's car. Simply put, it was the end of this chapter of our lives.

They "shelter-hopped" for a while. The thought of this made me crazy and I wanted so desperately to go rescue my grandbaby. However, once again, I wasn't allowed to interfere. It also bothered me that his girlfriend didn't really try to stay despite the fact that my son had to leave. I often wondered why she didn't plead for herself and her baby to stay. She knew I had a soft heart and I loved them. It was my son that was the problem. If I were in her situation I would have been on my hands and knees. I wouldn't have been put out because I would have caused a scene, acted a fool, cried, begged, and pleaded. She didn't do any of that. She just walked away. I was incredibly disturbed by all of it and was about to relinquish my power to Prozac, then God sent a Christian woman to rescue me.

I was so overwhelmed by the situation. I could not believe that after all my effort and personal sacrifice that it came to naught. That fact alone tore me up. My mind began to fog and my memory was becoming shorter and shorter. I was an emotional wreck and I could not stop crying. I felt like the worst person in the world. I knew in my mind that my son brought this on himself and his family, but I was the enforcer of the eviction. My job was also a factor. At the time, I was dealing with a new manager who was very dependent and exhausting.

One Tuesday, one of my bible class buddies called me asking if I was going to bible class. I meant to say no, but yes came out. I couldn't believe I said yes, I thought I was going crazy. I really didn't want to go that day because of how I was feeling. We went to class and afterwards I can't remember exactly what was said, but the truth of my emotion came pouring out. She guided me to a place to sit down and she let me cry until there were no more tears. She then asked me if I was through crying. I thought that was a weird thing to ask. She then began to share what God placed on her heart about my situation. She said that I was not God and that God will fix it in His time and not mine. She stressed that I could not do anything in my own strength, that I had done my part, and it was time to let go, and let God do His part.

She began to tell me that I did not need any drugs to regulate my mind and that I needed to allow God to regulate me. She said, "If you give power to another force to get you in order, then it would be to your demise." And then, she prayed for me right there on the street.I felt the power of God move through me like never before.

God healed my mind that day. God used this awesome, powerful woman as His instrument to direct me back to him, and because of His love, care, and direction I cancelled my doctor's appointment. I thank God for His loving kindness because He kept my foot from slipping.

> **For the Lord is your security. He will keep your foot from being caught in a trap Proverbs 3:26(NLT)**

Without God intervening there is no doubt in my mind that I would be on Prozac today. Don't get me wrong, medicine has its purpose and it's place, but it was not God's best for me. God best was to have another Christian pray for me. Through prayer and faith God healed me. Jesus suffered 39 stripes for the healing of His people and because of what he did I was healed.

> **Who his own self bare our sins in his own body on the tree, that we, being dead to sins, should live unto righteousness: by *whose stripes ye were healed*. I Peter 2:24(KJV)**

It is worth mentioning that as Christians we can become overwhelmed with our circumstances. Applying God's word and placing Him first daily is essential to our ability to endure trials and tribulations. We may not always know the "why" or the "how long", or even the "how", but we can be certain that God is in control. We may not see the fruit of our labor immediately or we may never see it. It does not mean that our part was not essential to the process. God works through His people and we all have our part to do. Paul writes in **I Corinthians 3:6 "I have planted, Apollos watered; but God gave the increase."(KJV)** Do not forget that what ever your part is, it is essential to the process.

21. The Father He Never Knew

After I evicted my son and his family, I assumed they would eventually land at one of her relatives, but they did not they landed in a homeless shelter. This deeply troubled me. Joey was working on my mother, trying to get her to let them move into her house. He was stopping by her house daily. On October 2, 2005 (Which happened to be Yom Kippur/ Day of atonement) my son received a call while at my mother's house. The caller asked, "Can I speak to Joey?" My son replied, "This is Joey, who is this?" The caller said, "This is Joey, your father." As I mentioned before, Joey, not knowing his father, had a devastating effect on him. I had been praying for a long time for someone to help my son. I longed for Joey to become a productive member of society, and for something positive to fill the gap in his heart, mind, and soul.

I know that God uses people and I was hoping for God to use the most capable person to help him out his dark place. I was hoping for a mentor to rescue him, or for my son to be an apprentice to a carpenter, or learn a trade. I wanted My son to sit at the feet of a wise person who would help to develop his mind, and repair some of the brokenness of his heart. I never thought, even in a million, billion years, that God would use his natural father to help repair him. I didn't even consider him as a viable option. Had anybody prophesied that God was going to use his own father to repair his brokenness, I would have considered that person a liar. It was as if he was dead.

I had not been in contact with his father for seven years. The last effort I made to get them together was not successful, and it furthered my son's pain.

As you read in chapter 18 when my son was 15, he was going through such a difficult time I exhausted every means available and I finally located his father. I sent his father a certified letter telling him that his son needed to see him. After a few conversations, Joey's father agreed to meet with us. During that time, my financial situation was tight. Plane tickets, and hotel expenses were an incredible sacrifice, but I was willing to spend my last dime to help my son get to a better place in his mind. I knew beyond a shadow of a doubt that my son needed to at least see his father with his own eyes. So we flew to Washington, so that he could finally meet his farther.

As you read Joey never saw his father. He never showed up. He stood us up. He never even followed up with a phone call.

After that experience, Joey's behavior became increasingly worse. He seemed to lose all ambition and to be set on self-destruction. I encouraged him to try to embrace the people in his life that loved him, but no ones love could fill the space in his heart that was reserved for his father. The rejection he experienced from the trip to Washington, turned into bitterness, which turned into anger, anger turned into self-destruction that ultimately all culminated into self-hatred.

During that time, I had to make a conscience choice to surrender my son to God, and trust that God was in control and could handle the situation. Once I gave it to God, I still tried to take it back every now and then, because I was not seeing any improvement. So, for his father to call at this desperate, homeless, dark time of my son's life was so perfect. For his father to even locate my mother's phone number was a miracle.

My mother's phone number has changed at least 10 times since his father had been a part of our family. Sometimes my mother's number was listed sometimes it was not. His father's ability to locate the number and call Joey was perfection. Joey, actually being the person to answer the call at my mother's house was beyond perfection. (**See**

Romans 8:28) I recalled the many times I tried to get my mother to move out of her house after my father passed. I also recalled how awful I felt when I evicted Joey and his family. But once I reflected over this most recent event, it all seemed so perfectly orchestrated.

As many mothers are, my mother is the matriarch and the staple of the family. If she had listened to me and moved, it would have been nearly impossible for Joey's father to locate him. Also, if the events had not led to Joey's eviction from my house, he would not have been at my mother's house to answer the phone call from his father.

I saw the hand of God so clearly. I witnessed the instant effect the call had on my son, and I embraced hope and possibility for him to become whole. Some of my family felt overprotective and bitter toward his father's effort.

I eventually expressed to them that I thought it was God in action and I asked them, "Did they not see God in this?"

All eventually agreed. Family can be very protective and meddlesome, and can harbor resentment and bitterness to those who have hurt their loved ones. These feelings are reflexes, but God is so powerful that He can even change that.

I told my son not to let anyone cheat him out of this opportunity, even if it appeared that their intentions were to protect him. I made it clear that the choice was up to him to have a relationship with his father or not. He was now the pursued and the power was in his hand to reject or accept what was being offered. Joey said, "Okay," to the opportunity, but I was not sure if he really meant it.

"Do you see God in this?" I asked my son.

He did not respond.

Since the initial call, they both have continued to build their relationship. His father sent gifts by United Parcel

Services (UPS) which, really meant a lot to Joey. I don't think he had ever received a package by carrier before. Plus, it was such a surprise. He sent money, a tape, and a letter. All gifts were helpful and all were needed. The timing of each gift was so perfect. My son did not know how to react to this new attention. His father was actually pursuing him. This felt weird to him and he became a little harder to read. His dark behavior continued, but God had a plan.

Joey shared the letter his father wrote with me. It touched my heart on so many levels. It was full of repentance, truth, and healing. I had made a choice long ago to forgive his father for everything… even the current state of my son. I was not harboring any bitterness. I recognized long ago that forgiveness is a choice and bitterness will kill you in very small increments. In the letter, he simply told the truth about the decisions he'd made. He gave Joey advice and completely bared himself, and owned the blame that was rightfully his to own.

They are scheduled to meet on January 1, 2006. My son is excited, but he is trying his best not to express it. He is afraid of being disappointed again. He is behaving nonchalantly, but he shows his excitement in very small spurts. I am looking forward to this chapter of his life to be over and for him to start a new one. I am also hoping to see his father to let him know that nothing bitter remains in me, and that everything is really okay. I'm writing this in real time on December 26. 2005. A week from this date God willing my son will meet his father for the very first time. Hallelujah!!!!!

> **Acts 26:18 "To open the eyes of the blind and to turn them from the power darkness to light from the power of Satan unto God that they might receive the forgiveness of sin and the inheritance amongst those who are sanctified by the faith in Christ Jesus."(KJV)**

The Lord led me to Act 26:18 and I prayed this scripture over my son's life. I am agreeing with this word and confessing it over my son daily. When people ask me, "How is Joey doing?" I respond, "I believe that Joey's eyes are being opened and he is being turned from darkness to light". I'm no longer sharing the stories of Joey's activity with the enemy. Therefore giving the enemy secret praise. I've asked my Christian friends to confess and agree with me Acts 26:18 over Joey's life. Since God led me to that scripture, and I prayed and believed, that it is already done, I have experienced Gods peace concerning it.

This time, I have not taken it back from God. I know for sure, beyond a shadow of a doubt, that God is able to do, and will do just what His word says.... open the eyes of my son and turned him from darkness to light. Until the manifestation of my prayer is materialized, I will confess what God's word says about my son and in doing this, I am stepping on the enemy's head and bringing my son out of the devil's captivity.

I have been on vacation since December 23, 2005 and I am writing on the evening of December 31, 2005, the last day of this year. I have had the most peaceful and wonderful vacation ever. It's weird, because who would have thought this would be one of the best vacations that I've ever had. I did not really go anywhere; my husband is unemployed, *and* during this very time of my life I'm facing a plethora of challenging situations. This is what the word calls "the peace that passes all understanding."

> **Then you will experience God's peace, which exceeds anything we can understand. His peace will guard your hearts and minds as you live in Christ Jesus. Philippians 4:7(NLT)**

I've never had peace like this before. This peace is new to me. It is special and awesome. I arrived at this place of peace by really trusting in God. Even now, several days later, I'm realizing it is God's peace that made this vacation so different. It moves me that it is mine. At 8:30 p.m. I remembered that my son's father was scheduled to arrive tomorrow.

It's funny, from the last time I wrote until now, I had forgotten about it. I don't know how, but I just forgot. Therefore, I did not have any anxiety. From the moment I remembered, I began to pray: "Oh Lord, bless that nothing happens that will keep this union from happening. Bless my son to finally meet his father. In Jesus name, amen."

I had a hard time staying up till midnight. I believe I was in bed by 12:17 a.m. The last thing I did was pray for a blessed union, and then I was out.

22. My Son Meets His Dad

The next morning, I woke up at 10:30 a.m. It was the first day and first Sunday of the New Year. I woke up late and therefore I would be late for church. I sighed jumped up to start getting ready, but my husband simply said, "No Linda." He did not want me to start the New Year off running around like a crazy lady. I soon felt the stress and pressure in my head from jumping out of bed so quickly that I had to lie back down. Then I remembered that this was the day for my son to meet his dad. The phone rang and my husband answered it. It was my mom. She informed me that Joey's father was in the city and that he would be at her house in an hour and a half. I was so grateful to God for His faithfulness. This chapter of our lives was finally going to be over!

My mother also informed me, that she could not locate my son and the number that she had for him was out of service. I told her I would call her back. Once I hung up, I knew I needed God to intervene immediately. I knew exactly what to do. I asked my husband David and our daughter Kaylin to pray with me for God to wake Joey up, wherever he was, and have him call me. I prayed, "In Your word it says when two or three is gathered together and touch and agree, You hear us. Your word tells us to believe when we pray and we would have the things we desire. I am making my petition known to you God."

> **Again I say unto you, That if two of you shall agree on earth as touching any thing that they shall ask, it shall be done for them of my Father which is in heaven. For where two or three are gathered together in my name, there am I in the midst of them. Matthew 18:19-20(NIV)**

I tell you, you can pray for anything, and if you believe that you've received it, it will be yours. Mark 11:24(NLT)

And we are confident that he hears us whenever we ask for anything that pleases him. And since we know he hears us when we make our requests, we also know that he will give us what we ask for. I John 5:14-15(NLT)

I prayed every scripture I knew related to praying, believing, and receiving, while we were in prayer the phone rang. It was my son Joey, God woke him up and he called me. God is faithful! I think my husband got goosebumps.

My son was so nervous and acting so strange, but really, he was just excited and needed to hear his mother's voice for reassuring. I encouraged him and my heart was rejoicing the entire time we spoke. I was so amazed at how God was setting things right the first day of the year. That meant so much to me that He loved us like that.

Once I tried to get up again, pain went through my face and down the back of my head. This was a familiar pain. It is called a migraine, and whenever a migraine happens it means a lost day. I lay back down and tried to remember where my sinus medicine and Excedrin were. This combination of medicine would sometimes work in relieving the pain, but sometimes nothing would work and I would throw-up and be in bed all day. While thinking about the medicine, God spoke to my mind so clear. He said, "Did you not just see the power of your prayer?" I replied, "Yes" God simply said, "Pray" I called my husband and daughter back and asked them to pray one more time. They prayed and then God did what God does. He answered, and INSTANTLY took all the pain away.

I need you to look back at both of those situations. The one related to my son, forced me to realize immediately that I had no choice, but to trust in God and to lean on Him entirely. So, I did and got great results, but when it came to my pain, I leaned immediately on my own power. It took God to remind me of what He had just done moments before. It was not automatic for me to lean on Him again. I had to be reminded within moments of His power and presence that is available only through Him.

When things are clearly out of my ability to control, I quickly rely on God. However, when things are within my ability to control, I tend to depend on myself. By default of being a human with lack of discipline, I automatically lean and depend on my own wits and human ability. God wants all of us to consider Him first and to depend on Him at all times for all things. **(See Proverbs 3:5)** Had I not just moments before experienced a miracle, I could have easily not prayed to receive His deliverance from that horrible pain. I rejoiced all day! It was an amazing day! The entire day was like a dream. God showed up and showed out for me that day.

My son called me from my mother's house to tell me that he was there with his father. I rejoiced again! Joey and I talked for a few minutes and then I asked to speak to his father. I told his father that I was so happy that he was there and what a blessing it was for our son. He replied, that it was a blessing for him too. I was rejoicing! I asked him how long he was going to be at my mom and he said not long. I told him that I was hoping to see him. He said that he was not going to be at my mother's very long because he had a lot of family to visit. I said okay and expressed that it would be nice to see him after all these years.

A little while later, my son called me again. This time it was from his paternal grandmother's house where he and his dad were visiting his father's side of the family. My son told me that he needed me to take him and his dad to the shelter where his girlfriend and baby were staying. That made my stomach flip. After the earlier conversation, I never really expected to see his father and that was cool, I was content with that. Knowing I was going to see him made me feel weird. I told my son to call me before they came. I went on with my morning loving my husband and playing with my children.

I was going upstairs for something and glanced out the window and saw a car parking in front of my house. It was them! I could not believe it. I was not ready. I was a mess. I told Joey to call me before coming. I had rollers in my hair. I screamed to my husband that they were there and ran upstairs. So there I was ripping rollers out of my hair and trying to find something to put on quick. You don't want to see somebody you haven't seen in 20 years in rollers, looking a mess. To my own surprise, I was able to pull it together fairly quick. I had the absolute perfect outfit to throw on. My employees had given me this really elegant and beautiful silk gown and robe for Christmas.

I looked in the mirror before going down stairs and I said to myself, "You look good." I went down stairs and could not believe it. He was standing right next to my husband, bald as ever. The ironic thing is, so is my husband. I ran over and hugged him tightly and said I'm glad to see you. Once I pulled back and looked at the rest of his face, I immediately realized that things had been hard for him. I could see in his face that seeing me was a painful experience. It saddened my husband and me. I felt confused and remorseful. This is going to sound really funny, but I felt so awkward. I wanted to take away his pain, which was so very evident in his expressions. It made me wish that I had a missing tooth or was fat, or something. You would think that I would enjoy this experience of him living and seeing the consequences of his choices, but it did not feel good at all. I almost wanted to vanish.

It took me a minute to recuperate. My husband noticed that I was uncomfortable and stepped in so graciously, being his hospitable self. I love my husband! He is a wonderful man! He demonstrated compassion and a confidence that I've never seen. I eventually pulled my act together and joined them in the living room.

It was a weird day. I could not have orchestrated a more perfect day. If I tried to pull things together for the benefit of getting even, it would have never worked so perfectly, even down to the miniscule things such as the fire in the fireplace being perfectly beautiful, my children playing their games on the computer, and my husband being so wonderfully hospitable. I felt all this was almost too much for my son's father and I wanted it to end.

Once we were alone, I asked him if he was okay and he just looked at me so weird. He was doing his best to keep his emotions in check, but it was a losing battle. I was just amazed that while he was sharing the truth of his heart, nobody came in the living room and that he had a chance to get some things off his chest. I just listened. I didn't know how to respond to what he was saying. He was full of repentance, regret, and remorse.

I took my son and his father to the shelter so that his dad could meet my son's girlfriend and his grandbaby. Later that day we all went to my mother's house where we spent the evening eating and socializing. My mother had called everyone in the family over and cooked a bunch of food. It felt really strange to be at my mother's house with my son's father. It was at her house where we said our tearful goodbyes when he went away to the army. It was at her house where we made our son. It was at her house where we got married. I tried to act as normal as possible, but it was very uncomfortable being in his presence.

I was pleased with the way the night ended. Everyone seemed to have enjoyed them self, and it gave my heart such joy to see my son with his father. I expected a little bitterness to show up from my son, but it did not. My son looked genuinely happy. We all hugged and said our goodbyes and parted ways. What a lovely day!!

23. God a Wasp and a Catalog

One day, I was getting ready to leave for work. During my normal state of frantic rushing in the morning, the spirit of God instructed me to pick up a magazine. I said, "No" and He replied, "Take it with you". I mumbled, "I'm not ordering another thing or spending any additional money that I don't have". God said, "Pick up the magazine and take it with you". I grabbed the magazine with all types of attitude thinking what is the purpose of this? I don't want anything in the magazine and it's just going to be another thing to carry on the train during my commute.

Once I got to my car, I unlocked the door, and in the reflection of the window I see a wasp flying into my wig. To say I freaked out is an understatement. I jumped up and down and screamed like I was a crazy person. The Lord then reminded me that I had the magazine in my hand. I began to beat my head with that magazine until the wasp fell dead on the ground. I'm quite certain I gave all my neighbors the laugh of their lives. The real beauty of this is that I could see that God cared for me even in the simplest thing, that day.

God knew that the type of wig I had on was attached with short combs that were inserted into my real hair, and if I had to remove it in a rush I would have ripped out a substantial amount of my own hair no doubt. God knows I'm afraid of bees, wasps, and spiders. Without that magazine to assist me in killing that wasp I would have ripped myself bald, but God had a better way. I know this story is funny, but it's true. It sure made me recognize that God loves and knows me on every level. I need to learn to trust His instructions without question.

God talks to His people, and when He talks He is not asking for your opinion. He is stating facts, or giving instructions. He is trying to guide you into His best. I have several of these little stories where God leads me with a thought and compels me to act right away. Most of the time I follow through, but with irritation and great annoyance because I don't understand the point. But He never promised to share the purpose, but I trust that He is guiding me and leading me into what is best for me.

> **O Lord my God, you have performed many wonders for us. Your plans for us are too numerous to list. You have no equal. If I tried to recite all your wonderful deeds, I would never come to the end of them. Psalm 40:5(NLT)**

24. Refinancing the House

While working, the Lord impressed upon my mind to get on the Internet to look up my mortgage account information. I rejected the idea because my mortgage was paid and I was very busy doing my job. The thought to check my account kept resurfacing and finally I gave in to the idea and went online to check it out. Actually, I was just doing it to prove to myself that I was right. Keep in mind that I believed that this was a total waste of my time. I was completely preoccupied with my workload that morning. Once I reviewed my statement online there was an erroneous charge on my account. This charge compelled me to call customer service.

During the conversation with the service representative, I was informed that my mortgage would be increasing approximately $400 due to an interest increase. I was completely shocked by this news. I had completely forgotten that I had an adjustable interest rate. ***God intervenes and makes us aware of the unknown. If I had continued to ignore His prompting, I could have found myself in a world of trouble.*** The customer service representative transferred me to the mortgage department to see if I qualified for refinancing.

The Loan Officer informed me that I did not qualify. Primarily, because my husband was unemployed and our debt to income ratio was out of proportion. She also stated that it would be very difficult to get refinanced with anyone under these conditions. While she was speaking, I could hear the enemy of our soul speaking fast and furious in my mind. I recognized that I was in a spiritual battle and I retaliated with every scripture I knew that applied to my situation. Keep in mind the initial battle is in the mind. I was doing my very best to give the enemy a black eye.

I told the devil that it was God's job to supply all my needs. **(Philippians 4:19)** I also recalled **II Corinthians 9:8** which says **"And God is able to make all grace abound to you, so that in all things at all times, having all that you need, you will abound in every good work."(NIV)** I politely thanked the customer service representative for her time and went to the Ladies room to pray.

Typically, when facing a problem, I would go to an Internet bible resource to print the word for the day for encouragement. I would take it with me to the Ladies room to read and pray. This method proved to be most effective for me in the past. The word for the day was typically relative to my current situation. For the first time ever, the word for the day was not about my current situation. I sat there for a moment thinking, "What's up with that?" The Lord spoke to my spirit theses words. "Why are you looking for a word on the word? I've already planted my word in your heart? My word is down in your heart and you've already used it. You don't need to look anywhere else. It's in your heart. You already extracted it and applied it to the situation. Now watch me work." I heard "You graduated, but you are following old habits."

> **When I was a child, I spake as a child, I understood as a child: but when I became a man, I put away childish things. 1 Corinthians 13:11(KJV)**

At this time of my life I was focused on memorizing the scriptures. I had made it priority to plant the word of God into my heart daily. Applying **Romans 10:17** says, **"Faith comes by hearing and hearing by the word of God."(KJV)** This is the only formula to get the Word of God into your heart. I shared with a few friends and family members my situation regarding the mortgage. I boldly confessed and believed God that I would never pay 10% interest because all grace abounds unto me!!!

That night when I got home I mistakenly answered the phone. I usually do not answer the phone because of annoying telemarketers. The caller was a loan officer. He stated that he could get me a better interest rate.

"It's funny that you called because today I found out that my interest rate is increasing."

"Let me take down your information and get an application started."

"Before we go through all the trouble of completing an application let me tell you about my unique situation, then you can decide if you can still help me."

I gave him the details of my situation. He said, "Let's try it". He then told me that he was a Christian and believed that his call to me was not by accident or coincidence, but that this was God's intervention on my behalf. We shared our thoughts concerning God's timeliness in our lives. In closing, he said, "I can't make you any promises, but *God is able.*"

> **Now unto Him that is able to do exceeding, abundantly above all that we ask or think, according to the power that works in us.**
> **Ephesians 3:20(KJV)**

It blew me away that God orchestrated the loan officer to call to me on the day that I found out my mortgage interest rate would increase. After which two other loan companies also called me promising to offer of lower interest rates. I applied for two of them in addition to the one with the Christian loan officer. The first two companies denied my application. The reality that both of these were unable and unwilling to offer me anything was very disheartening. When I spoke to the Christian loan officer he told me that without my husband's income, our debt to income ratio was the factor for not being qualified. I thought that was the end of the conversation, but he continued talking and wanted to go over my credit report.

I thought that was a funny thing to do because in my mind it was a dead deal. We went over the balances of my debt and monthly minimum payments. I informed him we did not have to make payments to our credit cards because of our insurance protection. He rolled this information over in his mind and said, "This will work. When could you fax me the credit card insurance agreement and the other critical paper work?"

"Tomorrow." I said

Amazingly enough that night I was able to pull all the required paper work together. I faxed everything over first thing the next morning.

There were several other obstacles that the Lord moved right out of my way. The Loan officer had a tough time scheduling the closing because it was month end. Finally, he called and told me where to go and how much money to bring to the closing table. On the night of the closing, I had a headache, a stomachache, and I still had to attend school. Not to mention the hectic day I had at work. When I got to the closing the closer was late. One of the female closers who worked there, but not on my closing asked, "Where's your husband?"

I said, "at home." She then told me "you are not closing tonight."

She spoke to me in a condescending manner and I almost took offense. I asked her to make copies of the RESPA forms (Real Estate Settlement Procedures Act) and she said, "I'm gonna give you copies of everything."

When she came back with the financial details, they were completely different than what was previously disclosed to me by the Christian loan officer. I was annoyed to say the least. The documents that I was reviewing required that I bring a lot more money to the closing.

She then asked if I was prepared to pay the required amount, and I said, "Yes." I shared with her that God was good and He saw this day long ago and He prepared it so that I would have provision for this occasion. I was well able to pay the closing costs.

You see a few weeks prior I received the biggest bonus ever in my entire career. God provided for me and met my need before I even recognized I had a need.

I said, “Well, apparently it’s nothing we can do today. My husband is not here, I don’t have enough money with me, and a really critical piece of paper work is missing from the file. I’ll have my loan officer reschedule the closing for tomorrow.”

She said, “I doubt if you will close anytime soon because we are booked solid for the next few days.”

This posed a great problem, because of funding requirements.

During my commute to school, I reviewed the copies of the closing papers line by line. I located several errors of double postings and payments that caused the increase of my closing cost. I contacted my Christian loan officer. I shared with him my closing experience and the errors I discovered in the documents. Of course he was agitated and a bit annoyed. He was very concerned about the funding deadlines and the difficulty he was going to face regarding rescheduling the closing.

The next day my calendar was extremely tight. I had one meeting after another at work and all this personal stuff to complete. It seemed hopeless, but I stood on His word. I thought to myself, God has a lot to do.

That day, I closed on my refinance! All my findings regarding the money were correct. The corrections were made prior to the closing and consequently, I paid less money at closing. The closer even backdated the paper work so that it funded on time. God made a way out of no way. He is a miraculous God and He never falls short of His Word despite our weaknesses.

25. The Devil Will Make a Fool Out of You

Many times in my life I've been in situations where I allowed the devil to make a plum fool out of me. I would be so caught up with the event itself that I did not recognize that a trap had been set and that I was caught in it. My initial response to a bad situation was natural and not spiritual. The reason I initially responded the way I did was because I felt liberated to do so. The thought, "What would Jesus do?" never crossed my mind. I felt totally right in my actions. At the time it seemed as though I was right until later, when the Word of God would convict me. The devil would then come and bring condemnation. He would make me feel embarassed and unworthy to be in the presence of God.

> **We are all infected and impure with sin. When we display our righteous deeds, they are nothing but filthy rags. Like autumn leaves, we wither and fall, and our sins sweep us away like the wind. Isaiah 64:6(NLT)**

Sin separates us from God and it makes us feel unworthy and unrighteous. According to God's Word, since Christ, my righteousness has very little to do with my actions. My righteousness is based on the blood of Christ and my relationship with Him. As a result of Christ being in me, right actions follow. Independent of Christ, I cannot obtain or maintain my righteousness.

> **May you always be filled with the fruit of your salvation—the righteous character produced in your life by Jesus Christ for this will bring much glory and praise to God. Philippians 1:11(NLT)**

God instructs us in **Hebrews 4:16, "Let us therefore come boldly unto the throne of grace, that we may obtain mercy, and find grace to help in time of need."(KJV)** Let me tell you about another incident.

During this time of our lives my husband was unemployed and taking care of the kids. It was Monday morning and I was getting ready for work. While I was getting ready I asked my husband to make a list of important things I needed him to do for the day. I yelled downstairs, "Are you writing this down?" and he said, "Yes." Then I asked, "Are you writing it down with a pen and paper?" And again he stated, "Yes." At some point I realized he was not writing anything down, but watching the kids get on the school bus and drinking his coffee. I asked him why he lied about making the list. His response was that he was making the list in his head and I went ballistic. There was a trap set. What I perceived David to be doing was lying. David perceived what he was doing as truth. Basically, it was just a difference of opinion, but it had the worst effect on me. Even though it made no difference to him, since there were just a few things, he thought he could remember them. As for me, it made all the difference in the world.

Several trying events happened over the duration of the weekend, but I was victorious. However, David and I had never discussed or resolved them. I counted them as victories; because I chose not to respond in the way the devil would have liked me to. David's lying to me about writing the list was the preverbal straw that broke the camels back. My lid was flipped and I verbally flogged him. The truth is that our enemy is on a mission to steal, kill, and destroy. The devil is cunning; he is consistently looking for, and creating ways to cause us to fall. My response was full of suppressed irritation and annoyance from the other previous events. I was not victorious that time. I gave the devil the steering wheel for several minutes.

I said, "We need to get a couple of things straight. You need to make a list because you are not that bright. Every time I ask you to take care something that is important to me you forget!"

"That is not true. What's wrong with you?"

"A smart person recognizes his limitations."

Out of frustration and at loss for words David replied, "You got bumps."

"What? What has that got to do with this? You thought that was going to hurt me? Well it did not. I know exactly how I look and I'm okay with it. The point I'm trying to make is that you need to write things down to get them done. You are easily distracted and I'm tired of being disappointed. You need a list to keep you on track. You kill me because you don't even realize you need help. A smart person would recognize their deficit and would make a list to help them manage what they need to do. But no, not you, you are in denial. You make the same mistakes over and over again."

Well, needless to say this did not go over well with him. He again asked what was wrong with me? He strongly argued his point that he could easily remember the few tasks I requested of him and that he did write them down in his mind. He kept asking me what was this argument really about? I said, "The lies" and he said, "That was not even a lie" and that really pushed me over the edge. I could not believe what I was hearing. How did he not understand what a lie was? I asked him a simple question and he lied. Now he is saying he did not recognize that it was a lie. At this point I had lost my cool and got right in his face arguing and yelling, continually stressing my point.

He was trying to keep his cool, but I guess my tone and body language set him off. He threw the coffee from his cup onto the wall. I could not comprehend the point of that reaction. I said, "So we can't talk without you throwing coffee on the wall? What sense did that make?" It splashed on our son's camera and I said, "You are going to ruin David's camera." He picked it up and wiped it off. After that he really looked angry. Right before he threw the coffee on the wall there was a split second when I thought he was going to throw the coffee on me, instead of the wall.

Due to that thought, my adrenaline was flowing and I was ready to fight. I said, "You made the right choice by throwing it on the wall." For most of our marriage I have been the one to calm things down and have been the voice of reason, even if I was the one who was wronged and I had a reason to be angry. My husband's temperament was short, and at that time of our marriage he did not deal with stressful situations well. Sometimes he would blow things out of proportion and yell and act out. He knew that I did not want to argue or act out, especially in front of our children. But this day was different. The children were at school and I was tired of being punked. I said, "We could tear up this whole mother f#*$! We can start with your computer and then to my curio cabinet."

These were our favorite possessions. I was so full of rage. I did not care if we tore up the whole house. I was determined to make my point at any cost. I was not taking it any more.

I said, "You want destruction? I'll show you destruction! So you wanna throw stuff on the walls huh? The next time you throw something on the wall I'm gonna s#@* on the walls!"

He looked confused. I was so completely enraged and out of character. I felt totally out of control over the words that were pouring out of my mouth. They flowed out of my mouth effortlessly. Now, I need you to keep in mind that I still had to drive 20 minutes to my train station to go to work, and get on with my day. I grabbed my stuff and said goodbye, but he did not respond.

Prior to that day, we never left the house without saying I love you and a kiss. I felt so strange when I left the house. The rage I felt lasted three days. At every opportunity I threatened him that if for any reason he made me mad I was going to s#!# on the walls. David was in constant, utter disbelief of my behavior. I broke down and shared this monstrosity with three friends. The first two just let me vent, but the third one was so shocked by the words that were coming out of my mouth that she asked,

"Who are you? I know you are not talking about your David like that!"

"Aren't you listening to what I'm telling you?"

"Yes, but who are you? Get out of my cubicle talking like that about your husband!"

Ooh, I wanted to smack her! When I got to the part about what I would do if he ever did that again, she asked, "What about your kids?" I responded that they would get over it! There's always therapy. She could not take it anymore and said, "You have lost your mind!" She knew how much I loved my kids and that I would never willingly do anything to destroy their happiness, or their well being. She knew the devil had a tight hold on me and that I was lost in my rage. I finally left her cubicle, irritated, and annoyed by her response.

The Lord orchestrated for me to be alone for a few minutes. I had to wait in the lobby to give something to a courier. During that time the Lord spoke to my spirit. He asked,

"Why are you still mad?"

"Because David still does not see that he is wrong!"

"What about you? You are wrong now and you have been wrong for three days. Surely, you can forgive him and over look his faults. You are expecting me to forgive yours. You know better than to behave like you have, but it has not stopped you. How can you be so harsh on David when you are so imperfect? You need to repent and confess your sin to everybody you shared this with and apologize to your husband."

It was hard for me to hold back my tears in the bank's lobby. When I called my husband he apologized first, which added to my underline irritation, because I wanted to be the first to say sorry and fix it. I just said, "Me too." I had a hard time holding my head up the rest of that day. I was so embarrassed and tired of the whole experience.

Two days prior to that argument we had experienced a major victory. Through prayer, faith, and the power of God's spoken word we were able to refinance our mortgage and secure a good rate despite great odds and many obstacles. Even though my husband was unemployed, our relationship was at an all time high. The enemy came quickly in an unexpected way to kill, steal, and destroy.

> ***The thief cometh not, but for to steal, and to kill, and to destroy*****: I am (Christ) come that they might have life, and that they might have it more abundantly. John 10:10 (KJV)**

The enemy came from a completely different angle and I was not ready. I fell for his trick, hook, line, and sinker. The devil made an utter fool out of me and he will make a fool out of anyone. No one is exempt. The only way you can avoid being a victim is to stay keenly aware that you are in a spiritual war at all times. Keep God's word in your mouth and do the very best you can to exemplify Christ's behavior at all times. The bible says in **Proverbs 24:16, "For a just man falleth seven times, and riseth up again: but the wicked shall fall into mischief."(KJV)** Falling is a part of the process. When and if you fall down, GET UP! Go boldly to the throne of grace, so that you will find mercy in the time of need.

26. Get Up and Write the Book

Over the last two years the Lord has used many people to encourage and influence me to write this book. Writing a book was the farthest thing from my mind. I had enough going on. I was working full-time, married with children, and going to night school. To add something else to my plate would be the last thing I wanted to do. One night when I was trying desperately to relax the Lord instructed me to get up and write the book. I thought, "I don't have anything to write about." After a few more minutes, I heard Him again. Get up and write the book." I reluctantly got up and went to the computer with an attitude. He said, "Get comfortable." So I did with an attitude. I was sitting there waiting on him to reveal to me what he wanted me to write, but nothing came. I sat for about fifteen minutes. I began feeling annoyed and sort of stupid. Why would the Lord instruct me to write, then not tell me what to write? My impatience kept prompting me to go back and relax on the couch.

More time went by while I was at the computer and the oddest thing happened. The next thought was, "You ain't got nothin' to say. Even if you did write a book nobody would read it. So, what's the point? I bet there's a double episode of 'Law and Order' on tonight. Get back on the couch and watch TV." I thought and agreed that I didn't have anything substantial to say. I felt nobody would read it anyway and I hoped there would be a new episode of 'Law and Order' on that night. At some point it hit me that I was talking to the devil and he was subtly trying to convince me not to write the book.

I thought, "What was that about?" Why did the enemy care if I wrote the book or not? The more I thought about this the more I began to recognize that it must be necessary for me to write this book. The enemy's effort to persuade me not to write the book was the pivotal event that convinced me of the importance and the need for me to write it. If writing this book were not important, the enemy would not have wasted any time trying to convince me not to write it.

I put my hands on the computer and wrote the first few lines. Then the enemy spoke to my mind sharper and clearer than I've ever heard him before. "You destroy my kingdom and I'll destroy yours." Needless to say this stopped me dead in my tracks. I thought, "What kingdom? I don't have a kingdom." Slowly, it became clear to me that he was speaking about my family. I was sitting there with tears in my eyes staring at the computer. I was outdone. I didn't want to write a book in the first place. On top of that I had additional, pre-existing insecurities about my ability to write. Many years ago I expressed an interest in writing and I was told that nobody was interested in what I had to say. Why is it so much easier to believe a lie instead of the truth?

> **The sinful nature wants to do evil, which is just the opposite of what the Spirit wants. And the Spirit gives us desires that are the opposite of what the sinful nature desires. These two forces are constantly fighting each other, so you are not free to carry out your good intentions. Galatians 5:17(NLT)**

Now there I was in that awkward situation. Trying to be obedient to God by writing this book and also facing the threats from the devil. I continued to sit there for a while wondering why this was my plight. I tried to figure out how I was going to get out of this terrible situation. While I was weighing my options, this question hit me like a ton of bricks. "Who are you going to listen to? God, or the devil?" The fact that the enemy was making such an effort to pressure me out of writing this book made me realize there must be something to it. There must be a real need for this book to be written, and written by me. I decided it would be in my best interest to trust God and to be obedient, no matter what the enemy threatens me with. I remembered that all power is in God's hands and that I could trust him with all things such as, my life, my children, and my marriage. I remembered the word of God in **(Psalm 91)** where He promised to protect me.

While writing around 2:15 a.m. the enemy repeated his threat. This time I responded with **Isaiah 54:17, "*No weapon that is formed against me will prosper*; and every tongue that shall rise against thee in judgment thou shalt condemn. This is the heritage of the servants of the LORD, and their righteousness is of me, saith the LORD."(KJV)**

I continued to write. A few minutes later I heard stirring upstairs and the pitter-patter of little feet. My daughter came down to the family room and she had blood all over her face. She was crying a bit, but mostly shook up. She asked me, "Why is this happening to me?" I knew it was the enemy attempting to actualize his threats. My husband and I cleaned her up and prayed over her. After that I recognized it might get ugly, but I made up in my mind to trust God's word in **Psalm 34:19 "Many are the afflictions of the righteous: but the LORD *delivereth him out of them all.*"(KJV)** I put my daughter back to bed and continued to write. That night I wrote the first 15 pages of this book.

> **Ye are of God, little children, and have overcome them: because greater is he that is in you, than he that is in the world. I John 4:4 (KJV)**

Be assured that God is stronger than the devil and He is able to preserve, and keep you safe. Ultimately, all your trials and tribulations are working together for your good. Purposefully follow God's will. In doing this, your victory is secured. As it says in **Romans 8:37, "... in all these things we are more than conquerors through him that loved us."(KJV)**

27. Heart's Desire

I was daydreaming while washing clothes one day about having a beautiful baby girl. I have always wanted a baby girl ever since I could remember. At that time money was very tight. My husband had gotten a promotion, to a better position, but he did not consider his current overtime while negotiating his new salary. So, basically he had a better position, but his actual salary was less. I was thinking I really would love to have a little girl and imagining how wonderful that would be.

Earlier that day when I was gathering the clothes together to wash, I couldn't find a pair of blue jeans that I bought for my son from Kmart. I searched the house high and low and nothing. This frustrated me to no end. Well, while I was daydreaming about my daughter the enemy started talking. He said, "You can't afford another child. You can't even keep up with the little bit you have." I almost started crying because that was so harsh and I didn't lose the pants on purpose. I was very careful about my son's clothes and I was doing the very best to manage what I had.

I really didn't respond to the devil in any verbal way. I just began to pray. I said, "Lord you know my heart and I really want a baby girl. That is a desire of my heart. Your word says that if I delight myself in you, you would give me the desires of my heart.

> **Delight thyself also in the LORD: and he shall give thee the desires of your heart. Psalm 37:4(KJV)**

The spirit of God responded, "I will send you a token of what I have in store for you." I finished up with the clothes and went upstairs. When I got upstairs someone was at the door. I peeked out and it was an old friend that I had not seen in years. I hesitated in answering the door, because I looked terrible.

You know how it is if you haven't seen a person in a long time. You want to look your best. Well, I looked awful, but I was more excited about seeing her than how I looked so I opened the door. We hugged then talked for about an hour. We had so much catching up to do. I really enjoyed that time with her. I realized while talking to her that I would have missed out on this joyous occasion if I hadn't let her in because of vanity.

At the end of her visit, she asked me what size my son was. When I told her she smirked. She asked if I accepted hand-me-downs, and I replied, "Yes." She went to her car and pulled out two big black garbage bags full of clothes. Guess what? They were all my son's size. I sat there in awe because the Lord had just told me that He was going to send a token and He sent it the same day. I frantically went through the bags. There were more clothes in those bags than my son had in his entire wardrobe. Most were brand new and had not even been worn. The tags were still on them and were all name brand clothes. My son never wore name brand clothes, because they were too expensive. He was well kept, but most of my shopping was done at discount stores. During that time of my life, buying name brand clothes was not an option.

I asked her where she got so much stuff, and she told me that they were gifts from her baby shower and her son's birthday parties. She told me she had been given so much that her son outgrew them before he had a chance to wear them. She then said she had packed them up months ago and had been trying to drop them off at the Salvation Army, but had never got around to it. She said she was in the neighborhood and I popped into her mind, so she came to pay me a visit.

Needless to say, I was crying and I shared with her my prayer about my baby girl, and what God said about sending me a token. Then miraculously, she showed up and blessed me just like He said He would. I would not have thought of the clothes as a token because there were so many. In my mind, a token is something very small. This was huge. It did not qualify as a token because it was much more than I ever expected. That just goes to show that my expectations and definitions of blessings and tokens are very different than what God has in store for me. I was blessed with so much that I extended the blessing to my sister who had a son the same age. God never ceases to amaze me. He showed up and showed out!

Once my husband got home, I told him everything that happened and I got busy trying to get pregnant. Once I got pregnant, I believed God would make it a girl. Two weeks later, I fell down a flight of twenty stairs. I even broke the banister. I landed flat on my butt and I felt a sharp pain in my belly. I began to bleed, so we went to the hospital. The doctors said I probably suffered a miscarriage, but it was really too soon to tell because I was less than four weeks pregnant and it was too soon to locate a heartbeat. I said, "I believe I'm still pregnant and that she is going to be fine." They looked at me like they felt sorry for me and that I needed psychological help, but they let me go home anyway. I claimed to anyone and everyone in earshot that my baby was fine. When I went back to the doctor's office for a follow-up visit, they heard my baby's heart beat. I wanted to say, "I told you so!" But instead, I thanked God for His goodness.

Soon after, it was confirmed I that I was finally having a baby girl. I was elated! Having a baby girl was my heart's desire. I was on cloud nine just knowing that I was finally going to be able to doll up my little girl. This was a wonderful time of my life. When I was about three months pregnant, I started to dilate. My doctor requested that I take it easy and sit as much as possible. I did, but I still experienced the cramping and the dilation appeared to stop.

At my sixth month doctor's appointment, I was told that I was dilated to 4 centimeters. This was, of course, not normal and they sent me home for complete bed rest. I was told not to do any walking. I could sit up, but was strongly encouraged to lie down for the next three months. I was not uncomfortable and I did not experience any cramping. I was, however, completely bored to death. I watched lots of Christian television, kept a daily journal, and forced my husband and my son to rearrange furniture, paint, and do all kinds of other stuff.

It was finally time to deliver my long awaited bundle of joy. I was cleaning out the closet and I felt a bit of pain. I watched the clock to monitor the contractions. They were very far apart. Later that night, around five, my mother and I went to Burger King. Right after the first bite I felt the first real pain, and I told my mother I thought it was time. She took me home so that my husband could take me to the hospital. Once we got to the hospital, wouldn't you know it, the pain stopped! They released me around 4 a.m. All I wanted in the whole world were Pancakes from International House of Pancakes (IHOP). On our way there we had to stop at the cash station to make a deposit and a withdrawal. While we were there I was talking to God. I said, "God, I need to know if I'm really in labor or not." A nano-second later, my water bag broke, and I felt a pain like no other pain I had ever experienced. I took in a breath so sharp I felt as though I almost punctured my lungs. The noise I made from the onset of the pain scared my husband and he asked what I wanted to do. I said, "Let's go to breakfast." We drove to IHOP, but to our surprise it had moved. Disappointed and in pain, I told my husband to just take me home. I didn't want to go back to the hospital too soon because we had just left.

My first step onto my porch was incredibly painful. Keep in mind I had been up all day with no rest. It was at least 5:30 a.m. and all I could think about was getting some rest. I laid there in torture for about 10 minutes. Finally, I was totally convinced, that it was time to go back to the hospital. My husband drove like a man with a wife who was about to give birth in the backseat of his car. Under the circumstances, I encouraged him because I felt like the baby was going to fall out on the car floor. Once we got there it was a completely different scene than our last emergency visit. It was helter-skelter! Lots of screaming on my part, lots of running and pushing me in the wheel chair on my husband's part, and lots of chaos on every one else's part.

I was wheeled directly into a delivery room where a nurse checked me and was yelling for a doctor. Apparently, from the time I left until the time I got back, babies were being delivered every few minutes so there was no doctor available to deliver my baby. She was doing the best she could. She told me repeatedly not to push. Well, at that time, all I wanted in America was an epidural. I was trying my very best to keep my cool. I asked anyone within two feet of me for an epidural. The anesthesiologist was in another room giving an epidural to some fortunate woman.

I, on the other hand, felt cursed with a curse. During this moment, an Asian nurse laughed and said, "It too late for you get epidural, it time baby to be born." I was so angry with the hospital's staff because if they had just kept me there at the earlier visit, if they had made me walk around a little bit, I would have gone into full blown labor while there. I would have had the opportunity to get the epidural I so desired.

My daughter would wait no longer. I screamed, "She is coming out!" They were screaming for me not to push. I wasn't, although she was. I couldn't hold her back even if I tried. The nurse looked completely unprepared and pitiful. In the next instant the doctor dashed into the room like in the movies and said, "Mother, on three."

At that moment, I actually thought I was going to die. The pain was so severe. I pushed on three and all of a sudden I would have sworn someone had set me on fire. I screamed fire with all my might and the doctor said "One more really good push." And just that second my daughter ran out of me like she was late for a train, hair appointment, or job interview. I could not understand my daughter's rush to be born. I was still screaming fire when a nurse dowsed me with a cool sponge and finally put the fire out, but I was still in a lot of pain because of her quick departure from my body. Before they had a chance to clean her up she was making a sucky face and looking around for some food. The nurse brought her over for me to nurse her. I was still experiencing a lot of residual pain and could not fully nurse at that time. I told them to give her a bottle until after my recovery.

When I got to recovery I was so exhausted and extremely hungry. My husband brought breakfast and I ate it hungrily. Right after my husband left I ask the nurse how much should I bleed. I felt like it was a bit heavy, but I was too tired to worry about it. So finally I rested. A dull pain awakened me. When I feebly tried to reposition myself, by putting my hand down on the bed, I heard a squishy sound. The sound confused me and my hand was cold and wet. When I looked at my hand it was covered in blood. My brain had a hard time comprehending what the blood was.

I had no strength and could barely reach the nurse call button. It seemed a million miles away. It was like I was moving in slow motion and I could actually feel myself losing consciousness. My hand literally just landed on the button. It was just like in the movies, when a person is right near the phone, but they collapse less than a half-inch away from it, and you're frustrated and screaming at the screen, "Try harder, just a bit more!"

In the distant corners of my mind I heard a nurse ask, "How can I help you?" I replied with barely audible whisper, "Blood."

This is what I remember hearing. "Code!" "She's losing too much blood!" I saw a lot of people. A young black doctor with dread locks, several black women and a white woman. There were more people in the room, but I don't recall their races, faces, or any specifics. I do recall thinking there were too many people in the room. I heard, "Find it. Stop it." I heard splashes of what sounded like water. Someone dragged something across the floor. I felt pressure and then pain. I cried. I don't know if tears were coming out of my eyes, but my heart was crying. At that moment, I realized my life was in danger. My next thought was, I couldn't die because I finally got my baby girl.

Then I thought about my husband raising the kids all by himself. Then I thought about my eldest, and then my baby boy. I began to pray. I recalled every scripture I could recall pertaining to long life and the desires of my heart. I remember saying my redeemer liveth. I recall asking God to save me from this attack of the devil. I rebuked the devil and said I will live and raise my children. I repeated my redeemer lives. The next thing I remember was seeing this lady who looked very sad, she was holding back tears and she walked away. I was thinking why is she so sad?

I didn't understand her sadness because I was living. I wasn't dead. I could see her face. Then another lady left the room and I was screaming, "My Redeemer lives! I'm raising my children and raising my daughter! She is my heart's desire! The Word says that if I delight myself in the Lord he would give me my hearts desire. She is my hearts desire and I will raise her and love her and praise God for this victory. My Redeemer liveth!"

For I know that my redeemer liveth, and that he shall stand at the latter day upon the earth. Job 19:25(KJV)

When I opened my eyes there was a nurse standing in the room. She said, "You really gave us a scare." She began to tell me that I hemorrhaged and lost a lot of blood because a piece of after birth was stuck in my uterus. She said, "You were really praying. You made all of us pray. Even people who didn't pray, or believe in God, prayed. We thought we lost ya. It's the saddest thing to lose a mother or a baby. That is when the job becomes almost unbearable, but you made it!!!" She was so excited. I felt like I had been hit with a ton of bricks, but I rejoiced, because God answered my prayer. I was alive! I was granted the opportunity to enjoy my daughter, raise my children, and love my husband. I was alive!

> **He that follows after righteousness and mercy finds life righteousness and honor. Proverbs 21:21(KJV)**

A few minutes after the nurse left, my mother came in the room and literally took one look at me and said, "You almost died." I began to share with her what happened. She said, "Girl, this is yo' last baby, right?" She was right. I was done!

The enemy is a thief. He comes to steal, kill, and destroy. He had made several attempts to steal my dream of having a baby girl, but the Lord delivered me each and every time. Jesus is a keeper and you can trust him to take care of you. I am a living witness that God honors His word. Jesus has an excellent track record.

Whenever I am troubled, or facing trials and tribulations that seem unbearable, it's important for me to remember to still my thoughts and to remember where He has brought me from and what He has brought me through. Only after I remember to do that am I able to rest in knowing that God will take care of it. *Remembering how God took care of you in the past is essential to your ability to rest and trust him with your entire future. You can only rest when you trust Him. And you can trust that God has your best interest in mind.*

> **For I know the thoughts that I think toward you, saith the Lord, thoughts of peace, and not of evil, to give you an expected end. Jeremiah 29:11(KJV)**

God knows that is an important for you to remember his faithfulness. As you remember what He has done for you in the past, will enlarge your capacity to trust Him with your future. That is why he instructed the children of Israel to remember how he took them out of Egypt. He wanted them to never forget what he had done for them. That is why he instructed them in **Deuteronomy 16:3** to, **"Eat it with bread made without yeast. For seven days the bread you eat must be made without yeast, as when you escaped from Egypt in such a hurry. Eat this bread—the bread of suffering—so that as long as you live you will remember the day you departed from Egypt."(NLT)**

Remembering His goodness takes the stress off of you, and places the responsibility on the God who says, "Cast your cares upon me because I care for you." Then, and only then, can you fully rest.

> **Give all your worries and cares to God, for he cares about you. I Peter 5:7(NLT)**

28. Pride

At one time in my life I thought I had no pride. I would always say, "I have no pride." But I was proven wrong by a small incident that panned out like this. I didn't have a lot of money, but I loved my children to be well dressed. I shopped for bargains matched shoes, jackets and cute little outfits. I always tried to shop in advance of the season. At the end of summer, I would shop for next summer. This typically worked out for me very well. After successfully finding all the great deals, I would pack up my treasures until the next summer. I was always so pleased with my purchases, and was exceptionally satisfied because I met my goal of staying within budget. The lengths I could stretch one hundred dollars would amaze you.

On the first summer day of the next year, I was excited to pull out my bag of goodies and dress my son up in his new little outfit. I went to the closet where I stored the new clothes and they weren't there. I only saw the bag of old clothes for Purple Heart, which I placed there a few months ago. I asked my husband what did he do with the bag of clothes that were in the closet? He said, "I gave them to Purple Heart like you told me." My heart fell to the ground. How could he do this? Why didn't he look in the bag? Why didn't God intervene and stop him from giving a way the wrong bag?

I was full of questions and irritated beyond words. I was very angry with my husband. He was also angry with me for putting the new clothes right next to the old clothes. To this day I have no explanation of why I would do such a thing. I believe it must have gone something like this. I bought the clothes and packed them away in the closet. Months later, I got a call from Purple Heart asking for donations, so I packed up the old clothes and placed them in the same closet. Subsequently, my husband grabbed the wrong bag.

Of course I was kicking myself thinking this is the trouble you get for trying to help somebody. If I had I just said no to the lady from Purple Heart, I would not have been in this predicament. The old adage came to mind, "No good deed goes unpunished." Boy was I livid! I cried on my commute to work that day. I couldn't find one good thing that could potentially come out of this situation. Walking from the train station to my job, I remembered that the clothes still had the price tags on them and that sent my blood pressure through the roof. For the majority of that day I was totally dysfunctional, unable to focus. I was entirely ineffective at work.

At some point, my friend Paula came over to my desk and asked what was wrong with me. I shared my angry story and busted out in tears. Then she said something that surprised me. She said, "Apparently, it was in God's will for some little boy who never experienced new clothes to have new clothes." I wanted to beat her down. Those clothes were picked out for my son through my effort, not for anybody else. But I couldn't express that, because that sounded so selfish. My indifferent response was, "I guess so." After giving it a few more moments of thought I was okay with it. I knew God well enough to know that he would take care of it. What I was not prepared for was how he would take care of it. Later that day, around lunchtime, my girlfriend Paula brought me two bags of clothes full of the cutest outfits in the world from Carson Pirie Scott.

I had a hard time receiving this gift. I didn't want her charity. I was a good mother and I had already taken care of my son's needs. I didn't need or want her to buy my son any clothes. It felt terrible. Plus, she paid full price for the clothes. She must have spent hundreds of dollars. Why didn't she just give me the money? I was sure I could have found better deals. I tried to be gracious, but she saw straight through me. I can't remember exactly how it came out, but it was brought to my attention that I had too much pride and I should be grateful that God blessed me, and should not consider the source of the blessing.

The root of my problem was that I was struggling to prove that I was capable of taking care of my business, no matter how limited the resources were. I was proven to be wise, because I was able to take little and make much. There was nothing in this experience for me except for humility. I was simply embarrassed. I wanted to provide for my family. I did not want any handouts. I did not want it that way. That was the reason why I made great efforts to take care of these things in advance. But in my ability to do this, somehow pride crept in.

Paula and I talked about it later and she stated that her only hesitancy in giving me the clothes was her awareness of my pride. It's a funny thing, because I was the last one to know that I had a pride issue. I always felt like I couldn't have pride, because I was always struggling financially. How could I have pride? Compared to others, I had so little. But God allowed a situation to reveal the actual state of my heart. I've learned that pride is not created through abundance. Pride is created when you think you are doing things on your own.

If I did not have pride, I would have received the gift graciously. You never know what is in you until a situation arises that exposes the truth of your heart. Typically, people on the outside see you clearer than you see yourself. There is nothing good about pride. It is classified as one of the seven deadliest sins. Pride takes God out the picture and displays only your efforts, accomplishments, and victories. Having pride will cause a person to act rude and miss out on God's blessings. Humility on the other hand is always honorable. Jesus himself was humbled unto death. We need to live by His example, get rid of pride, and practice humility.

Pride ends in humiliation, while humility brings honor. Proverbs 29:23(NLT)

Before his downfall a man's heart is proud, but humility comes before honor. Proverbs 18:12(NIV)

29. Girlfriends

Some people come into your life for a lifetime, some for a season, and others for only moments. Each has a purpose and a part to play in developing and shaping you. We are all works in progress. People, ideas, how we think, what we think about, are shaped by the daily interaction with people, the media, and those closest to us. Have you ever had a thought, and the next thought was, "I wonder what so and so would think about that?" So you reach out to that person and they have a totally different perspective on the matter. They have a completely different perception, idea, or approach. Sometimes, friends can influence in such a way that can bless you. Whether or not it felt like a blessing at the time is irrelevant. It is the outcome that is key.

My friends and family have all played important roles in my life. Some have saved me from trouble, some have pushed me to dream bigger, and others have challenged me to see things differently. Some have made me try harder, some made me take inventory of my life, and some guided me into God's best. Some asked really important questions, and some were used by God to remind me that He knows my situation. I thank God for my friends. They all have brought such richness to my life. Every experience was not pleasant, but the harvest made the labor immaterial.

Growing up I was a loner. Once I got pregnant all my teenaged friends went away. My eldest cousin was my one and only best friend for years. She has been my confidante sounding board, scale, and spiritual intercessor. She witnessed every up and every down of my life. She saw me cry a river after my first husband divorced me and rejoiced with me when my second husband divorced me. She was with me throughout my greatest happiness, joy, and consuming sorrow. She is one of the friends that God uses constantly to remind me that He sees me. Whenever I was in a situation that was taking me over the edge or causing me enormous stress she would call and say, "Hey girl, what's going on?" This spiritual connection is so deep for me. Initially, when this first began to happen, I would ask her, "What made you call me?" She would respond, "You were on my mind, so I called. What's going on?" I would then share my situation. She has been operating with this gift for many years, and the tripped out part is, I'm still amazed at the entire thing.

I was raised not to trust women. I cannot remember the entire conversations about it, but it was understood that having girlfriends were a "no-no". They were only good for stealing your husband and causing you pain. Women outside of your family could not be trusted and never befriended. To break this rule was to your own demise.

In my mid-twenties I met some wonderful women on my train commute to my job and at work. I found myself drawn to them and finding comfort in their company and council. When I first started interacting with them it was a bit strange. Sometimes they would share information or ask questions that I've never thought about before. All of these women had prior girlfriend experiences. I on the other hand, did not. I was totally clueless about girlfriend stuff.

I did not know how to interact at times and I felt the least bit knowledgeable about certain things. One of the sayings I heard my whole life regarding girlfriends was, "When mad day comes, and it will come, all your business will be in the street." I am not sure which woman in my family experienced this type of betrayal, or if they were the one who betrayed a friend's trust, but this saying is the core reason, a girlfriend was the last thing ever needed. I do not think that this rule applied to guys, just girls. My brothers had friends and I guess that was okay. Boys and men must have been viewed as more loyal and trustworthy. At least that was what I thought.

I went out on a limb when I first extended myself as a friend. It was un-chartered territory and I was watching my step. I'm sure they all felt my precaution, but they loved me past it. This band of women has blessed me so much and in so many ways that I cannot name them all. I had to come to a place where I trusted God to take care of my heart even when it came to the forbidden girlfriend factor.

I experienced some very hard times, stressful times and everything in between with these girls, but they blessed me far more than they ever hurt me. I recommend that every girl and woman should have at least two girlfriends. After I gave it some serious thought and looked into what the bible said about friendship I came to the conclusion that friends are a blessing. According to the bible there is only one way to get a friend.

> ***A man that hath friends must shew himself friendly*: and there is a friend that sticketh closer than a brother. Proverbs 18:24(KJV)**

Only the enemy would place the thought of having girlfriends as being harmful. Satan is the one that plants the seed of restriction and fear. That thought did not come from God. It came from a woman who was hurt by another woman, not a friend. This is an example of the world system that people live by, simply because the world system says so. If applied, to the world you are considered to be wise, but God's word says something different in **II Timothy 1:7, "For God hath not given us the spirit of fear; but of power, and of love, and of a sound mind."(KJV)** If we can trust God with everything else, surely He can be trusted to protect our hearts when it comes to our girlfriends as well.

30. Tithing

Before I became obedient to tithing we would give about $150 $300 a month; whatever we could afford to spare and even that was very hard. It seemed like something always came up to consume our money. One year when my kids were babies and funds were very tight, God caused a friend to treat me to lunch; of course I did not have lunch or money for lunch that day. During that time, I shared with her my financial situation. She asked me if we were tithing. I responded, “Sort of.” and explained how we paid. She said, "Well, you know, tithing is 10% of what you earn. So, if you are not giving at least 10% you are not tithing." She then quietly stated that I determined how long my “valley experience” would be and that I would be in the valley of “barely enough” until I became obedient to God’s word. I wanted to choke her!

I was very irritated and could not believe her audacity and it annoyed me that God orchestrated the encounter. He knew exactly what I was facing. If I tithed the 10% our mortgage or other bills would not be paid on time. When I got to my car that evening this preacher was on the radio screaming, "YOU EXPECT GOD TO DO THIS AND THAT AND YOU DO NOT TITHE. YOU DO NOT EVEN QUALIFY FOR A BLESSING!!!!!!!" I was so angry, I slammed the radio off and cried for at least twenty minutes. Well come pay day, I was forced to line up. I wrote the tithe check and began to believe God was going to work a miracle.

Since purchasing our home we had never been late on a payment. The very possibility of this was too much. I had to gain quick faith. I did not want the payment to be late. The very next day my brother-in-law met me at my children’s daycare. He said he had been looking for me and gave me a wad of money. I didn't know how to respond to him. He said, “I was told to give this to you.” Told by who was the question.

I never shared with anyone in my family what was going on. I had been a Christian for a long time; everyone probably assumed that I tithed. I did not want to be exposed and invite everyone into my affairs. So who told him? Well, the money he gave me was $55 more than what we needed. God showed up! The next two times were almost the same. Twice, money was left in my mailbox by a neighbor. I received checks that were unexpected “miracle checks”. It is a true saying, “If you never have a problem, you will never really know that God can solve them.”

The next situation was during the time my husband was unemployed. We were forced to trust God in a deeper and continual way. The unemployment checks were barely enough. Prior to that experience we faced a plethora of faith-building exercises. I was feeling as if I was on some type of accelerated course in faith building. It is amazing how much faith you can put into effect with the right set of circumstances. When you are unable to figure out, manipulate, work, rework, stretch or manage your own way, you will develop a greater confidence and trust in God.

During this time, we continued to tithe as if my husband still had a job. God was faithful as He promised. All of our needs where met and even some of our wants. We were able to go on vacation to Cancun and all our bills were paid on time. I was amazed by God’s faithfulness. When I received our financial statement from church and it said $10,000 I was floored. When my husband was working, our combined income was not $100,000 so how in the world did we give that much to God while my husband was unemployed?

God caused supernatural increase. We were obedient and paid tithes on every penny that came into our hands during that year. God showed us that He takes better care of us, when we trust Him, than we take care of ourselves. **(See Proverbs 3:5)** There was absolutely no lack, only increase and overflow. When my husband went back to work he asked, "What happened to the extra money?" Before I could respond he said, "God takes better care of us than we do." I smiled and thanked God for His faithfulness.

> **Now unto him that is able to do exceeding abundantly above all that we ask or think, according to the power that worketh in us, Ephesians 3:20(KJV)**

I learned a lot during this period of my life, but one thing stuck out in my mind more than anything. If I do what the Word tells me to do, then I will have what the Word says I will have. God is not challenged by His word, people are.

31. Try'em One More Time

The same week my tithing story was published in Christian Women's Magazine my husband lost his job. This was my first published article and it had been in the works for many months. Some may see the timing of these events as coincidental or think it is ironic. I call it PURPOSED. I felt like the enemy was saying, "Now that you have encouraged others through your tithing testimony, let's see if you can 'walk the talk' the second time around."

The enemy always overplays his hand because he is so proud. The simultaneous occurring of these events made it crystal clear to me that it was a test. I just didn't know to what extent my faith would be tested. Two things happened at once. First, the Lord told to me to forgive a debt that was owed to me. Second, was to maintain my integrity in a financial matter that appeared as though I could lose a significant amount of money.

In my mind, these situations were more than I was prepared to deal with independently, so this combo deal was a bit much. Regarding the debt, it wasn't very much money. But since my husband lost his job, it was time to call in all debts. The thought of not being able to depend on that money was annoying to say the least. At first, I tried to act like I didn't hear Him, but He repeatedly made it clear to me what His will was about the matter.

I tell you every time I opened my bible, or any bible related book, it would address forgiving a debt. Finally, after sometime, I do not know exactly how long it took me to cave and to finally become obedient, but I eventually did. The very day I decided that I was going to be obedient and forgive the debt, the word for the day in my daily reading was of course, about the same subject. I thanked God for being patient with me and for making His will clear. I had a full calendar that day. I had back-to-back meetings and could not even see how I was going to fit in time for a personal call. It was a hectic crazy day, but I was determined to get it accomplished. Once I made the call I had such a sense of relief and the gift was graciously received. I did shared how hard it was to be obedient to this instruction because of our current financial state. I even joked and said, "It had to be God cause I ain't that nice on my own." We laughed, and I went on with my stressed out day at work. I informed God that he had a lot of work to do. We needed money and we needed it quickly.

The second thing that I had to face was the financial matter regarding my childcare reimbursement account. Now that my husband was unemployed there was no need for our kids to continue to attend the after school program, which we could no longer afford anyway. $600 was automatically deducted from my paycheck each month for this service. The only way I could get my money out of this account was with receipts for services rendered for childcare. The thought of living without the money made me dizzy, and the thought of leaving it in a reimbursement account that I couldn't touch was even more dizzying. Since the kids no longer went to the after school program, I didn't have a receipt to get reimbursed. The only option I thought available was for me to falsify a receipt. The Lord made it clear to me that was not an option. I said, "Well then what?"

I could not foresee how we were going to make it without the $600. Now keep in mind that this was happening simultaneously to my forgiving the debt that was owed to me. I called a good friend to share my dilemmas. I was actually balling my eyes out, because I was completely overwhelmed with my reality. She listened quietly. She is a very good listener. She shared her thoughts regarding my situation and reminded me of the God that I serve, and how faithful He is. She then stated that I amazed her because I always lined up and did the right thing. This time I really felt like doing the wrong thing. I felt utterly desperate and out of control.

While we were talking, it became crystal clear to me that this was an issue of trust. The question was: Did I really trust God to do His part? When you are being tested your initial reaction is natural. You begin to ask yourself, "How am I going to fix this?" Depending on how far you allow the Holy Spirit to guide you, determines how you react to such trials and tribulations. This situation opened my eyes. After I had this moment of clarity, I was embarrassed. I'm talking about the God who created everything I see, who also called me out of darkness into His marvelous light. This event would not have been the first time that God did His Godly "thang". He did it often and excellently. This moment I would not soon forget, because I recognized a significant deficiency in the trust factor in my relationship with Him.

I knew from that moment that I was going to trust Him and do His will. It was just a matter of how quickly I would do it. During that conversation, my friend asked if I had called the reimbursement program.

"No, for what?"

"You never know. Just call. Maybe there is way out."

"Okay, I'll call when I get back to my desk."

Once back at work, I went online and struggled to find the information that was buried deep in the website. When I called, the representative stated that if I had waited another week, I would have exceeded the allowable time to notify them of a life change. My husband losing his job qualified me to discontinue my contributions and to receive the money in the account. If I had waited any longer to share my situation with my girlfriend, I would not have been able to drop out of the program. They would have continued to withdraw money from account and I would have been unable to qualify for any reimbursements.

The notification window to inform the reimbursement program of a life change was relatively small. Without God's intervention I would have missed it altogether. I never thought to call or look into it, because I assumed I had to remain in the program for the duration of the year. It never crossed my mind that there was a way out of the program. God's requirement for me to maintain my integrity was pointing me to the solution to my problem the entire time. I love how He loves me. I'm striving to love him back just as well.

The last time my husband was unemployed, the lesson was about learning to trust God, and learning that He is Jehovahjireh **(See Genesis 22:14)**, my provider and He takes the most excellent care of His people. This second time it was about that as well, but combined with exercises in obedience, and giving.

It is easy to give when you have extra, but when you only have a little bit, or when what you have is already accounted for it is a very different story. Initially, God provided all we needed to get us through this period via my annual bonus. I received this bonus two months after my husband lost his job. What perfect timing! All was going according to my plan until one day one of my sisters in Christ lost a family member, an infant niece and it was shared that they didn't have any insurance or money to pay for the funeral. I prayed about it, and God said to give her $1,000. Instead, I sent around an email asking for donations for her cause and started the donations off with $100.

The card went around. When I got it back there was still very little money in it. I said out loud, "I know these fools ain't gonna make me have to give $1,000!" So, I went back around to the majority of the people and solicited money. I was so pleased with myself. I was half way there. When I went back to my desk, so pleased with my efforts, The Lord said, "Give her $1,000" I was so out done. I said to myself I have already taken up this substantial collection to prevent from having to give $1,000 and now He still wants me to give $1,000!

I asked Him why this was necessary, and if I could just make up the difference instead of giving an entire $1,000. He did not respond. I also wanted to know why He was requesting this of me. Why wouldn't He ask one of the other Christians? We had plenty of them around for Him to ask! I had even gone so far as to name their names, as if He didn't know who I was referring to. From my perspective, they were all chilling, and I was the one constantly being tested and tried. I never received an answer from Him and I became a bit resentful toward God because it felt like He was picking on me. Later, He reminded me to keep my eyes on Him and not to compare myself to others.

I tried to rebut by saying that I was not comparing. I was just making sure He did not forget that they also needed developing. I think He laughed. Here I am with my mortal self, trying to pull the wool over the eyes of the omnipresent, all-knowing God. What foolishness! It is laughable. I used such a weak argument to disguise my real motives for mentioning them, and to top it off there I was reminding God almighty what not to forget. I cannot even keep up with my own little life. I was attempting to substantiate my actions with a lie.

The truth is misery loves company. I did not want to be in this alone and He knew it. He also knew about my lie. I would have been better off saying nothing. I told my Christian friends that I mentioned to God not to forget about them, that they needed developing too. Of course, they did not appreciate it and responded something like, "Don't pull me into your mess! That's between you and God! I have my own issues!"

God made this request the Monday after Easter. I remember it so well, for two reasons. The first reason was because the Christian who lost her infant niece had purchased the child's first Easter dress. The second reason was because the most unusual thing happened at my mother's house at Easter dinner. During dinner my sister and I got into a physical altercation.

I recognized early in the evening that my sister was not in a very good mood. I thought she would eventually come around to her normal self. She sat to my right and we were all enjoying each other's company joking around and stuff. My younger brother told us this super, funny story and while laughing, I hit my sister on the arm. I did it half on purpose to pull her into the camaraderie. What I didn't fully take into consideration was the extent of her bad mood and how extremely heavy handed I am. My sister retaliated with a ninja-like move. She quickly circled my wrist with her hand and grabbed it with a force and speed I didn't know she possessed, and proceeded to forcefully dig her nails into my wrist.

I was so shocked, hurt, peeved, angry, and ready to beat her down! I said,

"Let me go!"

"Why did you hit me?"

"I was just playing. Now let me go!"

She kept squeezing and glaring at me like a crazy person. The room became silent and everyone's eyes were on us. By this time I couldn't believe she really was trying to hurt me. My feelings were hurt, but that quickly changed into anger. Anger rose up and I retaliated with equal force, but I was being careful not to dig my nails into her skin. Looking her straight in the eyes I said, "You are digging your nails into my skin, you're hurting me, now let go of me!"

My mother was yelling for us to stop. My younger brother was saying, "I got five on Linda." Finally, my sister released her crazy hold of my wrist and I then let her go. Then she started to cry. I didn't understand what she was crying for. She hurt me. My wrist bore the marks of her force. I had several crescent moon-like scars on my wrist. I then recognized that my bracelet was missing. It got knocked off at the initial blow. I found my bracelet and stood up. My mother was so embarrassed and hurt by this unexpected display of disdain. She tried to get us to apologize. I was infuriated and the only thing I wanted to do was beat my sister down for leaving marks on me. I said, "I don't owe her an apology, she hurt me!" My sister finally gave me a cold, dry, sorry and ran upstairs.

I started to get ready to go. The dinner was over and I was so ready to leave. While getting my kid's coats on my sister came back down stairs and said she was sorry again. She looked so miserable. I said I was sorry too and I hugged her. During the embrace I asked her, "Why did you want to hurt me?" She then broke the embrace and walked away pitifully. I was standing there looking stupid and feeling sorrowful. The enemy had made a fool out of both of us.

Later that night I had several conversations with family members who expressed what I should have done and what she deserved. I was ashamed of my behavior. Nobody else thought I did anything wrong, but I did. I retaliated with the same force. I didn't exemplify Christ. I let my anger combined with the pressure of people effect my behavior. That night, I earnestly prayed for my sister deeper than I've ever prayed for her before.

The situation weighed so heavily on my mind that I had to call her before I went to sleep. It was late I got her voice mail. I left her a heartfelt apology and I said we needed to talk. As soon as I got to work the next day I called her again. No answer. Again, I left another message. She returned my call later that day. She sincerely apologized and began to share with me her day and her feelings that ultimately led to our altercation. She also shared that I annoyed her. My sister was dealing with feelings of jealousy toward me. She had shared that she was jealous of me years ago. I assumed that she had gotten over it.

I'm the only little sister she has, and I love my sister and I have always admired her. She went on to say how it appears that everything always works out for me because of my obedience. She sensed that I was reaping a good harvest. I was amazed at the words that were coming out of her mouth. I was right in the middle of being disobedient by not giving the lady the $1,000. I interrupted her and said, "Nothing is easy for me, and I'm not obedient all the time. Rarely am I quickly obedient." I told her that from the outside, things look totally different from reality. I shared some of my struggles, and then I shared my current situation. I said,

"See, I ain't so faithful or obedient. I struggle like everybody else."

"How do you know it was God who told you to give the $1,000 to her?"

"I know God's voice. Plus, Satan wouldn't have me do anything nice for anyone."

"You're right."

"God is so good and faithful, and His word says that I will reap what I sow. I can't out give God."

"Well, knowing all that, why haven't you done what He told you to do?"

"Because it feels so foolish to give away the little bit I have when there is no more coming in."

"But you just said, 'You couldn't out give God!'"

"I know. See how I struggle? There's a difference between knowing the word of God and applying it. I'm having trouble in the area of doing what the word says."

"Well, what are you going to do?"

"The right thing."

"Good."

I sat there for a few minutes after our conversation thinking about how God took a bad situation and worked it out for the good. Prior to that conversation with my sister I had not shared what God told me to do with anyone. I was purposefully planning not to share it and then God, in His infinite wisdom, used this fight, the situation and the conversation to verbally expose His will and confess my disobedience to my sister, who thought I was all that.

It's so tripped out because my disobedience was about a lot of things. I cared about what people thought of me. I didn't want anyone to think I was a fool for giving away money during the time of my husband's unemployment. I really just wanted to keep my money in my pocket. I could see it there. I didn't have to wait for a miracle to be performed to get it there. It was already there. This had everything to do with me feeling in control of the little bit that I had. The little money I had was not even enough to meet all the needs at the time. This was a very frustrating time for me.

On the way home I made up my mind to follow through and do what the Lord told me to do. It was evident to me that I was not a cheerful giver. I only surrendered, because I'm no match for God, and I saw first hand how He orchestrated and confirmed His will. I was like, plain ole, "Okay, I give." You'd think the next day I would have hurried up and took care of business? But oh no, I dragged it out another day. The Spirit of God woke me up with: "This is your last chance." I sat straight up in the bed and looked around. I thought my husband must have heard it too. I looked over at him and he was sound asleep. I sat there for a minute thinking, last chance! I thought you gotta be kidding. I said I was going to do it. I got in the shower and I heard it again. My heart was beating so loudly, I thought it was going to crash through my chest bone.

I then repented for my delayed response to His will. I could not wait until I got to work to get the cashier's check and finally get this thing behind me. This must have been what Jonah felt like when he got the opportunity to be obedient to God after his stay in the belly of the fish. Funny thing was that I felt overwhelmingly embarrassed, even though God was the only one watching.

As always, I read the daily word during my commute. I was dreading reading it because I thought it would certainly have something to do with disobedience, or God's wrath for disobedience. This happens more times than you would believe. The word for the day typically applies to whatever situation I'm experiencing. Some would say that's uncanny, I say it's God once again showing up in everything.

When I started to read the word for that day I was initially relieved because it appeared to have nothing to do with disobedience, or the wrath of God from disobedience. I literally exhaled after reading a few lines thinking thank you Lord for this word not being about me. I really got it and didn't really need anything else to top it off. For real, I got it! Then I kept reading. To my chagrin the story had everything to do with disobedience. I had to stop reading for a few minutes because the story upset me to tears. I never read this story from the beginning. The story is about an unnamed prophet who is given explicit instructions by God. He is told to deliver a message, how to enter, exit, and not to eat or drink while there. He followed God's instructions to the T. He even rejected a lucrative offer from the King, but in the end he was killed because another prophet deceived him into disobeying God. **(See I Kings 13)**

Once I got to work I called my sister who was a bit shocked by the fact that I had not yet been obedient. I told her about the word for the day and I told her I was on my way to get the cashier's check. I was an emotional wreck to say the least. I told her that I didn't want anyone to know the gift was from me. I wanted the gift to be anonymous. I didn't want any praise for the gift because it took me forever to become obedient. My guilty conscious was getting the best of me. If people knew the monetary gift was from me they would naturally respond like what I did was so great, and I was so good, but for me that was the farthest thing from the truth. It was all God's goodness and not my own. I felt unworthy of the least amount of praise because I'm not good, not at all. Only God in me is good. Linda is automatically set on self-preservation.

My sister informed me that I could request a blank cashier's check. I was happy to hear it and immediately went to the bank to finally get this thing behind me. A nice, young man asked how he could help me. I told him that I wanted a blank cashier's check. He asked why, and I told him for an anonymous donation. He then went to the back to ask his manager if that was possible. You would not believe what happened next. The enemy showed up, in a big way, he begin to speak to my mind. These were his words. The enemy said,

"You are a fool! You don't even have enough money to carry your family from now until the end of the year!"

"I replied, "God will supply all my needs according to His riches in Glory." **Philippians 4:19**

"What do you plan to do? You don't even have a plan!"

"God will take care of me. I will reap my harvest if I faint not." **Galatians 6:9**

"You are the biggest sucker!"

"I'll be a fool for Him." **Psalm 34:22** supports this response.

"Who's going to help you when you have a need?"

"God is a very present help in the time of need." **Psalm 46:1**

"Are you sure that was God who told you to do this?"

"Yes! It was God because you would never tell me to help anyone; you are the god of selfishness. You would only tell me to ignore the urge to help somebody; to only take care of me and mine." **James 2:15-16** supports this response.

I won the battle and the war that day by successfully appropriating God's word. The enemy was under my feet!!!.**(Chapter 1 Read and Apply)** The word of God is the only weapon we have to use against the enemy

The man came back with the check in hand. I thanked him and I was about to walk away when I remembered I was giving it anonymously. I asked him to write his name on the check. My handwriting is very distinctive and I didn't want to be found out. On the elevator, the enemy attacked once again. He said, "She ain't even coming in to work today. They already gave her the card and the money when she was in yesterday." That thought instantly irritated me and almost took me over the edge. Then I finally regained my composure and asked the Lord if she was coming in today. He quickly responded, "That's my job. Don't worry about that. Just do your job." That word from God gave me an immediate bounce to my step and I went to the believer's desk looking for the card to put the cashier's check into it, but it was not there. No one was there. So I put the envelope on her chair and walked away.

While I was on a conference with an attorney I heard a big raucous. I wanted to put the call on hold, but it was at an inappropriate time, so I tried to ignore the noise and focus on the conversation. As soon as I hung up the phone one of my co-workers came running down to my desk smiling and crying happily. I asked her what happened. She said,

"Girl, somebody gave a big cashier's check and forgot to sign it. Wonder why they didn't sign it?"

"Usually when people don't sign something they want to remain anonymous." She then looked at me most peculiarly and said,

"That's from you?" I hushed her and told her I didn't want anybody to know it was not from me because it was from God. I think I said that three times during our small conversation and I asked her not to tell anyone. She said, okay, smiled, and walked away.

Later on, when I was on another call she came back over. Her face was wet with tears again, she was there when the young lady showed up and picked up the other collection that I initiated in disobedience, along with the cashier's check from me. She was saying, I should have been there to see her reaction. She said it was so moving. I could only imagine. I was so happy this entire event was behind me. During the mid point of this experience, I shared my situation with one of my Christian friends. When I told her I gave anonymously, she asked,

"Why?"

"I wanted to be anonymous because I didn't want any undue praise. It took me too long to become obedient. God really gave it. I didn't."

"Was that part of God's instructions?"

"No."

I explained to her again my reasoning and she said, "That's your guilt; not His instructions. I believe it is God's will for her to know it was from you."

The funeral happened on my off day, but I had a strong urge to go. I had to travel a great distance and traffic was horrible. When I got there the funeral was over. I almost had a conniption fit right there in my car. I sat there for a minute about to cry. I heard, "Get out of the car." I did. I walked toward the church. A few people walked past me. I couldn't believe it. The young lady came walking out of the church. I was so happy! My trip was not a total waste. I could hug her and let her know that I was there for her. She looked so happy to see me. She squeezed my hand so tight and she just held on to it. For a minute there were no words.

I told her about the traffic and how I tried to be there for the funeral and she responded, "Thank you, I'm so happy to see you!" She didn't look sad at all. She looked strong and sturdy like a tree planted by the river. I was amazed at her strength. We talked a bit more and then said our goodbyes. The ride home was very long, but not entirely unbearable because the mission had been accomplished.

I can't remember how much time passed, but one day the young lady asked if she could speak to me in private. When we got into the conference room she said,

"You know why I want to speak to you, right?"

"Yeah, I think so."

She then went on to thank me for the gift and expressed to me the most amazing thing. She said the entire time she was taking care of the funeral expenses she never prayed or asked God to help her pay her bills. She just did what had to be done. While she was taking care of God's business, He took care of her business through me. The money that I gave and the extra that I collected met her needs exactly. While she was talking I was once again amazed at His awesomeness. He took my disobedience and turned it around and used it to provide for her. God is awesome. I am constantly awed by His ability to turn bad into good.

At the closing of our conversation she confessed how she would give me the cold shoulder, sometimes. She also shared that God instructed her to stop acting like that. She initially thought if she was not saying anything bad she was safe. But then God made her know and understand that He was not pleased with that type of behavior. She said she was working on it. We hugged and laughed. We are friends to this day.

When God woke me up with, "This is your last chance." He knew that she was coming in early that day and afterward she would be off. He was speaking of the last opportunity for me to do His will. It's a choice. I thought He was speaking about my last chance before He did something drastic for my disobedience. Then, once I read the word for the day, my feelings of doom were compounded. But make no mistake; it was God's will for me to read that story to recognize His mercy on me. I thanked God for His mercy. Without it I would have been in deep trouble.

A few months later while speaking to a woman at work about God's ability to do exceeding above all we can ask or think **(See Ephesians 3:21)** she shared that she believed God for a new house. I instructed her to write her dream down on paper and to list everything she wanted her house to have in it. I told her that writing it down would keep the vision before her and would help to increase her faith.

It was challenging for her to put her dream down on paper. I asked her why was it hard for her to write it down? She admitted it was because of fear. I told her that God did not give the spirit of fear, but of power, love, and a sound mind. I also shared my vision of my new house with her.

> **For God hath not given us the spirit of fear; but of power, and of love, and of a sound mind. II Timothy 1:7 (KJV)**

After our conversation, I was so engrossed in my work that I forgot to warn her that once she wrote down her dream and believed God for it, the enemy was going to make an attempt to steal her dream from her. The enemy does this through whatever means he can to distract the person from praying and standing on God's word. The Lord reminded me later that she was not prepared for the upcoming attack.

A few days later she was very upset and I pulled her into a conference room and asked her what was wrong. She informed me that since she prayed, and believed God for a new house, things began to go wrong. She had recently purchased a bed and her daughter had spilled something on her mattress. In her daughter's attempt to clean it, the entire mattress was ruined. She was very upset. She then said it seemed like every time she prayed, something bad happened. I told her that it was the enemy's job to try to quickly remove God's word and any developing faith. She told me of several bad things that had happened since she prayed. For each of the additional negatives I shared a positive. She responded that she had not considered the positives and she began to see God's hand protecting her even in what the devil presented as negatives.

I asked her, "Have you asked God for a new bed?"

I told her that she needed to make her request known to God.

> **Don't worry about anything; instead, pray about everything. Tell God what you need, and thank him for all he has done. Philippians 4:6(NLT)**

She replied no, so I told her what God's word says about Him supplying all her needs, and then we prayed. **Philippians 4:19, which reads, "And my God will meet all your needs according to his glorious riches in Christ Jesus."(NIV)**

On the way home I was thinking about what miraculous means God was going to use in meeting her needs. Then God said, "You do it." I replied, "No, not me, I meant somebody else." He said, "You do it." I said, "Okay." I agreed a bit quicker this time to His instructions because I was making a concentrated effort to apply what I had recently learned about obedience. When you know better you should do better. Just keep in mind it was a struggle from that point until God's mission was accomplished.

The next day when I saw her I asked her where did she sleep last night. She said in her daughter's bed with her other children. I told her that the Lord wanted me to buy her a bed. She looked at me oddly and said, "For real?" and then she said, “Okay.” She did not express a lot of excitement about it. She was almost indifferent. When Friday rolled around, she left without giving me her information.

When I got home I shared with my husband what God instructed me to do. I was scared to tell him, because I was afraid of his reaction. We were still surviving off one income and he was having trouble understanding how we were able to do everything we needed and able to bless other people in any monetary way. I told him the entire story and the truth of my heart. After listening to what I had to say his attitude changed. The truth was, I was having a hard time being obedient and understanding God’s purpose as much as my husband was, but I just had to trust Him.

The money that I was planning to use to purchase her bed was specifically allocated for the month of December, yeah Christmas. So, to use my kid’s Christmas money to buy someone a bed seemed crazy. The Lord did not ask me to use our mortgage money, He asked me to use something that was stored up for later. David and I had bible class that night and God pointed us to every scripture supporting His will for us. God constantly amaze me at how he does this. I know He is God and He created everything I see, and even the things I cannot see, but it is still amazing how He leads us in our personal bible class time.

The next morning, while I was out I realized that I still did not have a way to get in touch with her. I said, “Lord, she left work without giving me her information.” and He replied, “Look in your phone.” I thought, what? Sure enough her number was in my phone. This freaked me out for a minute, but then I remembered putting her number in my phone a while back in case I needed her assistance. She worked really close with my manager and I thought it would be a good idea to have her numbers in my phone. I called her a few times on Saturday, but she never answered.

My husband and I woke up pretty early Sunday morning and began to talk. He walked over to the chest where his bible was open. He looked down and began reading. Then he said, "Linda, this scripture is for you." I said, "Read it to me." He began to read from **II Corinthians 8:7-15(NLT) "Since you excel in so many ways in your faith, your gifted speakers, your knowledge, your enthusiasm, and your love from us I want you to excel also in this gracious act of giving I am not commanding you to do this. But I am testing how genuine your love is by comparing it with the eagerness of the other churches. You know the generous grace of our Lord Jesus Christ. Though he was rich, yet for your sakes he became poor, so that by his poverty he could make you rich. Here is my advice: It would be good for you to finish what you started a year ago. Last year you were the first who wanted to give, and you were the first to begin doing it. Now you should finish what you started. Let the eagerness you showed in the beginning be matched now by your giving. Give in proportion to what you have. Whatever you give is acceptable if you give it eagerly. And give according to what you have, not what you don't have. Of course, I don't mean your giving should make life easy for others and hard for yourselves. I only mean that there should be some equality. Right now you have plenty and can help those who are in need. Later, they will have plenty and can share with you when you need it. In this way, things will be equal. As the Scriptures say, those who gathered a lot had nothing left over, and those who gathered only a little had enough."**

I needed those words from God that morning. It confirmed that I was doing exactly what I should be doing. I called the young lady and she answered the phone. I was so happy to hear her voice. She sounded a little bit surprised to hear from me because she knew she left without giving me her phone number. We talked on the phone for a while. I shared how God had dealt with my husband's heart during our bible time along with the scripture he read to me.

The odd thing about that particular scripture was that it was not highlighted in my bible. My husband had the New Living Translation and I read from the Kings James Version. I typically understand the Kings James Version just fine and I have most scriptures memorized from that version. However, this scripture was very difficult for me to comprehend in the Kings James Version.

I called her before I left the house and told her I was on my way and she said,

"I just told my mother that you were coming over to buy me a bed."

"Is she the first person you told?"

"Yeah."

"Oh."

She then said, "My father is trippin' he was suppose to come and get my kids, and now all of a sudden, it is a problem."

"That is just the devil acting a fool because you are about to get a new bed. Don't worry about it. God will work it out."

While I was talking to her I spotted my debit card on my jewelry box. I thanked God for letting me see it because if I had gone that far, and was not able to purchase the bed it would have been angry. I picked it up and went into the kitchen to get some coffee and food to eat in the car. I was on my way out the door and my husband asked, "Do you have everything?"

"Yeah, I think so."

I went back into the kitchen and my debit card was on the counter. I thanked God again and this time, I put it in my purse and thanked my husband for asking me if I had everything. My husband said, "Linda, slow down and pray." We then said our departure prayer, "May the Lord watch between me and thee, while we are absent one from another, in Jesus name, amen." Then I left.

I was so excited to take care of this for God. I had $750 to buy her a bed and my intent was to replace the exact one that was ruined. She lived a great distance from my house and I was not familiar with her neighborhood at all. I passed her house several times before I finally pulled over and called her on the phone. She asked if that was me sitting in the car across the street. I said yes.

I busted a 'U', and pulled in front of her house. She got into the car and off we went to take care of the business. Everything worked out better than ever. The bed only cost about $450.00 and was scheduled for delivery the very next day. We were so happy. The Lord's will had been done and she had her bed. Praise the Lord!

Once we got back to her place we talked a bit more about God and His ability to take care of us. Then the Lord told me to ask her if she died that day where would she spend eternity. I thought that was an odd question to ask, since I thought she was a Christian. After a few minutes of reluctance, I finally asked her the question and to my surprise she said, "Hell."

"What?"

"Hell."

"I thought you were saved?"(Accepted Jesus as your Lord and Savior)

"No. I use to be, but I backslid."

"Oh."

"I've done bad things."

"We all have."

"I've murdered."

"In what sense do you mean?"

"I murdered my baby. I had an abortion."

"So did I; I had two."

"Really?"

"Yes. You have not done anything that God will not forgive you. If you ask Him for forgiveness, He will forgive you. After you acknowledge Him as your Savior, and ask Him for forgiveness, you are a Christian. "Do you want to go to hell?" (By default of not choosing to accept and acknowledge Jesus, as Savior, one has chosen to go to Hell)

She replied "No."

"God is not expecting perfection. Becoming like Christ is a decision and process. It is not an instant thing and it is a lie that Satan uses to keep people away from God. People think they have to become perfect before they can give their lives to Him or even join a church. You can't clean yourself up. That is impossible. Only God can clean you up. It is actually a transformation from your image to His image. He takes out the old, which is the world system, out of you and He builds you up with His word, God's system. This is how you become like Jesus. Really nobody is expecting an over night sensation and if they are, they shouldn't be. In this process, you sometimes fall down you get up, you fall down you get up. The most important thing is to get up. Don't stay down. The more time you spend in the word and in prayer you will get to know God's character and you will build a relationship with Him. Just like you are getting to know me. Prior to the time we spent together you had no idea of what type of person I was. You probably figured that I was different than what I actually am because people look at the outside and judge."

I asked her "Am I anything like you thought?"

"No. I would have never thought you would have done and have been through the things that you've shared with me."

“The truth is the truth and continuing in God’s truth is freeing. Do you want to give your life to Christ?”

“Yes.”

I led her in prayer and she gave her life to Christ that Sunday afternoon in my car. God is awesome! I had no idea that was part of His plan. She looked and behaved like she was a Christian, but God knew the truth. It is so funny to me in retrospect because I had other things I needed to do for myself that day. I needed to prepare for my daughter’s birthday party, which was the following weekend, and get my hair washed, but God had other plans for me that day.

I thank Him for allowing me to be His instrument. Know that the enemy fought me all the way. Doing God’s will is a matter of choice. God talks to each one of us and tells us to do things. It is up to us to choose if we will do them or not. God is looking for obedience. God is looking at your willingness to obey Him and to do His will over your own. To tell you the truth, there was a great sense of fulfillment after His mission was accomplished. Everything worked out for my daughter’s party and my hair survived another week. Don’t get me wrong, I was tired and the enemy was mad, but I was victorious in Jesus.

The next day I found out that the young lady did not believe me when I told her that I was going to buy her the bed. She had been so let down in the past by close family members and church folks that she lost confidence in people. So this mission that God sent me on was three-fold purposed. In doing His will three needs were met. A practical need, a spiritual need, and an emotional need. A practical need was met by my gift of buying the bed for her. The spiritual need was met because she was led back to Christ and the emotional need was met by my keeping my word and not lying to her. In all my efforts Christ was demonstrated. Without God in me, none of this would have been accomplished.

For if the willingness is there, the gift is acceptable according to what one has, not according to what he does not have. II Corinthians 8:12(NIV)

God speaks to each of us. He is the tug you feel in your heart to do something kind or generous for someone. That is God directing you to action. Some people think they should pray at this point. I would never say that prayer is a bad thing, but it makes me wonder. Does anyone actually get around to praying about it? If so, did God say no or stop? Or, is the opportunity to be a blessing to someone is forgotten or altogether missed? Only God directs you to bless, help, or assist someone.

The fact is you were born selfish, and like me you are not good, at least not on you own. But, God in you is good. You have a choice, a free will to respond or not to respond. I am aware that there are scheming people looking to take advantage of others. Maybe that is why people hesitate and miss plenty of opportunities to be a blessing to others. People fear being made a fool of. It would be great if people worried less about being made a fool of and was more concerned about being obedient to God's tug on their heart's. He is such a powerful God that He can, and He will, and He does protect you in every way. So you are covered! Relax, take a deep breath, and be a blessing.

No weapon formed against you should prosper. Isaiah 54:17(KJV)

It is always an excellent idea to measure all things up against God's word. Such as considering the poor, the orphaned, and the widows are no-brainers. These things are covered in the word. Some may not know theses scriptures, but they are all covered in His word especially in the book of Proverbs. God typically does not ask you to mortgage your house, but he may ask you to feed a family, pay a bill, or spend some meaningful time with the sick, the prisoner, or elderly.

God is love and He takes care of His people through His people. He moves through people and that includes you. God is also judging the reason you respond or not to His will. You are an open book to Him. There is nothing that He does not know about you. Down to the intent of why you do or don't do what He says. So start today, listen for His direction via that tug on your heart and bless somebody.

A few weeks later I was asked to do something that I have been counseled against by the world all my life. My cousin needed me to co-sign on a loan he needed to continue college. Needless to say, I tried everything I could think of to get out of this request. Even though he is a Christian, a family member, and the only young person I know going to a major university on an academic scholarship, I still could not bring myself to do this. I shared my dilemma with my husband and surprisingly he replied, "Doesn't the bible tell us, 'As we have opportunity to do good, to do it especially to other Christians?'" **(See Galatians 6:10)** I replied, "Yes." I stood there in absolute amazement. Didn't he have any concerns about how hard it was to establish our credit, and didn't he remember that I use to be bankrupt, and that my credit was all we had because he was not working? Simply put, I was annoyed.

I wanted my husband to fight me on this. I wanted him to say "Absolutely not!" and get me off the hot seat. But no, he got all spiritually deep on me. Great! This request was different than the others because of the size and the amount of time associated with it. I prayed, and prayed, and prayed, and heard nothing, but what my husband said. During the course of these conversations I was impressed with my cousin's ability to follow up, and do his part no matter what I asked him to do. He never displayed any annoyance or irritability to me. I knew he must have been on pins and needles, and tired of me as well, but he held himself together.

Sometime later I mentioned to my husband that I was still waiting on God to reply and he said, "I already replied. I told you what to do. What more do you need?" I did not understand what he was talking about. I was talking about God not him. Then he looked at me and said, "Linda that part is in the bible. I'm surprised you are struggling like this." I was mad as a mad hatter! The very next day I was on the Metra train praying and reading the word for the day and guess what the scripture was for the day? It was the one that my husband mentioned earlier from Galatians 6:10. I was saddened and frustrated. My husband was on target the entire time, but I had the worst time lining up. I reminded God how hard I worked to get and keep my credit good, and He replied, "I know. It was for such a time as this." Finally, I got it and signed the papers.

God sent the final confirming message through the word of the day. God knew I needed to hear directly from Him because that is what I was accustomed to. He wanted my cousin's need to be met and He wanted them met through me. God was speaking through my husband the entire time. But I could not receive it that way because I was not accustomed to him moving in that way. It is very easy to put God in a box and expect him to operate in only one way, but those are caps and limitations that we place on God. I have learned from this situation that He can move in any way He wants and can use anybody He wants, simply because He is God. Due to God's will I was able to be a blessing, my cousin was able to continue his education, and he did not miss a beat. My cousin is such a wonderful, positive progressive young man. I am very proud of who he is and what he is striving to accomplish.

32. The Sweetest Surprise

I found out that I was pregnant with my son David, the day after burying my father; it was the most unexpected thing. My husband and I had given up on having any babies together. We had miscarried two and had conceded that we would not have any of our own. After the second miscarriage, I had an exploratory surgery, but was not give any definitive reason for the miscarriages. I was told miscarriages were nature's way of dealing with unhealthy fetuses. That did not help me. The first one, we lost at three months and the second one, was closer to five months. One day the baby simply stopped moving.

My husband was content to raise my son Joey as his own. He never complained about my inability to carry a baby to term. I felt enormous guilt. I believed in my heart the reason I could not have his baby, which I wanted so badly, was because of the two I aborted before I met him. I did not keep this a secret from him. Amazingly, he never held a grudge about it, and if he did, he never showed me.

The day I found out I was pregnant, you could have bought me for a broken penny. The pregnancy was a complete unexpected surprise. My son Joey was getting ready for school. He came in my room and said, "Mom, you look so terrible! I'm not going to school unless you go to the hospital." My husband told him to go on to school, and that he would make sure I saw the doctor. I really did not want to go to the doctor because my dad had just died of cancer, and my period had been missing for so long. I could not even remember when I had the last one. In my mind, the only news they could have given me would be bad news.

Once we got to the hospital, my husband remained in the room with me. The doctor walked in behind the nurse and did their thing. They were gone for a long time. When the nurse came back she said, "Mother?" I was wondering how she knew I was a mother. I was thinking I probably looked like somebody's mother. Because of the lack of my response she said, "You are pregnant." I responded, "How?" She then started to laugh. My husband was behind me doing the 'Toyota shout' and I felt so confused. I said, "We haven't even 'done it' in forever. How could this be?" Then my husband said sort of jokingly, "I did what I had to do when you were asleep." I couldn't believe what he was saying. I was totally embarrassed. Then he said, "I had no choice. The only things you have done for the past two years is cry, pray, and sleep. I got my time when you were asleep."

He was right. I could not remember the last time we were intimate. I was totally engrossed with my father's illness from the onset, until death. He said, "You were so tired from all that running around and worrying, you slept through all of it. He was just smiling like he was so proud of himself. I was mortified. I wanted to bash him in the head! Nasty self!!! How could he do that? Yuck!!! I found out later that a lot of babies have been made this way. Who knew?

I was four months into my pregnancy when I found out I was pregnant. God covered me with His grace, to unknowingly get past the first trimester. But I had a hard time adjusting to accepting that I was pregnant. I could not get my mind wrapped around the fact that I was having a child. Especially, since my father had passed, I really did not want to have a baby. He was the pivotal male figure in my eldest son's life. I felt as though it was not fair for my new baby, to be raised, without the luxury of having a grandfather.

My father was the most exceptional grandfather. He was much better at being a grandfather than a father. I do not remember much about his fathering ability, but I recall so many excellent things that he did as a grandfather. I am not sure if that was because I needed him, and he was there for my son and me, or whether it was because he got older, finally realizing what was really important in life.

At that time in my marriage, I had not fully realized the quality man I married. After several weeks of battling, what I now know was depression; I told David "If you ever leave me, I will staple the baby to yo back! Cause I ain't raisin' any mo' babies by myself! If this goes bad, I'm doing the walking this time around. I'll visit and pay child support." He looked at me with such love in his eyes, placed his hand gently on my face, and said, "Linda, that's crazy talk, and I'm gonna look over what you just said because that's the hurt from your past talking. I am not going to leave you, or hurt you."

From that day forward, I believe David made it his primary mission in life to love me deeper, and harder, and more purposefully, than he ever had before. I am not sure if that conversation sparked this deeper love, or was it just the fact that I was finally having his baby. He became everything I ever wanted a husband to be, but I still held some of me in reserve, just in case things didn't work out. I was living in a place of extraordinary wonderment and dreaded anticipation of the bottom dropping out. Because of this fear, I was afraid to shop for maternity clothes. I felt if I allowed myself to get excited, it would jinx me. But God planted a person near me to help me during this transition period.

We were an unlikely pair to become friends. We had nothing in common, and she even felt inclined to let me in on that fact during one of our conversations. When I first met her I felt like she needed a long, sincere hug. I felt like something really bad had happened to her. She came off condescending, arrogant, and a wee bit harsh. To me, all of that screamed that she needed to be befriended. She initially resisted my friendship, but she wound up loving me. She watched me very close after she found out I was pregnant. She knew I was still mourning my father's death. I think his death hit me harder than anyone expected. She noticed that I was not buying any maternity clothes, then one day she said,

"Let's go shopping. You need some maternity clothes."

"No, I'm good."

"No, you are not. It's time for you to buy some maternity clothes."

She practically dragged me there, but a wonderful thing happened while I was there. I recognized how pregnant I was. I couldn't stop looking in the mirror at my belly. I was actually pregnant. I was having a baby. I was having David's baby. I was having a baby by my husband and I looked so pretty. I purchased several outfits and was glowing from that day forward. God blessed me through this dear friend that day.

God has used her to assist me in so many monumental moments of my life. This is the person who said, we had nothing in common, and really did not want to be my friend. God uses whomever He wants to do His will.

One day, during lunch, she asked me, "What is the theme for your nursery?" For a minute, I did not know what she was talking about. I never had a nursery, or knew anyone who had one. I was not aware that this was something I had to do. I had just gotten excited about being pregnant, and now she is informing me that there is more to be expected that needed to be done. The more she talked, the more I listened, and finally, these conversations got my creative juices flowing. Needless to say, the nursery turned out exceptionally wonderful. Even today, when I look back at the pictures, they bring me certain joy. I think to myself, wow, that was my son's nursery.

Everyday during my pregnancy was sweeter than the day before. I was getting all this special love from everyone. Everyone was so happy for me. This is also when I fully realized what a great husband I had. I had no idea what an exceptional father he would be. He tenderly loved me during my pregnancy, but after the birth of our son I felt his love even more and he constantly doted over our son. He took the most excellent care of me. I had never been taken care of in that way before. That time of my life was like a fairy tale. I cried a lot because I could not believe how happy I was; the great experiences I was having; and the wonderful feelings I was feeling. I said to my husband, on more than one occasion, "I wish my mother and sister could feel this type of love. This kind of love would heal them." It was like having something tasty that you wanted to share with those who are closest to you, so that they can share in that same experience.

This love, that I experienced, had healing attributes. Prior to getting pregnant with my son, David, I was emotionally bruised and bitter. Not to the point where I was unbearable, but on a deeper, hidden level. The damage was most apparent to my husband. I was married twice before David. My first husband was my eldest son's father. My second husband was a fellow I married after only knowing for six months. Both failed for many reasons, and my heart bore the scars. I felt like if I could hold back from loving hard, then my heart would not get damaged any further.

For seven years, my husband David received reserved limited love. In my heart and mind, I was doing what was necessary to protect myself from future hurt. In retrospect, I recognized how much I cheated both of us. It is nothing short of a miracle David stayed with me. He felt my half-love daily, but he continued to love me anyway. I did not surrender my heart completely to David until a month after our son's birth. That is when it finally sunk in that he was not going to abandon me.

During a heartfelt conversation, I shared with David why I was so upset about having a baby, since my father had passed He replied, "It was necessary for your father to be there for your first born, because there was no one else. Now, I am here. It is my job to be that pivotal, male, role model for our son, no one else's. You do not have to worry about anything. I'm gonna take care of you. This child is mine too, and I'm taking this job very seriously."

This pregnancy was a tremendous blessing because it was through this child that God healed me. God used this situation to reverse all the pain I had experienced in my past. He offset all the bad I had suffered with good. Actually, it was more than good. It was amazing! Through the love, my husband continually expressed to me during this time, God enabled me to open my heart and to truly love again.

The bitterness, resentment, pain, and fear all went away. Slowly, I began to understand that God could protect my heart along with the rest of my life, and He did a fantastic job. I had no idea of the joy that was set before me. Having a baby in a loving, committed relationship was nothing I had ever experienced. It was better than I ever expected. It was so wonderful to share this little bundle of joy with my husband and not be alone. My husband was every bit involved in every aspect of this newborn's life as I was. I was amazed at my husband's level of interest in areas that I thought were specifically for mothers.

At the 2 a.m. feeding time, I would get up and go to the rocking chair, to relax and nurse our baby. My husband would get up too. He would always bring me something good to drink, and adjust the pillow behind my back or feet. His demonstrated love was beyond anything I ever thought about or even asked for. It was this type of expressed, demonstrated love that assisted in my healing process. Never discount the power of love. God is love, and expressed love is powerful. It has healing components.

One morning I was having a very difficult time nursing the baby, because my breasts were engorged. This happened as a result of our baby not waking up for the 4 a.m. feeding. So there I was, trying to get my son to latch onto my engorged breast. I was not having much success, and it hurt. My husband came into the room with a glass of orange juice and asked, "What's going on? Why can't he get a hold of it?" I told him the problem and I kept trying. Finally, I came to the conclusion that I needed to release some of the milk. I pressed my upper breast, and the hot milk sprayed across my baby's face. I was shocked. I never expected that much milk to come out, and especially with that much force. My baby gasped for air, and my husband yelled, "What are you doing? You are drowning him!!" I responded, "I'm not trying to! I was trying to get some of the milk out so that he can latch on!" My husband said, "Well let me hold the baby until you get it together." I was annoyed, tired and frustrated, but a part of me was so happy to have someone there who cared and was up with me trying to help.

Finally, my breasts were supple enough for the baby to latch on. My husband had cleaned his face and neck, wrapped him in a fresh blanket, and brought him over to me. He asked, "Are you ready?" I replied, "Yes." Well, now the baby is really hungry. He smells the milk and he excitedly tried to locate my nipple. It was the most hilarious thing to see. His little face moving around in such excitement, it reminded me of the excitement a little puppy displays. Instinctively, he turns his face to the extreme right and latched on with perfection.

Now everyone's happy, and I leaned into the rocking chair to relax my back, and my husband yelled, "Linda he can't breathe! You're smothering him!" My body immediately responded to the tone and loudness of his voice. I jerked down to see what was he talking about. The baby was fine. From my husband's viewpoint, it looked like my breast was completely covering the baby's face, but it was not. I told him that the baby was fine, and asked him to go back to bed. He would not.

That was the first time my husband's concern about our baby irritated me to the point of no return. I went on to explain to him that I knew how to breastfeed and I did not require any more assistance. Despite my dismissal, he still hung around until our baby burped. There were many more of these instances because I was not used to having anyone around to question me, or to give their opinion. This took some getting used to. Eventually, I learned to consider his viewpoint, opinion, and concerns, but it took awhile before it became second nature.

We had three distinct goals we wanted to accomplish in our marriage. Buy a house, change his name back to his birth name, and renew our wedding vows. I thought it was amazing that all three goals were accomplished before we were allowed to have children. I also find it remarkable how easy things are when they are in God's perfect will instead of in His allowable will.

In my opinion, I classify His allowable will (free will) as God giving mankind the power to choose, to follow His instructions or not. When we choose to go our own way and not listen to God's instruction, then the results of our actions fall into the realm of His allowable will. God allows us the power to choose our paths and experience the results of our choices. We are not puppets because He has given us the power of choice. His perfect will is for a married couple, to have a baby, and to share in the responsibility of raising and providing for the baby. God's allowable will is when a baby is created out of wedlock. God allowed us the power of choice. The choice or decision to have a baby out of wedlock may, or may not, result in the parents sharing in the responsibilities of rearing the child.

Another example of His allowable will is when a baby is created and the mother decides she does not want to keep the baby, and aborts the baby. God allowed the mother to choose. He did not make that decision for her, but He gave her the power to make her own decision. The latter two examples are very hard, and they come with dire consequences, repercussions, regrets, struggles, and some aspects of guilt.

In God's perfect will, He designed marriage and the covenant relationship between a man and a woman to raise children together.

My son David was blessed from inception to birth. Our son's life has brought us significant joy; that we never knew existed.

> **The blessing of the LORD, it maketh rich, and he addeth no sorrow with it. Proverbs 10:22 (KJV)**

33. Put the Slippers On

One day, when I came from work, I was in an exceptionally great mood. My family was pleased to see me in such a great mood. I was going through a tough time at work with yet another new manager, and dealing with other standard irritants. On most days, I was not the happiest camper. I cannot remember what triggered this exceptional mood, but the difference was clear to my family.

My husband was busy cooking dinner, and the children were drawing at the kitchen table. My kids could occupy themselves for hours on end, as long as they had a supply of paper, makers, and crayons. We talked a bit about their day, and then I went upstairs to change into something comfortable. After changing clothes, I heard in my mind, "Put on your slippers." I thought, "No, I do not like slippers. I like to be barefoot." I proceeded to join my family in the kitchen.

My husband announced that dinner was ready, so I started setting the table. I stumbled over something on the floor, but ignored it cause it did not cause me any immediate pain. My daughter was moving the artwork from the kitchen table to the dining room table. I asked my husband where our son David was, and he said, "I think he went outside." I went to the back door and called for him. He replied that he would be right in. I tripped over the sponge like object again. This time I looked down to see what was tripping me. It was poop. Dog poop!

We'd had our puppy Brownie for three months. This puppy came with two house rules. The first was that the kids would check the house, and clean up any of Brownie's surprises before I got home. The second was that Brownie's surprises would be placed in the outside garbage. On this particular day, both kids forgot to do the Brownie poop check. My son David remembered once he saw me. He immediately went to take care of it after I went upstairs to change clothes. He was trying to be discrete because he did not want anyone to know that he had not taken care of his responsibility. In doing so, he had to handle this monumental task all on his own. He had to open the back door with one hand and balance the hot, steaming, pile of poop in the other. Well, while he was struggling to take care of this, all by himself a piece of dog poop rolled off the napkin. Now keep in mind, this was a hard task because the back door is located in the kitchen where his father was cooking dinner.

Once I realized there was dog poop on my bare foot, I remembered what I heard, in my mind, upstairs. I started laughing, and I could not stop. My family was looking at me in utter confusion because laughter was not my typical response to something as disgusting as that. My husband almost flipped his lid, when I quickly explained that it was not a big deal. He had a hard time understanding why it was not a big deal. He had stepped in it too, but he had on shoes. I said, "I'll be right back." And I hopped upstairs, to the bathroom, to clean my foot. I could not stop laughing. I laughed so hard that my back started to hurt.

When I looked behind me, my family was standing at the bathroom door. I think they thought I finally lost it. They thought my stepping in the dog poop had taken me over the edge. I explained to them why it was so funny, and the clear instructions I received to put my slippers on, before I came down stairs. My son David asked why didn't you listen? I replied the same as I did before. I did not like slippers, and I liked to be bare foot.

The moral of the story is this. Listen to your Inner Voice. Yes, you have heard it. You have one too. You might have referred to it as intuition, Holy Ghost, Holy Spirit, or Inner Voice. What you really need to understand is, its purpose. It is there to help you.

My dog poop episode led me to ponder why I did not listen to it. Well, for me, it was because it instructed me to do something I did not want to do and appeared to be meaningless. Sometimes, I did not listen because it took me out of my comfort zone. Other times, because I simply wanted to do things my way. I had a plan, and I wanted to stick to it. Out of ignorance, I ignored it because I did not fully recognize its power and purpose. Now that I understand it, I'm more inclined to heed its instructions.

When you listen to it, it saves you a bunch of trouble. When you ignore it, you typically wished you had listened. This voice is nothing to be ashamed of. It is a gift, and we just need to learn to listen to it when it speaks. It would be ashamed if we ignored this awesome, supernatural, built-in, cool tool that is there for our good. The only one, who suffers when the voice is ignored, is you. Let us embrace this nifty, hidden treasure. It is there for our benefit.

> **But the Counselor, the Holy Spirit, whom the Father will send in my name, will teach you all things and will remind you of everything I have said to you. John 14:26(NIV)**

34. Use Me

At church one Sunday, my pastor asked, "Who wanted to be used by God?" I raised my hands. This service was exceptionally emotional for me. In retrospect, I do not know why I was raising my hand. I had just begun a season of peace. Later that night, as soon as I lay across my bed to relax and watch a bit of TV, I received a call from a relative of my son's, girlfriend. She was notifying me that my grandbaby was just born. My brain had a hard time comprehending this because she was only six months pregnant, and it would mean that my grandbaby was born three months premature.

No child in our family had ever been born premature. So, I had nothing to draw from. I was terrified for my son's girlfriend, for me, and for my grandbaby. During the Memorial Day weekend, she had come to visit her family. It was during this visit she went into labor, and my second grandson was born. I called the hospital to get information regarding their status. The nurse asked,

"Are you a relative?"

"I'm the grandmother."

"Are you her mother?"

"No, I'm the paternal grandmother."

"We are trying to contact a relative."

"What is going on? Is she okay? Is my grandbaby okay?"

"We can only share that information with a relative."

"I'm like her family! Is she okay?"

"I'm sorry ma'am, but it's a matter of privacy. Can you contact a relative and have them call us?"

"I'll try."

I was livid! Why wouldn't they tell me if she was okay? Was she dead? Was my grandbaby okay? Was the baby dead? I was going nuts! My mind was racing, and I could not figure out my next move. I flopped down on the bed and asked God to help me. I prayed, "Lord, please bless her and my grandbaby." I remembered that I had some of her family's numbers in my cell phone, and I began to make calls. I finally reached the aunt, who had initially called me, and told her what the hospital said. I asked her to call them, and to call me right back with the information. She sounded a bit annoyed, but she said okay. While waiting for her call, I lay across the bed, prayed some more, cried, and drifted off to sleep.

The phone woke me up. At this point, my nerves had gone bad and I was shaking. When I opened my mouth to speak, my voice sounded strange. It was the hospital calling to say that they really needed to get a hold of a family member to sign for the baby's transfer to a neonatal hospital. Okay, now I knew the baby was alive. "Thank you Jesus!!" I told the lady on the other end that I informed her aunt to call. Then it hit me like a ton of bricks, why would anyone, other than the baby's mother, need to sign for the baby's transfer? I once again asked about the condition of the mother, and the lady's response shocked me. She said, "She is unable to sign at this time." I did not understand what that meant and she did not give me any details.

"In order to get the baby the proper care, we need to get him to Neonatal at Rush." Okay, now at least I knew it is a boy. I broke down crying, and then asked, "Was he born early because of the mother's diabetes?" She replied, "I think that could have been a contributing factor."

"Is she alive?"

"Yes, but unable to respond at this time."

"Is she in a coma?"

“Ma’am, I’ve already shared too much. I need you to try to contact a family member.”

“Okay, just one more question. Does my grandbaby have all his fingers and toes?”

“Yes.”

“Oh, thank you Jesus! I’ll try my best to get a hold of a family member.”

“Thank you.”

I called her aunt again, she replied that she went to the hospital, but they would not let her see her niece. So, she refused to sign for the baby’s transfer. I was extremely irritated because I did not understand her position. After getting off the phone with her I called the hospital, they informed me the baby was being transferred to Rush Hospital. I was satisfied with that and felt completely exhausted.

The next day, we were originally supposed to have a barbeque, but I spent the first half of the morning trying to get answers from the hospitals, regarding my grandbaby and his mom. It was the most annoying thing. I could not believe the run-around. In all the chaos, my brain recalled Northwestern hospital instead of Rush. So, my first call was to Northwestern, neonatal unit. They informed me that they did not have my grandbaby there. I freaked out and began to ask a slew of questions.

“If he died in transfer, would you have a record of that?”

“Yes.”

“Can you please check again? They said they were transferring him there.”

“What hospital was he transferred from?”

“St. James.”

"That's not a receiving hospital."

"I would have guaranteed they said Northwestern."

"Call St. James Hospital and ask them what neonatal hospital they use."

"Okay."

I called St. James Hospital, and they informed me it was Rush Hospital. I could not believe the unnecessary stress I went through. So I started over with Rush. The first call was dropped after I was on hold for several minutes. The second call, I was transferred to the wrong department. The third call, I was transferred to the wrong department again. The fourth call, I was finally connected to the right area, but placed on hold for a long period of time. I patiently waited. I was determined not to hang up until I got some answers. Finally, a lady with a very pleasant voice answered the phone.

"I'm calling to see if my grandson is in your care. He was transferred last night from St. James."

"And you are?"

At this point, I was so tempted to lie because my first experience taught me that paternal grandparents did not have any rights to information, and I really needed to know how my grandbaby was doing.

"I'm the grandmother."

"What's the child's name?" I told her my grandbaby's name.

"Hold please, he is here."

"How is he doing?"

"Well ma'am, I can't share much information with you because of the privacy laws. All I can say is that he is here and he's stable."

“I know, well maybe you can just say, yes or no, to some very simple questions.”

No response. I went on.

“His lungs are developed right?”

“Yes.”

“His genitals are fully developed right?”

“Yes.”

“He’s very small?”

“Yes.”

“Do babies his size usually survive?”

“Yes, you are asking all the right questions.”

“Thanks, can I visit?”

“Yes, but the mother has to give permission.”

“But she is unable to at this time.”

“Oh well, you’ll have to wait.”

“That doesn’t make much sense. What if she never comes around? He’ll have to be there alone without any visitors?”

No response.

“What’s your name? Can I call you tomorrow and inquire about my grandbaby?

She told me her name. When I hung up the phone I was a sweaty mess. I had to sit down for a few minutes. I was completely drained. I thanked God for the lady who served as my connection to my grandbaby until his mom woke up. In between my inquiry calls about my grandbaby, the aunt’s daughter called about dropping off my other grandbaby. I told her that she could drop him off. I then called St. James to inquire about the mother, but they were extremely vague. I called her aunt and she said she would check on her. I asked when I should be expecting her to bring my grandbaby. She replied in a bit. He was down for a nap.

My mother and my sister came over to lend a hand. My mother had recently retired, and said that she would help to take care of the grandbaby for a few days. My son lived with my mother, so that was perfect. He would be the person to take care of his son. I was bringing them up on current events, when I received a call from the niece. She said that the mom wanted the grandbaby to be released to another family member. I replied, "She's woke?"

"Yes."

"Great!" I then called the hospital and spoke to her. She sounded extraordinarily well. I could not believe it. This girl has escaped death more than anyone else I knew.

My mother, my sister, and I went to the hospital to visit her. It was a strained visit because we all felt that if she took better care of herself, the baby would not have been born early. She told us that she accidentally left her medicine bag in her uncle's car, and she was unable to reach him by cell phone. After our conversation, she agreed that it was in the best interest of her son to be with his father and great grandmother. We went and picked up my grandbaby. I was so excited and exhausted at the same time. He remembered my mother. He smiled and reached for her as soon as he saw her. She soaked it all up. I enjoyed watching them bond. The ride home was extremely difficult. It was a hot, rainy day, and adjusting my 5 year-old daughter's car seat to fit him was hard. He was hot and tired, and once again on the move. I felt so stressed out for everybody, especially him. I had to keep reminding myself that God was in control, and that his mother was capable of raising him.

The next day, I went to work feeling exhausted. I had several meetings, and was having a hard time focusing during them. After my last meeting, I shared the news about my grandbaby with a good friend. I told her that I did not know where the hospital was located, or the best way to get there. She knew the area very well, and gave me instructions on how to get there by bus. I was leery of riding the bus because I never seem to wind up in the right place. She told me that I could use her bus pass anytime I needed to visit my grandson. That was such a wonderful, selfless act and it touched me deeply.

A month before, this good friend shared that she had been informed not to put any more money on her bus pass. They told her that she had too much credit on the bus card and needed to use up her current balance. We both thought it was odd because she rode the bus often, and should not have any overage. Plus, she told me that she gave rides away to people who appeared to be digging for change. She said that she would sit near the front of the bus looking for an opportunity to bless someone with a ride. I believe this is why she is so blessed. The more you give, the more you get. It is a foundational truth, a spiritual principle.

> **Give, and you will receive. Your gift will return to you in full—pressed down, shaken together to make room for more, running over, and poured into your lap. The amount you give will determine the amount you get back. Luke 6:38(NLT)**

The first time I went to visit my grandbaby; I tried my best to find the correct bus stop. After I stood there for about 15 minutes I lost my patience and hailed a cab. I was frustrated because, I only had an hour and a half to get to the hospital and back.

When I got to the hospital my nerves were wrecked. I obtained a visitor's pass, along with the labyrinth like directions to the Neonatal Unit. I carefully followed the directions and arrived at the nurse's station in record time. The receptionist was very pleasant and helpful. However, she informed me that I was not on the visitor's list. She proceeded to contact the mother to request permission. I was waiting with baited breath because I should have phoned first. She got the approval she needed, took down some information from me, and took my picture.

Funny thing, I can remember the exact outfit I had on that day. Let me just say that it was an experience that I'll never forget. The receptionist gave me some instructions on what to do, and I followed them as quickly as I could. I washed, scrubbed, and robed, and was finally being allowed to see my grandson.

When I entered the room, I was amazed at the technology. There were so many pumps, wires, and screens hooked up to each baby. I was a bit overwhelmed. When the nurse came over to ask whom I was there to see, I could hardly answer her. She walked me over to my grandbaby's space, where he was sleeping so peacefully. I stood there, in awe at God's creation, watching him breathe for a while, until the nurse broke the silence and asked if I wanted to sit. I accepted the seat and sat down. She began to tell me about his status. Being three months pre-mature, he weighed in at 1lb., 8oz. He looked much bigger to me. The preconceived picture I had in my mind was much smaller and more pitiful looking. He looked whole. I counted all of his fingers and toes. Then I began to pray for God's continual intervention on his behalf. I introduced myself and told him a bit about his mom and dad, and that it was time for me to go back to work. I had a really hard time leaving him. It was a strange, difficult experience. Before I walked away, I told him that I would be back Thursday.

I found my way through the maze, back to the main desk, and exited the building. Surprisingly, a bus was approaching the bus stop, so I was able to catch the bus back without waiting. When I got back to work, I was completely wiped out. My manager came over to ask me something I thought she should have known. I must have given her an odd look because she asked me if I was okay. I told her about my grandbaby. She responded appropriately, and I answered her question. I did not realize the affect this experience was having on me.

During this time, I had to remind myself often, not to show my frustration to people. It seemed like everyone really got on my last nerve. Everyone appeared to be complaining, needy, or spoiled. My patience ran thin, and I had a hard time relating to anyone. I had too much going on at work and at home. On top of that, now I had the additional stress of my grandbabies well being.

My second visit, I tried taking the bus again, but the one that I was waiting for never came. Again, I hailed a cab. Once there, everything went really smooth. I was with my grandbaby again. I told him his whole name, and everything God said about him. I told him he was blessed and favored, and that everything on his body was blessed. I told him that he had perfect lungs, bones, skin, blood, breathing, and everything in between. I blessed him from the top of his little head to the bottom of his tiny feet, and then he grunted. Before I knew it, it was time for me to go. I asked his nurse a few more questions and left.

Once again, I was on the bus stop trying to get back to work. The bus took forever, and I was frustrated. I was looking for a cab, but all were occupied. Finally, the bus came, and the driver informed those of us waiting, that the other bus had broken down.

My next few visits were more of the same. One day, while my grandbaby and I were bonding, he opened his eyes and looked directly at me. The nurse, who was present, asked me if I wanted to hold him. I did not think that was an option. While I was holding him, she informed me that he was classified as a healthy, growing preemie. No one knew the joy this particular day had brought me. I was on cloud nine.

Each visit had it's own set of obstacles. There were always complications with the bus, and getting back to work in time for my meetings which were always a challenge. Sometimes I visited late, and sometimes I visited early. No matter what, I was committed to going as often as I could. I tried to visit him at least twice a week, but sometimes it could be only once. When I couldn't visit, I would call and ask to be informed about his status. It was always good news. His dad and I were his primary visitors. Due to the mother's distant location of where she lived, she was only able to visit twice. I was amazed that I never ran into my son during one of his visits. We did not have a schedule, but it worked out. It seemed he would be there whenever I was unable to make it. I knew when he visited because there was only one admission card. I was able to see his signature and the date of his visit.

During one of my visits, the nurses informed me of how appropriate my son handled his new son. She stated that a lot of fathers do not interact with their little babies because they are afraid that they might hurt them. She said that my son was not scared at all, he acted like an old pro. She then also said that he talks to him too. I was elated to hear this. His dad and I were all he had. It was necessary for the both of us to interact with him, and love him into coming home.

On my second to last visit, my grandson began to make cute, little sucky faces, and I took a lot of pictures of him with his eyes open. I enjoyed seeing him. Seeing him made me feel so good. The commute was always dreadfully awful, but his face was worth the trip. He was growing and progressing by leaps and bounds. I shared his progress with everyone within earshot.

The next time I went to visit, he wasn't there. I had just learned the right bus to take. It is amazing how well things work out when you follow instructions. When I got to the hospitals main desk, I followed my standard procedure to get the hall pass. I gave my grandbaby's last name. The receptionist clicked into the computer and said he is not a patient here. I thought my ears were deceiving me, and I repeated his name again. Again, she repeated herself. At this point, I began to think. I asked her to search by my son's last name. She replied, "Nothing in that name either." I then asked if the baby died, would it show in the system? She paused and replied, "I think so." I then requested for her to call the Neonatal Unit and to speak with their receptionists. I told her what to say to the receptionist, and she did, verbatim. This was all I had the luxury to hear.

"Oh."

"Mm…"

"Really?"

"Okay."

"Uh huh."

"Alright."

"Okay."

"Thank you."

"Good bye."

I was about to lose my mind. I said, "What?"

"He's been transferred."

"Where?"

"I can't tell you that. You would have to call the mother."

"Why would they transfer him? Was he healthy enough to go home?"

"The only way babies are transferred, is at the mother's request."

Just hearing that statement broke me. Why would she do that without telling me? She knew that I visited him often. I was hurt to the bone, and more livid than I have ever been. I cried openly at the lobby desk. The lady tried her best not to make eye contact with me. I tried to pull myself together, but could not. I went from the emotional high, of the anticipation of holding my grandson, to being very distraught, disappointed, and confused. My mom was supposed to visit my grandson for the first time that day. I called to let her know what happened. She could hear that I was upset, and did her very best to try and comfort me.

After I left, I sat at the bus stop for an extended period of time, when someone informed me that the bus route had changed. They pointed me in the right direction, just in time for me to catch the bus that was now rolling to a stop across the street. It took all I could to not cry on the bus. It was tough.

I decided to go to my favorite pizza joint to pick up a slice. When I arrived, there was a sign on the door saying they had moved. That of course had the worst affect on me. It seemed like it went from bad to worse and I could not stop crying. I called my grandbaby's mom to find out what happened. The number was disconnected. I could not get any answers. I stewed in my irritation, and then the Lord showed up.

The Holy Spirit informed me that I did what He needed me to do. He told me to forgive her and go back to work. I cried some more, dried my eyes, and went back to work. When I got back to work it was evident to anyone who knew me that something awful had happened. I really could not talk about it. If I did I would have broke out in tears. How I got through that day was a miracle.

I was not instantly over it, though the Lord had made it clear to me that my work there was complete. My pain was like a dull ache, and I had to fight through every negative thought. I believe it was Friday night when my grandbaby's mother called. I was so happy to hear her voice. Before I could ask any questions, she began to explain that she had been in the hospital. Once she was released from the hospital she was informed by the hospital that was caring for her baby that he was doing so well he could be released to a hospital closer to her.

I was so happy for her, and my grandbaby. She only had seen her son three times since the day he was born. She lived several hours away and did not have any means to get to him. She called daily to check on him, but as you know, that was not the same as being there.

This experience has shown me that God is faithful. My grandbaby could have been sent to any hospital in the greater Chicago area, or surrounding suburbs, but God saw fit for him to be transferred to a hospital near my job. He trusted me to see after my grandbaby, to pray for him, and love him. He placed the right people within my path to help me provide insight, instructions, and the means. This entire event was by divine design.

Finding the time to visit my grandbaby was nearly impossible. One time, I could not find an hour and a half to go see him. I had to rearrange my schedule for the entire day. This was a tough choice because my manager was fairly new and we were in the "getting to know you" phase. There were a lot of stressful and difficult moments. I knew the devil was trying to cause my good friend, who was letting me use her pass, to rethink letting me use the pass. I felt it in my spirit a day before it happened, and then of course, pride tried to spring up in me to say that I did not need her funky pass. I saw the devil's plot from a mile away, and she did too. Neither one of us fell for that trick. We talked about it and then laughed at the devil. That really felt great.

Thanks to God, He gives me the victory! All of my grandbabies are healthy and thriving!

> **But thank God! He has made us his captives and continues to lead us along in Christ's triumphal procession. Now he uses us to spread the knowledge of Christ everywhere, like a sweet perfume. II Corinthians 2:14(NLT)**

35. Why Am I Here?

At this time of my life, I was working at the bank in the Confirmation Department. There were two seasons in the year when the work was extremely heavy. These seasons were referred to as peak seasons. During these seasons, we typically hired a few temps to help out with the work. I went to pick up the new temp from the Human Resources Department. I introduced myself to her, and when we were on our way to the elevator she asked,

"Why am I here?"

"Didn't the agency tell you about the assignment?"

"Oh yeah, but I'm talking about the real assignment. I'm trying to understand why I'm really here. Do you know Jesus?"

"Yes."

"Are you in a relationship with him?"

"Yes."

"Good, I thought so. Well, the reason I am here will be revealed to me soon."

I was thinking, "Oh no, why everybody gotta be so deep?" I wanted to end her assignment before we got to the department. I was pre-exhausted. We had so much work to do, I did not have time for her deepness. I quickly trained her and got back to my work. During the first few days, I thought she was watching me, which made me uncomfortable. I could not imagine what she could possibly be looking for. We went to lunch and we had small talk a few times, but nothing more.

One day I was overwhelmingly frustrated. My manager was filing her fingernails while I was busting my butt, trying to meet our deadlines. I was completely unproductive that day, and I could not hide the truth of my feelings anymore. As soon as my manager left for lunch, I shared with the temp how I really felt about her. She had already picked up on my vibe. She asked me why did she bother me so much. I told her if she had been sitting in my seat watching this behavior, day after day, she too would find it unbearable as well.

She said, "Well, what are you going to do about it?"

"Nothing, I'm just venting."

"Oh, I thought you were unhappy enough to do something about it."

"Like what?"

"Like find a new job, you've been here long enough."

I was so out done. How could she, the temp, tell me what is too long to be in a department? She did not even have a permanent job, and furthermore, she did not know that I had already been rejected 9 or 10 times looking for a new job. Yeah, I went through all those painful interviews and someone else was always more qualified. I was always rejected. Now here, Ms. Temp is sitting across from me saying, find a new job, like it's a piece of cake. How to get a new job were a complete mystery and an utter chore to me.

To fully understand the uncomfortable mess of the matter, I need to describe the office space in which we worked. It was very small. It was literally a hole in the wall. There were three regular sized desks, one long table and several file cabinets. There was absolutely no privacy. If anyone talked on the phone, everyone heard the conversation. My manager sat to my right and she was constantly on the phone taking care of her personal business. From that initial conversation, Ms. Temp would challenge everything I did.

Any venting was received as a cause for her to suggest that I reflect on what I could do, instead of what I was talking about. She got on my last nerve. I wanted to fire her 100 times. The only real reason I never did was because she was good at her job, and it would be too much trouble to start over with someone else. So I put up with her. At the end of one of my complaints, she asked me if she could see my resume. I looked at her like she was crazy. She said,

"I know you got one."

"I do." I was lying. I felt like I did not need a resume to apply for a job internally, but she made it seem stupid if I did not have one.

"Let me see it."

"I don't have it here." More lies.

"Well, bring it tomorrow. I want to see it."

"Okay." I think she knew I was lying, but she played along.

I dug out my old resume and updated it. I was so proud to give it to her the next day like, "BAM!!!!" When I gave it to her she replied,

"Can I write on this?"

"Sure." I was annoyed. She revised my resume, and I had to admit, it looked so much better. Then she asked about my references, thank you letters, and wanted to interview me. I was overwhelmed. I knew on a subconscious level that I was her assignment and that she was sent by God to help prepare me to get my new job, but dag, she was gettin on my last nerve! Having someone constantly scrutinizing and critiquing everything I did was awful. I could not stand her, but over time I started to love her. After awhile I dropped all pretenses and the real me showed up. From that point we became good friends.

One day out the clear blue she says, "You're ready. Start looking for your new job." I was flattered and terrified at the same time. All of the prior rejections I experienced affected my confidence.

While applying for jobs, I remembered my husband's words of wisdom about being rejected. He said, "Please don't see these rejections as rejections. See them as practice interviews. These interviews are practice for the real interview, and for the job that God has for you." I had not looked at it that way at all. It is so funny how those words came back to my mind, to help me move forward. Fear had almost paralyzed me. The word of God states in **II Timothy 1:7,"For God hath not given us the spirit of fear; but of power, and of love, and of a sound mind."(KJV)** I felt completely unmarketable. I started at that bank with only a GED. I called it my "God Enough Diploma". I started as a teller for eight months, transitioned to security guard for eight months, after that, I was a confirmation specialist for two years, all within the same bank.

When Human Resource called me for an interview, I was terrified and ecstatic at the same time. All of these dual emotions were wearing me out. I told Ms. Temp about my upcoming interview and she was so excited. She claimed that job to be mine. She asked, "What are you going to wear to the interview?"

"My blue suit."

"Why a blue suit?"

I thought it was a trick question. What else would I wear? I replied, "It's Corporate America and that's expected. As you know this is the most snooty booty prestigious bank in Chicago. What would you suggest that I wear?" At this point she is getting on my very last nerve. Why is this so important to her, and what did she expect me to say? She replied, "Yeah I know everyone wears blue suits to the interview and that's the problem. You would blend in and disappear. You want them to remember you. I think you should wear your burnt orange suit. You know the one I'm talking about, the long pencil skirt and bolero collared jacket. You should wear the brown, crocodile pumps, and your hair pinned up.

She had it all planned out and it was all wrong. "Who in Corporate America, in their right mind, would go to an interview in an orange anything? I told her that was the craziest advice she ever gave. I called and asked my mom what I should wear and she said, "Wear what makes you feel pretty and confident."

"What outfit would you suggest?"

"The burnt orange suit." I was outdone!

I told her that was the suit Ms. Temp suggested as well. I shared my many concerns about wearing that suit and she said, "Wear what you feel comfortable in."

You need to know that I trusted my mother's opinion more than any other person in my life, and for her to say the burnt orange suit meant that I should wear it. I was also thinking why would Ms. Temp purposefully sabotage her assignment. The more I thought about it, the more courageous I became. I need you to understand that wearing this orange suit was a totally outrageous, bold move on my part. This was the opposite of everything I learned since my first day in Corporate America.

Per advice of Ms. Temp, I sent a letter to the hiring manager pre-thanking him for taking the time to interview me. When I got to the location for the interview, he was standing there waiting. I walked up to him, looked him straight in the eyes, smiled and introduced myself. He said, "You're Linda Soboski?"

"Yes."

"You're hired!" He laughed and began to small talk. It was not in anyway, a typical interview. He said that he was very impressed with my resume and letter. He said the letter separated me from the other candidates. I was very pleased. I got the official job offer later that day. I was overjoyed and amazed. It was finally my turn. I got the job. Wow!!!!

I was not able to get the jobs before for several reasons. I was not prepared. All of my focus, attention, and energy were spent on being angry. I had developed a victim's mentality. I did not have a plan and I was a "player hater."

God assigned Ms. Temp to help me get my eyes off other people. She helped me to strategize and execute my plan. I did not talk anymore about my manager once Ms. Temp challenged me. As a result, I was able to refocus my energy. My manager was no longer the center of my attention. Plus, Ms. Temp was not having it. She would check me even if I appeared to be going there. She would say, "We ain't got time for that." I loved the fact she held me accountable for my actions. As a result, I became more aware of what I was doing, and not so concerned with what other people were doing.

My new job was the job for me. God placed me right where he needed me to be. After eight months I was approached by management and promoted to supervisor, and later to manager. In that same position, I was promoted to Officer, Assistant Vice President, and Vice President. While managing my team, I was also allowed the opportunity to mentor several young people, in the same way Ms. Temp ministered to me. I was the ambassador Christ called me to be. I purposefully affected those, within my realm of influence, with living the Gospel of Jesus Christ.

Ms. Temp left immediately after her spiritual assignment was complete. I never saw her again. I reached out to her by phone and mail several times. We talked a few times on the phone, but never actually got together in person again. I love her, and I wanted very badly to keep her in my life, but she was only there for a reason and a season. I eventually got over it and recognized that God was working His plan. I'm sure she is probably on another assignment, blessing and ministering to someone else.

36. Your House is Beautiful Too

I was giving a tour of my home to a really good friend of mine. Her little daughter was in tow absorbing everything her eyes and ears could capture. After the tour, I took her over to a mutual friend's house, who also recently purchased a home. Her house was just built. I did not remember what I said exactly, but it prompted the little girl to get my attention. She said with all power and authority, "Your house is beautiful too!!!" Boy, out of the mouth of babes! Her words were so powerful. I said, "Thank you. I know." The "I know" part of my response was mixed with the realization that my house was beautiful along with the embarrassment that this child somehow saw the truth of my heart. God spoke through that little girl to set me straight.

I'll give you some background information to help you understand my mind set at that time. After my daughter was born, I wanted her to have her own room. I shared this desire with a dear friend, and she replied that I should buy a bigger house. I told her the challenges I thought I would have in selling my house. She replied, "It can sell. You bought it. It's a beautiful house and someone else will think it's beautiful too." At the time, I thought her idea was crazy.

My husband and I had been in that house for almost five years. It was home to us. The idea of putting it on the market was ludicrous. We had already accomplished a major goal by purchasing a home in the first place. Everyone I knew that purchased a house lived in it for the rest of their lives. Nobody in my family had ever purchased a second home. I felt like that only happened for other people. Buying two or three homes, what was the purpose of all that moving anyway? Why couldn't people settle down and get satisfied?

The mere idea of selling a home, which I had never done before, finding a new home, packing and moving was all overwhelming to me. The only thing that drove me to seriously consider this idea was my little girl having her own room. I finally had the little girl of my dreams and I wanted to prepare a beautiful princess room for her. You probably already figured out that the desire for this room was more for me than my daughter. Most parents want to provide their children with better than what they had. But what drives that desire? Sometimes, it is simply to say we provided. Sometimes, it is guilt for not doing other things that we should have done. And sometimes, it is to live vicariously through our children. To give them some of the things we always wished we had. I had always wanted a princess room. The princess room was the motivating factor, which became more powerful than all my fears combined.

I was fearful that my house would not sell. If it did not sell I would be a failure, and the laughing stock of my family. I was afraid that we would not get approved for the needed loan amount to purchase a new home. I was afraid that if we were successful at selling our home, we would not be able to find a house within our budget that met our criteria. I was afraid that if we moved too far from my mother that I would not be able to make it on my own. I was full to the rim with fear. Of course, God being who He is placed His people around me to guide me, to encourage me as needed, and to cheer me on.

I had always lived in close proximity to my family, and moving far away was not an option. We helped each other out, and thought it was best for everyone if it remained that way. God thought differently. My mother and siblings were not very supportive of the idea of us moving out of the vicinity. My children were small, and my mother thought this was a bad idea. Plus, everyone thought my house was beautiful. My mom thought that I was moving to escape her, but really, she was not the motivation for the move at all.

In the fall, we put our house on the market and it sold before we found a new house for us to move into. We were busy looking for a new home. We placed several contracts on homes that we liked or loved, but each time, the deal fell through. My intent was to stay near my mother and family, but we could not find a house in, or near our community. My husband and I were getting very nervous.

This was a very stressful time. I was exhausted and upset. I could not understand for the life of me why all the contracts were falling through. Didn't God see us and care that we didn't have a place to stay? We kept looking, all the while going more, and more south. The south suburbs were attractive because the houses were larger for less money. At this point, desperation was kicking in, and I didn't care so much anymore about how far away I would be from my mother and family. My immediately family needed a house to live in.

The dear girlfriend who planted the seed for me to sell my house also put her house on the market in March. It was sold the month after. She was trying to get me to buy a new house in the subdivision where she was purchasing her home. At that time, I could not fathom purchasing a home in that price range. It would have been almost $100,000 more in price than what we paid for our first home. We did not have any liquid money for a down payment to secure a lot. We broke perfectly even from the sale of our home and we needed to be out by the end of March.

The first available houses in her subdivision wouldn't be ready until late August. That would mean we would have to move in with relatives for many months and that was not an option. The desired goal was to find a home, which met our criteria, that was move in ready.

Time was running out, and we still hadn't found a place to live. We were frustrated and at our wits end. The same dear girlfriend was searching the Internet, trying to help find me a house. She brought over a printout of a house that met our requirements to perfection. We contacted our realtor to schedule a showing. I figured, let's put a contract on it right away. If the house were not meant to be ours, the contract would fall through like all the others. Also, the purchase price was significantly under our original budget. Once we placed the contract on the house, I was secretly hoping the deal would fall through, because it was so far away from my family.

The idea of being so far away from my mother and family was very disconcerting. I had never ventured so far out. The only time I had been to that suburb was on official bank business with my manager. I drove there and commented on how nice the community was, but that it was too far away. We laughed about it and I sarcastically said, "We should have packed a lunch for our road trip." The drive seemed ridiculous.

If the deal went through, I would no longer be able to depend on my mother for her support. Well guess what? It did not fall through. It was a 'go'! I had so many mixed emotions. The challenging part was when we found out that we would not be able to move into the house until June. This added insult to injury because it meant that I would have to do the one thing I did not want to do. We had to move in with relatives for two whole months. Ugh!

My eldest brother was nice enough to let us move into his basement. This was a particularly low point in my life. I had tried so hard to avoid this, and yet, there I was doing the one thing I did not want to do. I never stayed in anyone's basement before. I was trying hard to make good out of what felt like a bad situation. Plus, I felt like my mother and family were laughing at me. We had to put all our furniture in storage. We called and ordered some extremely large crates from a big box storage company. They dropped off a couple of huge crates and we packed our belongings into them. The storage company picked them up and stored them until we moved into our new home.

My girlfriend also had to temporarily move in with a relative. She lived in the basement of her in-laws for five months until her new house was ready. We had that one experience in common, but that was all we had in common with our house buying experiences. She was comfortable and enjoyed her time at her in-laws house. I, on the other hand, was uncomfortable from day one. I appreciated my brother and his wife letting my family move into their home, but I was absolutely uncomfortable most of the time.

My brother had a full sized, furnished basement, with a half bath. It was more than adequate space for a temporary living arrangement, but it echoed terribly even though it was furnished. I was constantly concerned with the amount of noise my kids were making. I was on pins and needles the entire time. My brother and his wife did all they could to make our stay comfortable. My misery and uncomfortable ness was solely due to me not wanting to be there in the first place.

On moving day, I was extremely elated. When we pulled up to our house, the storage crates were already there, and I was jumping for joy. I was so excited to get inside because I could not remember any of the details of the house. All I remembered about the house was that it had the base criteria listed on our specifications. Here is the short list of our specs. Four bedrooms: three upstairs, and one on the lower level for our teenage son. I needed my son's room to have at least one real window, or a door. This requirement was for my peace of mind in case we ever had a fire. I wanted him to have an escape route. We wanted two and a half baths, with one being in the master bedroom, a family room with a wood burning fireplace, a living room and dining room with large windows, an eat-in kitchen, central air, and a two and a half car garage.

When I opened the door the house looked so dark, and smelled a bit funky. I walked through the house rather quickly to check out each room. I was so disappointed. The reason I could not remember much about the house was because there was not much to remember. The people we bought the house from had lived in the house for about 20 years, and it looked like it. It was so outdated and dirty. I immediately felt regretful, but I did not want to show it. God gave me the ability to make the best out of a bad situation. So I decided to do just that.

My husband felt different. He was so happy to be out of the city, away from the riff-raff, the drama, my family and the things he perceived that had the potential to hurt our children, or threaten their growth. He was glad to be away from things that could potentially harm our marriage, and anything that could possibly harm him. He felt that living in the city was being over exposed to all the wrong things.

My husband was glad that he was able to provide a better environment for our children and that this experience would bring us closer together. The community was beautiful. It had a great school system, and a big library on the same block as the park. He thanked God for our new home.

I, on the other hand, was just trying to be content with what we had. I immediately became concerned about what my friends and family were going to think of this old, dirty house. So I got to work. David and I scrubbed and cleaned twenty years worth of grime, grease, and dirt from cabinets, and every other place with an actual surface.

Another really dear girlfriend came over to help me, and was a great help indeed. I had many friends that would have helped me, but she was the best friend for the job. She was the brutally honest friend. She was not afraid to make critical decisions that would make it better, and she took matters into her own hands to get the job done. I needed that particular friend at that time because I was completely overwhelmed, and almost paralyzed by my situation. We all worked together, like the three amigos. We pulled down the curtains, pulled up carpet, and dismantled homemade bookshelves that were all throughout the house. The prior owner must have been a big book collector, or librarian.

I laugh when I recall my friends and family's initial reaction to my house. They all shared similar reactions and sentiments. Their responses were like, "It's bigger than it looks from the outside." "It has potential." and one person said, "You must have a great vision." David and I worked tirelessly to make the house feel and look like home. God also sent people to do the work that we could not do. It came together nicely, but we worked very hard to get it there. The renovation took a total of eight months.

The entire experience of selling our home and finding a new home was awful and overwhelming. Throughout the process we faced a plethora of constant obstacles and challenges. Our new home had a bittersweet affect because of all the prior negative experiences, and the hard work we had to put into it. At the same time, I was painfully aware of the contrasting experience my dear girlfriend was having.

It was clearly obvious, to both of us, that she was having a much better experience. This is what I remember: Her home was on the market for one month. My house was on the market for six months. She made money on her sale. I did not. Her house was new, built up from the ground. Mine was very old. She had many exciting experiences: breaking ground, watching the house as it was being built, going to the design center to pick out finishes and she actually enjoyed the time she stayed with her in-laws. Due to the simultaneous contrasting experiences I became jealous. All of her good experiences magnified my bad experiences. She recognized the difference as well. Therefore, she tried her best to downplay her excitement about all the good things that were happening in her life.

My dear girlfriend moved into her house a few months after I moved into mine. Her house was absolutely beautiful. Since it was brand spanking new, there was nothing for her to do, but move in. I almost exceeded the allowable amount of 'player hating'. Her home was spacious, and it had every amenity and luxury I desired. Due to her eye for detail and beauty, her home looked like a model home.

In comparison, my home was not beautiful. I got so caught up with looking at what she had, I could not see or be grateful for what I had. God used that little girl to deliver His message. It was effective and it penetrated my heart down to the core. From that day forward, I purposed to do my very best to keep my eyes on God and His provisions for me.

Initially, it took a lot of concentrated effort, but over time I got better at it. Biblically, coveting is modern day player hating. It is a sin and in that state it is impossible to be thankful or to be grateful.

> **You must not covet your neighbor's house. You must not covet your neighbor's wife, male or female servant, ox or donkey, or anything else that belongs to your neighbor. Exodus 20:17(NLT)**

Coveting other's possessions makes your own things look inadequate or worthless. Jealousy and envy are destructive forces and should not be attributes of Christians. Christians need to be able to sincerely thank God for what they have, with a true sense of gratefulness and contentment for what God has provided for them.

> **Then I observed that most people are motivated to success because they envy their neighbors. But this, too, is meaningless like chasing the wind. Ecclesiastes 4:4(NLT)**

Your perception is very important to your ability to praise God. It is nearly impossible to praise God if you feel entitled to something or if you have a sense of expectancy. With the entitlement perspective, you feel you earned it and have a right to it. If you receive what you desired you are not very likely to praise Him because you feel as though YOU worked hard for the reward and you deserved it. With the entitlement perspective you probably will not view the reward or gift as provisions from God at all. You may not even have God factored in the equation. You may have forgotten that it was God who enabled you, opened doors for you and equipped you to so call earn it.

> **Death and Destruction are never satisfied, and neither are the eyes of man. Proverbs 27:20(NIV)**

It is also difficult to praise God if you have a specific expectancy. If the desired thing (reward/item) does not come in the way in which you desired, you are not very likely to praise God for His provision. You probably will feel cheated and disappointed. You can become bitter and angry. Let's use the example of receiving a bonus from your employer. Let's say it is customary for bonuses to increase annually. So you probably would have a sense of expectancy that the upcoming bonus will be bigger than last year's bonus. Well you get your bonus and it is less than the previous years bonus. If you had an expectancy perspective you would be disappointed and unable to praise God for the bonus you received.

> **Look after each other so that none of you fails to receive the grace of God. Watch out that no poisonous root of bitterness grows up to trouble you, corrupting many. Hebrews 12:15(NLT)**

It is also very difficult to praise God for what He has provided for you, if you are aware that He provided or blessed someone else with more. Typically, this becomes more of an issue if you feel that the person who received more was not deserving, less qualified for the blessing according to your perspective or if they appeared to be unappreciative or ungrateful for the blessing that they received. In this situation it is very likely that your initial praise for what God provided for you will turn into ungratefulness, annoyance and irritation.

But if you harbor bitter envy and selfish ambition in your hearts, do not boast about it or deny the truth. Such "wisdom" does not come down from heaven but is earthly, unspiritual, of the devil. For where you have envy and selfish ambition, there you find disorder and every evil practice. James 3:14-16(NIV)

It is imperative in all of these situations for you to keep your eyes on God and His provisions for you and be grateful and praise Him for what He has provided for you. Everything else is a waste of time and life and God is not honored in it. Remember the ole saying, "Count your blessings." This is really an important component to being truly content. Stop right now and look around you. Count your blessings and give God some praise. Know and accept that there will always be somebody with more, and somebody with less. Your job is to be grateful for your blessing. I am still amazed at how much my perspective has changed since God spoke through that little girl. Now I am able to see Him in everything, even the little things. Sometimes when I open my garage door I tear up because I have always wanted a remote controlled garage door. I now have one and I am very grateful. I am still in the same house today, writing this book, and I cannot count how many times in the past five years I have walked through my house, in absolute contentment and thankfulness and it is good!

But godliness with contentment is great gain. I Timothy 6:6(NIV)

37. Destiny

I was working as a teller at a bank on the far, east side of Chicago. Prior to that, I was an agent at an insurance company. It seemed as if I took a step backward, but I was not content with the ethics, or the constant pressure of selling insurance. The South Chicago Community was predominately Latino. I was one of the ten African American women who worked for the bank. Due to the pressure I was under at the insurance agency, I quickly accepted the teller job without negotiating my salary. I made the assumption that the pay would be the same. To my surprise it was just a bit over minimum wage. I was unaware of this fact until I received my first paycheck three weeks later. I was completely devastated. I think I cried that entire day. My sister was the supervisor and was very instrumental in my being hired. She thought I knew it was an entry-level position. I did not, and with those wages, I could barely make ends meet. I had to pay rent, a car note, and my son's tuition all on minimum wage. This was as insane as it gets.

One morning while I was at my teller window waiting to serve a customer, I began to think about my situation. I was in an extremely unhappy, unhealthy marriage, working as a teller, earning minimum wage at a place where I did not fit in. While standing there, I began to talk with God. I asked "Why am I here?" If there was a response I did not hear it.

A couple of days later, I walked into work chatting with an associate. I noticed this handsome, young man who was walking by with one of the Banking Officers. I pulled my sunglasses down to my nose to try to get a better look. We made eye contact and I smiled. They proceeded to walk toward the back of the bank by the manager's offices. I said, "That's my next husband." The young lady that walked in with me said, "No fair. How many husbands do you want? Aren't you still married?" I smiled and laughed.

I went inside the teller area and began to prepare my window for opening. I was a couple of weeks into training a young Mexican guy. He was not getting it at all and I was so tired of trying to make him understand. The cute guy that walked in was still in the back talking with one of the officers. I wanted to get another look. Suddenly, my supervisor was trying to get someone to deliver a package to the officer where the cute guy was. I readily volunteered and grabbed the package before anyone had an opportunity. But, she stopped me and said, "Never mind, I'll take it. I gotta go that way anyway." My attempt was foiled. Well, I went back to training that guy, and then destiny happened. My supervisor said, "Linda, you are going to be training David, our new hire." When I looked up I could not believe my eyes, the cute guy was standing right there, in front of me. My mouth went instantly dry, and I mentioned something about the confused kid I was already training. My supervisor instructed the confused kid to go to the back and help with counting coins.

David and I had an instamatic attraction that even a blind man could see. My heart was beating so loudly I thought he could hear it. I was trying my best to appear calm, cool, and collected. I began to show him around to help him get oriented with the place. I put on my professional hat and began to train him. I tried my best to mask my attraction because I was married. I was married, but completely miserable, and trying to figure out how to leave.

I married my second husband after dating for six months. This was a bad decision on both of our parts. I don't think either of us got married for the right reasons. For me, marriage symbolized success, and I wanted to be seen as successful. Everyone and their mama tried to talk us out of getting married. We were rebels without a pause. Hell bent on destruction. I never really knew what his motivation was, but mine was to keep up with the Jones's. All of my friend's and associates from previous jobs were getting married and I was too.

My second husband was an extremely attractive guy. He was not a bad person, just not good for me. We both knew it and were sort of just going through the motions. I felt like, "Oops, I made a mistake that's all; making a mistake is never wrong." During our courtship and marriage he never bonded with my son, who was a young boy at the time. This had a tremendous impact on my interest and ability to continue in the marriage

I was ashamed to admit that my marriage was failing. I had been fairly warned, but I still did it. I was paying the price for my actions. I did not have many options. If I left him I would have to move back in with my parents. At that time I could not fathom that. So, I just stayed with him until I could not take it anymore. When I left him he made no effort to locate me, to reconcile our differences, or to save the marriage. I think he was secretly relieved. The weirdest thing is, I never saw him again, even until this day. We lived together as a married couple for a total of eight months. He later divorced me. I was so happy the day I got served the divorce papers because it marked the end of that awful chapter of my life.

I was so relieved. I do not think we ever loved each other. It was a mistake. My ex-husband was not very nice to me. He had an awful temper, and quite frankly he had begun to scare me. I remember praying for someone to love me. I wanted a man to love me more than I loved him. I know that sounds selfish, and a mess, but that is what I prayed for. I wanted to be essential to his life, the apple of his eye, his boo, his sweet thing, key to his world, and his one true love. I was not any of those things to my husband, and that is just how it was. In my prayer, I only had one requirement and I never went back to modify it.

During the time I was training David, he was so distracted because of all the flirting we were doing. I was becoming concerned that he would not be able to do the job once he was on his own. We went to lunch together a few times and were quickly becoming good friends. One day, I was in the break room, upset about my surmounting debt. David came in and asked what was wrong. I told him, and later that day he offered to help me. We really liked each other, but at that time we had not even kissed. His kindness was so attractive to me. I knew he had a bit of a hidden agenda, but so did I.

According to my assessment I met David at the absolute worst possible time. I was a twenty, year old African American girl, with a five year-old son, in an unhappy marriage. I had already been divorced once and almost 100% sure I would be divorced again. I was already planning my exit from my second husband, but I was afraid. So no matter how much I liked him it was not the time to begin a new relationship before ending the other.

I knew David, and I would eventually hook up because I liked him so much. I had no intent on becoming serious, or ever marrying anyone ever again. I had proved to everyone watching, and myself, that I was no good at marriage. I did not know anyone else who had been married and divorced twice before 21, and was not trying to go down that path again. When David and I began to date it was purely for fun. I was not trying to fall in love or anything like that. That part happened all on it's own, and quite frankly it upset me. I felt tricked. I was David's first love, so he was much more open and honest about everything. He was like a breath of fresh air and he fell for me hard. I was trying my best not to express my true feelings for him because that carried the potential for more future failure for me.

David got fired from the bank Christmas Eve of that same year for a money order error. He worked for the bank a total of four months. I quit two months later, when I was approached and recruited by a Latino lady who worked for a prestigious bank, in the downtown area.

David and I have been together for seventeen years and married for fifteen. We have suffered our share of ups and downs, and survived every imaginable high and low one could expect to experience in a marriage. I almost missed out and messed up because of my past when David asked to marry me. I was so afraid of being a failure again. I would have preferred to continue to live in sin. He had asked me twice before to marry him, but I declined. Then in December 1991 he asked me again. He said, “If you say no, I will never ask you again. You are going to miss out on a good thing, thinking about those knuckle heads in your past.” And with that, I said yes. But I threatened him a bit and made him swear on a stack of bibles that he would never leave me. He responded differently than I ever expected. He said, “Linda, I would never divorce you. You would have to leave me.” I had very little confidence in men keeping their promises, but he sounded so sincere.

We have experienced many situations where divorce could have been the option, but that was never really on the table for us. David would always say that’s the devil trying to steal our marriage. A couple of times when we both were responding and listening too much to the world system, we almost got caught up and made bad choices (sin). This would have significantly damaged or killed our marriage, but only by the grace of God, He saved us from following through on any intent. His grace appeared in the form of a timely word from a friend, a prayer, a push, or a shove.

> **There hath no temptation taken you but such as is common to man: but God is faithful, who will not suffer you to be tempted above that you are able; but will with the temptation also make a way to escape, that you may be able to bear it. I Corinthians 10:13(KJV)**

I thank God daily for my husband, and our exceptional love and commitment to one another. I can honestly say that I am essential to David's life, the apple of his eye, his boo, his sweet thing, key to his world, and his one true love.

I share this story because it is unusual, not perfect, and probably not what you expected. Real life is not perfect. When people tell the absolute truth it is unusual. Exposing myself in this way is unexpected. The purpose and intent is to make you understand that this life is a journey. You fall down you get up. You make mistakes you pay the price and God is there through it all. There is no fantasy or perfection here in this world. I do not have all the answers today, but I am striving to become more like Him. I am not ashamed of my past. My past is just that: the past.

> **Brothers, I do not consider myself yet to have taken hold of it. But one thing I do: Forgetting what is behind and straining toward what is ahead, I press on toward the goal to win the prize for which God has called me heavenward in Christ Jesus. Philippians 3:13-14(NIV)**

God, in His infinite wisdom, used the pain from my past as preparation for my destiny. God was able to pull me back together after I messed up so quickly. He is using my life experiences as testimonies to His greatness. I believe in my heart that God orchestrated my working for that bank for the sole purpose of my meeting David. Some might argue the fact that I was already married and the whole thing was wrong and they are free to do so. When I spent lots of time thinking about the past, I considered the fact that I never divorce any one. I was always the one who was being divorced. I'm not saying that over time if they had not divorced me that I would not have eventually divorce them. I honestly don't know. What I am saying is they divorced me. I have struggled with the fact that I have committed adultery in my past marriages and was an adulteress, but I'm not anymore. I asked God to forgive me for my two failed marriages, and guess what? He did. His forgiveness freed me from the shame and guilt that shadowed me for many years.

A dear friend shared her perspective concerning my marital past. She said,

"David is actually your first real husband."

"How can you say that? I've been married two times before him."

"You were seventeen when you married the first time and you all never even lived together. The second time you married, you all did not even love each other and was separated after eight months. You and David, on the other hand, have been married for many years in a committed (covenant) relationship. He is really your first real husband." After I thought about it, I agreed.

38. Applewood Lane

After I moved into my house on Applewood Lane I learned to trust God. I really learned more of His character and got to know Him on a deeper level. Applewood Lane is such a cute name. I liked to say it Applewood Lane it had a nice little ring to it. Once, when I was shopping, the cashier asked me for my ID. I gave it to him. He sarcastically said, "Applewood Lane. Oh, you're just having a perfect, little, suburban experience aren't you?" I could not believe he said that. What was that suppose to mean? He had no idea of my reality on Applewood Lane.

Applewood Lane symbolized the painful development of Godly character in me. I experienced a plethora of tests and trials in obedience on Applewood Lane. This is where I believe every fruit of the spirit was conceived in me of love, joy, peace, longsuffering (patience), gentleness (kindness), goodness faith (faithfulness) meekness (humility) temperance (balance).

> **But the fruit of the Spirit is love, joy, peace, longsuffering, gentleness, goodness, faith, Meekness, temperance: against such there is no law. Galatians 5:22-23(NIV)**

So many events, situations, and trials happened on Applewood Lane. These events and situations all brought me closer to God and gave me a deeper understanding of Him, which is in essence His Word. Godly character was developed in me on Applewood Lane. My friends and family would inquire about the state of things at my house, they would say, "What's going on, on Applewood Lane?" If I shared the truth of my experience, they would reply, "It's always off the hook on Applewood Lane." One friend would just shake her head and say, “It’s always something going down on Applewood Lane. Applewood Lane, Applewood Lane.” They were right.

> **In this all-out match against sin, others have suffered far worse than you, to say nothing of what Jesus went through—all that bloodshed! So don't feel sorry for yourselves. Or have you forgotten how good parents treat children, and that God regards you as his children? My dear children, don’t shrug off God's discipline, but don't be crushed by it either. It's the child he loves that he disciplines; the child he embraces, he also corrects. God is educating you; that's why you must never drop out. He's treating you as dear children. This trouble you're in isn't punishment; it's training, the normal experience of children. Only irresponsible parents leave children to fend for themselves. Would you prefer an irresponsible God? We respect our own parents for training and not spoiling us, so why not embrace God's training so we can truly live? While we were children, our parents did what seemed best to them. But God is doing what is best for us, training us to live God's holy best. At the time, discipline isn't much fun. It always feels like it's going against the grain. Later, of course, it pays off handsomely, for it's the well trained who find themselves mature in their relationship with God. So don't sit around on your hands! No more dragging your feet! Clear the path for long-distance runners so no one will trip and fall, so no one will step in a hole and sprain an ankle. Help each other out. And run for it! Hebrews 12:8-13(MSG)**

Job Loss

After the second year of living on Applewood Lane, my husband lost his job. The loss of my husband's job taught us how to trust and depend only on God. God always showed up and He never let us down. During my husband's unemployment, we were miraculously able to go on vacation to Cancun, and I even went on a girl's trip to New York City. God would not allow me to change my lifestyle one bit. God wanted me to know that He was my provider, and that I should not put any confidence in anything or anyone besides Him. I learned that if I had a need, I could ask Him, and He would provide.

During this time, I decided it would be practical to take my lunch to work, instead of buying it downtown. The Lord told me not to. He provided lunch everyday. Whatever the need was, He provided. I had gotten to a place in my relationship with God that I was completely stretched out in His arms. God took care of me, and my family during the nine months my husband was unemployed. We never got behind on any bills. The Lord provided for each and every one of our needs. God remained faithful.

But my God shall supply all your needs according to his riches in glory by Christ Jesus. Philippians 4:19(KJV)

Flood

After returning home from a hard day's work, I opened my front door, and smelled the beach. A strange noise was coming from the family room, which is located in the lower level of the house. The noise sounded familiar, but I could not exactly place what it was. I told my kids to wait upstairs so that I could go investigate. I was a bit scared going down in the darkness alone. I wished a million times that my husband was home to investigate the strange noise and smell, but he was at school that night.

So, there I was, all alone, by myself, going down the dark stairs. I was also concerned about leaving my kids upstairs by themselves. I was a complete wreck! I slowly and cautiously descended the stairs. When I got to the second or third step, I slipped, and whoooosh! I landed on the floor, but it really did not feel like the floor. I was so disoriented by my sensations that it took my brain a couple of seconds to figure out what was going on. I did not understand how it was possible that I could be cold and wet in the family room. I screamed, jumped up, and flicked on the light switch.

My chest tightened with fear once I fully recognized the gravity of my situation. I was standing a little over ankle-deep in ice, cold water. I could have been killed! I could not believe my eyes. I did not understand how this could happen. I followed the sound into the den, and saw water gushing out of the wall. I ran upstairs screaming, "Oh no!! Oh no!!" My four-year-old son asked,

"Mama, what happened?" I flopped down on the kitchen chair and told him,

"The basement is flooded."

"What's flooded?"

"Down stairs is filled with water."

"How did that happen?"

"Water is pouring in from the wall, and I don't know why."

I was cold, wet, confused, and alone. I called my husband and it went directly to voice mail. I was freaking out! The water was still pouring in and I didn't know what to do. I cannot remember who I called, but whoever it was told me to locate the shut-off valve for the water. I was really crying now. Why wasn't my husband home to take care of this? I went back downstairs and after a few minutes of complete frustration, I finally located the shut-off valve. I repeatedly thanked the person on the other end of the phone. I then sat on the stairs and cried my eyes out.

My son sat next to me, and my daughter sat next to him. My son said, “Mama, don’t cry. It’s only water.” I looked into his sweet, little face and said, “Okay.” He had no idea how much damage water could do. I pulled myself together, changed clothes, and figured out my next steps. I called my insurance company and they were able to get somebody out to my house licitly split.

The damage control team came in, pumped the water out, and removed all of our wet property. I could not quite get it together. I was just sitting there looking completely traumatized. They got all the standing water out a few minutes before my husband came home from school. I was so exhausted and annoyed by that horrible ordeal. I was constantly running smack dab into drama, and quite frankly, I was sick and tired of it!

Over time, the insurance company had everything just as it was or better, but it was a long, nasty, stanky process. Before the big flood, it seemed as though the family room was possessed by a manifestation of evil. There were spiders, ants, flying ants and other unidentified bugs centralized in my prayer area. I would wake up at 5:30 a.m. lay prostrate on the floor, in the family room and pray. This was sanctified time for me to talk to God. It was very special. Satan knew it, so he sent a new tormentor every day to drive me out. Everybody who knows me knows that I hate bugs, especially spiders. It was the most insane, consecutive, insect event I had ever seen. I pressed beyond my fear of bugs and continued to pray daily, and then the big flood happened. That’s when I began praying in the living room. We also had squirrels. They took up residence in our attic and were not satisfied with those accommodations, so they attempted to move into the main quarters of the house. We paid a great deal to have them removed.

For Sale

After the initial big flood we suffered three additional floods. Each time causing us to have experiences that otherwise we would have never had. The third flood took my husband over the edge and he insisted on moving. I could no longer tolerate his in contentment and frustration. I wanted him to be happy and shut up so I found a realtor and put Applewood Lane on the market. We only had a couple of weeks to fix up the place to help it to sell. The realtor knew a contractor and through Gods grace and goodness he was able to work on my house immediately. I told the realtor that I did not have the money to make the repairs, but it's amazing the money came. I was able to pay for all the many little repairs. The kind of annoying broken things around the house that just needs to be fixed.

We looked around and found a house that was newer and very pretty, but was actually the same size as Applewood. I was not in love with it, but it was newer and appeared to be in better condition. It was not my hearts desire by any stretch of the imagination, but it was shinier and newer. It also lacked curb appeal and I had already looked into Nova brick facing the front elevation of it.

There were five or six houses in my neighborhood that was also on the market to sell. My realtor told me that my house showed better than the others because it was very pretty. We had to sell the house relatively quickly because I wanted to be settled in by August before school started. The week before our open house my husband asked me, "Why are we selling our house again?" I could not believe my ears. He started the entire fiasco and I told him that and then he asked the weirdest question. "When did you start to listen to me? I was just mad at the time. We have such a pretty house." I was so mad. What was he talking about? He had me doing all this work and if he knew he really was not serious about moving why didn't he stop me. We had already put a contract on the new house so we were just waiting to sell our house. I could hardly respond I was so angry. I finally replied, "If it's not God's will for us to move it won't sell anyway."

My open house was a success lots of people came to see it, but not one offer was made. My real estate agent was baffled was completely outdone. She told me that everyone would comment on how pretty the house was and asked questions about the furniture. The very last showing I did myself because the lock box had already been removed and I just happened to be home that day. The perspective buyer was a middle-aged lady. She was very pleasant. This was the first showing I actually did and it happened the last day the house was to be on the market. Of course David and I were very excited because it was the eleventh hour and very possible this could be the person to buy our house. I greeted her and began showing her the house. She smiled and said, "This house is beautiful." As we entered each room she asked what upgrades had been done. I shared the information with her and each time she would reply. "Wow, you've done quite a bit here." When she got to my daughter's room she said, "Now this is a little girl's room. How cute is this. It looks like you've just painted. Did you?

"Yes. Not that long ago."

It was much of the same for the rest of the showing. When we got to the family room she said, "Now this is a family room. Is that a wood-burning fireplace?"

"Yes"

"How nice"

"Where do you put the Christmas tree?"

I pointed to the corner where I always put the tree

"Wow, this is really cozy. You have those big picture windows upstairs do you put a tree up there too?"

"Yeah"

"In the living room or dining room?"

At this point her questions were getting on my nerve. I did not understand the point of them.

"I bet that's pretty."

"Do you let the kids help you decorate?"

"Yeah, I let them decorate the tree down here in the family room. The one upstairs is mine."

"You're blessed with two trees huh?"

"Yeah."

She then looks in the den and laundry room and said, "It even has a separate den. This is really cute."

"You can also use it as a bedroom."

"Have you used it as a bedroom?"

"Yeah, when my oldest son lived here. This was his room."

"Oh, and after he left, you converted it into a den. That's nice."

"You spend a lot of time in here?"

"No, but my husband does."

"It's nice to have your own space and a place to get away and unwind."

"Yeah, I guess so."

We went back upstairs and she asked to look around one more time. She quickly went from room to room. She came down the stairs and said, "This is a really beautiful house. It has a very inviting comfortable feel to it. Where you're moving must be really, really nice."

"Yeah, it's nice."

"Where are you moving?"

I told her.

"It's nicer than this?"

"In some ways."

"What's nicer about it?" I couldn't come up with any thing specific and then I finally I said, "It's newer."

"Newer doesn't always mean nicer."

We thought so, enough to put a contract on it, I thought.

"Seems like you have put a lot of time and effort fixing up this place. Have you even enjoyed this place? Seems like a waste to spend all this time fixing up a place just to sell it." I was so mad. What in the world was she talking about? What did that have to do with her buying my house? Why did she want a showing, if she was not really interested in buying? Why was she wasting my time? That was last day for my house to be on the market and she was wasting my time. I wanted to curse her out and push her out the door for coming by here and getting my hopes up for nothing. She was saying the same thing the realtor shared with me that everyone said about my house. How nice and pretty and beautiful it was, but nobody put a contract on it; how incredibly frustrating. It was clear to me that she was not going to buy my house.

Then she asked, "What are you going to do if it does not sell?" I thought, what an odd question. I started to laugh and replied, "Odd that you said that because this is the last day the house will be on the market. If nobody puts a contract on it today we stay."

She smiled and said, "You really have a beautiful house thanks for showing it to me."

When she left the house I cried like a baby. I was mad at God. I was already hurt and embarrassed that my house did not sell and I felt like He let me down. The lady who came to see the house on the last day gave me false hope. I could have accepted that my house simply did not sell better, if I had never had that experience of showing it to that woman. I felt like I had been toyed with; I was livid. I did not talk to God for a few days. I had nothing nice to say.

After my family returned home I went shopping I bought all kinds of little things that I had wanted for the house. I was so amazed that I was able to find everything I wanted at such reasonable prices. That was the best angry shopping I ever did. I felt like God was blessing me despite my being mad at him and the thought of that softened my heart. I realized that I was acting like a fool. Who was I to be mad at him? But I could not shake what I was feeling. I knew in my heart that God does not play with people's feelings or emotions, but I still felt like my having to show the house to that lady was an unnecessarily cruel thing that God allowed to happen.

Sunday morning I woke up and went to the living room to pray and the Lord said to "look in the Bombay Chest". I did not know what I was looking for and then I saw this book my mother had given me called "The Art of Abundance." I opened it and began to read. This was an amazing little book. It was about enjoying everything you have. Being and living in the moment every moment. The first scripture I read in the book was **Jeremiah 29:11** it read, **"For I know the plans I have for you," says the Lord. "They are plans for good and not for disaster, to give you a future and a hope."(NLT)** Hot thick tears began to roll down my cheeks. God knew that I was hurting and I felt betrayed. He sent His word through this book to remind me that He was not trying to hurt me, but save me from hurt. He then played back in my mind everything that lady had said and her message was "You have a beautiful house that you clearly have put a lot of work in, you should enjoy this house."

He revealed the purpose of the third flood, which led to David acting crazy, putting the house on the market that led to us fixing all the things that were broken. Without the incident of the flood and the subsequent events that followed we would have never invested the money to make it comfortable and He was right. He made it clear to me that we needed to be content and enjoy what He provided and that was Applewood Lane.

Saved By An Angel

I was speaking with a sales consultant in the dining room while my children were outside playing. There was a huge crash. It was the kind of sound that makes your blood curdle. It was the most awful sound. I was momentarily paralyzed with fear. In that moment I waited to hear a cry or something to let me know they were still living. The crash sounded like death. I ran what seemed to me in slow motion outside to see what happened.

My son who was six years old was in the garage hitting the punching bag, he leaned on the utility shelf and a 35-50 pound rim fell from the top of the10 foot shelf. When I got outside I saw he was at the far left back of the garage and my daughter was in the driveway. I could not understand how he did not get killed. I asked him how did he get out the way and he said he heard it and ran as fast as he could to the other side. His story did not make any sense because if something that heavy was falling from at that distance one typically would not be able to move quick enough to escape.

He escaped without even a bruise. God was good to us that day. I believe an Angel moved him out the way. God had just instructed me to enjoy what I had. How could we enjoy our home if our son was dead lame or even hurt? I felt extra blessed. If anything had happened to either child I would have been to blame. My husband was at school and I was supposed to be watching them. I usually did not let them play in the garage or out of my sight. If any tragedy were allowed it would have been beyond difficult for my husband to get over. I believe God spared our son that day, for the keeping of His promise.

Harvest Party

My husband and I decided to celebrate God's goodness by having a Harvest Party to celebrate the blessings that we had received from God, and it was a wonderful party. It was one of the most memorable moments of my life. I dressed the tables in white linen, decadent candles and fall ornaments the chairs were also covered with white linen with satin tie back bows. I also hung an additional chandelier, which balanced the room and bathed us in natural glowing candlelight. The table was set with white plates, silver, and green goblets topped with a colorful autumn linen napkin.

Everything was absolutely beautiful and to top it off I didn't have to cook. I hired a chef to cook and serve the food. The food was outstanding and the service was exceptional. I have never had an adult party before, only parties for my kids. Every thing went as expected and everyone enjoyed themselves. It made me happy to see my friends enjoying their time in our home. It was a momentous occasion and a phenomenal night. Momentous, because it gave us an opportunity to celebrate what God had given to David and Linda. It was phenomenal, because I had never experienced a dinner quite like it. It was a beautiful, elegant, personal, intimate dinner shared with couples closest to us. We were served like kings and queens.

Treat Her Like She's Your Daughter

Five months after our Harvest Party my son's girl friend went into labor to have my first grandbaby. My son informed me that she took the bus to the hospital and just hearing that completely stressed me out. I was very upset on the drive to the hospital just imagining having to take the bus to the hospital to have a baby. When I got there her labor had just really begun to kick in. I was amazed that she was alone and it stressed me out to no end. I was so overwhelmed with emotion I almost could not hold back my tears. At the hospital the Lord instructed me to love her like she was my own daughter, so I stayed. My son, her aunt, her two cousins, my mom and my sister all came to the hospital, but I still could not leave.

She had the worst labor with lots of screaming crying and plain old suffering. Finally, they decided to take the baby and all was well. After I heard about how many stitches she received, I offered for her to stay at my house until she healed. Where she was living had a lot of stairs that would be hard for her to manage. My son also wanted a chance to come home to get his life in order. I let them move in. It was more about her than my son, but he needed a chance to get his head together as well. It was a package deal. We let them move in our home, which was against every traditional religious instruction that I had received. You know the shacking up factor. My inviting her to stay was not about my son and her shacking up, it was about loving and guiding a young woman who desperately needed love and guidance.

I helped her in everyway I could and there was nothing that she needed that I didn't provide. This was a challenge for me because she didn't know how to receive my love. She did not give me big hugs. She expressed her appreciation by hanging around me and talking. She also had a health condition that added another layer of stress that complicated things on an ongoing basis. They stayed in my son's room for about four months and then they moved into the family room for the rest of their stay. Sharing space with two additional adults and a newborn was an exhausting thing. I continued to show love to my son, his girlfriend, and my grandbaby until I was relieved of this responsibility.

It is required of us by God to love. Loving can be very trying. It is not always comfortable, but it is Gods will for us to love one another unconditionally.

If I speak in the tongues of men and of angels, but have not love, I am only a resounding gong or a

clanging cymbal. If I have the gift of prophecy and can fathom all mysteries and all knowledge, and if I have a faith that can move mountains, but have not love, I am nothing. If I give all I possess to the poor and surrender my body to the flames, but have not love, I gain nothing. Love is patient, love is kind. It does not envy, it does not boast, it is not proud. It is not rude, it is not self-seeking, it is not easily angered, it keeps no record of wrongs. Love does not delight in evil but rejoices with the truth. It always protects, always trusts, always hopes, always perseveres. Love never fails. But where there are prophecies, they will cease; where there are tongues, they will be stilled; where there is knowledge, it will pass away. For we know in part and we prophesy in part, but when perfection comes, the imperfect disappears. When I was a child, I talked like a child, I thought like a child, I reasoned like a child. When I became a man, I put childish ways behind me. Now we see but a poor reflection as in a mirror; then we shall see face to face. Now I know in part; then I shall know fully, even as I am fully known. And now these three remain: faith, hope and love. But the greatest of these is love. I Corinthians 13:1-13(NIV)

These are some of the experiences that happened on Applewood Lane. Each taught me some aspect of the fruits of the spirit. All were learned in some element of discomfort and most were dreaded experiences. For the most part I resented these lessons. Each experience revealed the truth of my heart. In most instances I was so devastated because I was walking by sight and not by faith. I also felt that I should be exempt from these troubles because of my relationship with God. However, it was in these troubles that God's character was conceived and developed in me. He never said that I would be exempt from troubles. He said, **Psalm 46:1,"God is our refuge and strength, a very**

present help in trouble."(KJV) From these experiences on Applewood Lane I learned that I could do all things through Christ who strengthens me. **(See Philippians 4:19)**

39. My Truth & My Choices

I met my first love at church when I was fourteen years old. He was seventeen. We thought we had life figured out, as most teenagers do. The church I attended was a very small 'sanctified', legalistic church on the south side of Chicago. One of the elders of the church, who lived in a south suburb of Chicago, invited my 'would be' first love to church one Sunday, hoping to bring him to Christ. He and I were instantly attracted. He wooed me from day one. I wooed him back, and we fell head over heels in love.

I was introduced to Christ at thirteen years old, which is when I learned about sin. I was amazed at the things that were considered a sin. The ironic thing was that, my sister's schoolmates had come by my house one evening to witness to her. However, my sister had tickets to a Stevie Wonder concert and informed them that she was not intending to miss it for anything. End result, my mother and I were witnessed to instead. At thirteen, I was still innocent, but not completely, because we were all born into sin and shaped in iniquity.

> **Behold, I was shapen in iniquity; and in sin did my mother conceive me. Psalm 51:5(KJV)**

They made it very clear to me that I was a sinner and that I needed a savior. This led me to accept Christ into my heart and I received the gift of the Holy Ghost that night. When I received the gift and impartation of the tongues I did not know what it was. My mother and I had never seen or heard anything like it before. It really freaked her out. My dad came home during this experience and explained to my mother that it was a normal part of Christianity.

I was not raised up in the church, but I had a good sense of right and wrong. My neighbor, who lived across the street, would sometimes take me with her to church. It was a Baptist church. I really enjoyed the music, but I had trouble understanding all the hollering and shouting, and sometimes ladies would jump around and cry, and that confused me. I found out later that it was called getting happy. To me, it seemed like they were getting sad, wild, and out of control. Quite frankly, it scared me.

The witnesses used a lot of really big and unfamiliar words like fornication, lust, and idol worship. All of them sounded strange to me, mainly because I had not yet committed these sins. I did not even know what they were. I had lied, cheated, and felt jealousy and envy, but not yet committed some of the sins that they mentioned.

So, by the time I met my first love, I was well aware of what sin was. I knew sex before marriage was a sin, and it was called fornication. However, the more time we spent together the more intimate we became. It became very hard for both of us not to fornicate. To my surprise, he wanted more than just sex. He wanted me to have his baby. At the time, this idea was so romantic. All I could think about was what a pretty baby we would have. It was so weird because before he came into my life I never thought about having a baby. My plan was to be the first person to go to college in my family, become a doctor, and make something of myself.

He continued to persuade me that having a baby was a noble idea because then, my family would allow us to get married. Because I was so young, I would need my parent's permission to get married. Once married, we would no longer be living in sin and we would be together forever. While he was busy convincing me that having a baby was a good idea, I was extremely confused about the messages I was getting at the church. During that time, the message at the church was about Jesus coming back, and that He was coming back soon. I did not consider Jesus coming back to be good news and it saddened me. I had just started to live. I had just fallen in love with this wonderful, handsome, young man who brought so much love and joy to my life. The love I experienced with him was so great, I could not compare it to anything that I had ever experienced in my fourteen-year old life. So, Jesus coming back was a downer, and if He was coming back soon, I had to hurry up and start living my life. So, I agreed to get pregnant and we changed the course of our lives forever. I was determined to get pregnant. We tried several times before we were successful.

Some family members thought his behavior was controlling and dominating. However, other family, friends, and neighbors described his behavior as true love. He did some things that proved both dominating and marked by true love, but of course, the romantic in me focused on the positive. My mother in particular thought his behavior was excessive and it always concerned her. I thought she resented him solely for getting her little girl pregnant. Therefore, I did not give much thought or credit to her concerns regarding his negative behavior.

I was pregnant and we were in love. No one could deny our love. We radiated it. It was a glorious time in both of our lives. Our plan was working and people were finally treating us differently. Once the baby was born, things started to change. He could not find or keep a job. This caused extreme stress on our relationship. My mother and grandmother always had something negative to say, and our plans were falling apart. It also seemed that he was not bonding with his son and was sometimes a bit jealous of the attention our son was getting. I had great expectations of him since having his child was his master plan.

Due to the frustration surrounding his inability to keep a job, I suggested that he sign up for the army. We reworked the plan. He was to join the army. Then we would get married and move on with our lives. Things began to work out according to plan. We persuaded my parents into giving us permission to get married and then, he signed up for the army. As soon as we got married, he left for basic training. We never lived together as a married couple. Before he left for the army, we spent one night together as a married couple. The night he left was the saddest moment of my life. I felt like I would never see him again. We kept in touch by writing. We wrote often and talked as much as we could about our plans for our lives.

With the money he sent monthly, I opened up a savings account for our future. I was so excited about buying things that I thought were necessary for our new beginning. I purchased a brass hope chest and over time, I filled it to the brim with things for our future. I got increasingly excited as time drew near for me to join him. My mother was being as supportive as she could, but she sometimes expressed her sense of foreboding to me. Everyday, I was busy preparing to move and then the calls and the letters stopped. I became really concerned then finally, after a long period of time, he called me. He sounded so far away. He said, “You would never guess where I am. I’m in Germany!!”

“What? Germany? Why are you there?”

“They put me on a plane and I’m in Germany. I don’t have much time to talk so let me give you the address. I have to put in for our housing and then you can come. I miss you so much. I can’t wait to see you. I love you.”

“Okay… I can’t wait to see you too.”

“I gotta go, I love you so much.”

“I love you too.”

“Kiss my boy for me, bye.”

“I will, bye.”

I was excited that I finally heard from him, and that I was going to be with him soon in Germany. I excitedly told my parents the good news. My father said something like, “That’s far away baby.” My mother said, “That is too far away." For the next several weeks my mother made me understand how far away Germany really was. I told them I did not care about how far it was and that I just wanted to be with him. She suggested that, if I decided to go, then I should leave my baby with her. Since my mother didn't have any confidence in my husband to begin with, she would say things like, "What are you gonna do if you get there and you find out he's really crazy? We can't help or rescue you in Germany. It is too far away! You would be on your own. You can go if you want to go, but leave the baby here until you get settled in." In the same breath, she admonished repeatedly that I should not go. This went on for weeks. I was confused, lonely, sad, and now scared. I couldn't decide, then one day my mother decided for me and said, "You can't go, that's just too far!"

In retrospect, if this was my daughter, I can't say in honesty that I would have done anything different. I'm pretty confident that if this was my situation, it would be nearly impossible for me to send my daughter, and my grandbaby off to another country with a young man I had no confidence in. I totally understand that she was protecting me. I was not an adult and my not leaving validated that. Adults leave when they want to leave. I was a teenager in every sense of the word and she was doing everything she knew to guide me into my best. Who could be mad at that?

I had never been on a plane and did not even know how to get to the airport. I needed my mother's help to get to him and she was not willing to assist. My mother had a hard enough time getting okay with the idea of me marrying him and moving to North or South Carolina, or Virginia. Germany was never in the equation. It was a complete surprise to everyone, and it was out of the question. He called again to inform me that it was finally okay for me to come. That is when I told him that I could not come.

He was outdone. He could not comprehend the meaning of the words that were coming out of my mouth. He reminded me that I was his wife and pleaded for me to come. He expressed his constant concern that my mother had too much influence and control over me. He was furious! He told me that he expected me to pack up and leave. He reminded me of the reason he went to the army in the first place. So he expected me to keep my end of the bargain and come. I told him that I needed more time, and he said he was out of time and tired of waiting. He said he was not waiting any more and that I had to come. I was in a really tough spot, and did not know what to do. His tone threw me off and scared me a bit. Then I started to wonder if my mother was right, what if I get there and he mistreats me. Fear gripped my heart and paralyzed me. I couldn't figure out how to purchase a plane ticket or how to get my mother to change her mind. So I stayed. I cried everyday for a year.

Our plans had failed, and I was all alone raising my son without a father. Our plans had backfired. I never envisioned raising my child alone. This scenario never crossed my mind. Nothing was how it was suppose to be. Fate had tricked us. I fell into a deep depression and watched the seasons change from my bedroom window. I did not want to go outside for fear of being seen as a failure, because in my mind, I was a loser. All everyone knew is that I was alone raising my son. I didn't hear from my husband for a while, and the next time I did he sounded totally different. He sounded mean and bitter unlike the person I knew. After a while the calls, letters, and money came to an end.

My husband made very little effort to keep in touch with his son, and each time we talked, we argued. He served me the divorce papers himself at my job, which I thought was cruel to the grave. For the longest time I thought he hated me because I abandoned him, and he thought I hated him for giving up on what we had, and for abandoning our son. We both believed this for twenty-two years. Then October 5, 2005, he reached out to our son. After their initial conversation, he wrote two letters to our son attempting to explain himself. My son shared the letter with me. When I read it I could not believe some of the things he was saying. He was remorseful and said that I was his one true love.

January 1, 2006 my son met his father for the first time, face to face. See (Chapter 22) After their initial meeting, my son's father wrote me several letters. We began to communicate through emails on a regular basis. For nine months he never said anything that overstepped any boundaries, but then in an email, he asked if he could spend some time with me alone when he came back to visit. I responded like a married, Christian lady should and I shut him down. I told him that it wasn't appropriate and he apologized. A month or so later, I received a call from him saying he was coming to Chicago because he had a death in His family. I was excited to hear that he would be in Chicago and I secretly hoped to see him.

After he arrived in Chicago, he went to see his family and spent the majority of his time bonding with our son at my mother's house. Of course, I was happy to hear it, but I still wanted to see him. During a conversation with my son on Thursday night he mentioned that his dad would be leaving Friday, about 2:00 in the afternoon, which happened to be Friday the $13^{th.}$ I could not get it off my mind that he was in my city and I did not get a chance to see him. Every night that week I was occupied with something or another that prevented me from being home.

Friday morning I could not shake the need to speak to him and to no avail, I tried desperately to remember his mother's phone number. I even called directory assistance to get her number. After a while I called my mother's house with the intention of getting his mother's phone number under the guise of wanting to share my condolences. To my surprise he was there. We talked about our son and I shared some things that were troubling me about him and I said, "It would have been nice if we could have gotten together to talk about these things."

"We can. I didn't know that was an option."

"I thought you were leaving at 2:00 today?"

"That can be changed."

"I can't be anywhere until 6:45-7:00"

"I'll wait. Where do you want to meet?"

"Some place public. How about Borders?"

"Okay."

"See ya then."

I could not focus after that conversation. I had a sense of foreboding, but I wanted to see him. Now this is going to sound crazy but the main reason I wanted to see him was because I had a new look. I was sporting a new hair do and I looked like 'the bomb'. Plus, since I knew how he felt about me I thought it would be a good idea to get together to get closure on the matter. I did not feel threatened by meeting with him in any way. I told my husband in a round about way that he might come by, and he did not seem very concerned. I was extraordinarily nervous on my train ride and I purposefully did not tell anybody what I was up to. I knew that if I told anyone that I was going to see my ex-husband alone they would try to talk me out of it because it was a bad idea.

I thought I was strong enough to deal with anything. I just wanted him to see how cute I was with my new look, that's all. Vanity is a terrible thing. I would have been satisfied even if he had come to my house. Vanity is not a Christian attribute. When I got to the location I spotted him in the car and I pulled beside him. He smiled, got out of his car, and got into mine. I parked the car and we began to talk. We talked about our son, which ultimately led to his regrets.

We had not spent any meaningful time talking alone in twenty-three years. He began to share his thoughts and heart with me. He told me things that I never knew, which changed my perspective about our failed marriage. The information he shared surprised and moved me in a way that was completely unexpected. After which, I shared the sentiments of my heart with him. I told him I agreed that fate had cheated us. At that point, my heart was grieving as if someone dear to me had just died. I said, "If ever given the opportunity, I would love you like I intended to love you years ago, but it can't happen at this time, because I am committed to my husband." His emotion was getting the best of him, so I reached out and touched him in an attempt to console him. He touched my hand, and from that point on, I was totally caught up in an emotional state I could not explain.

He took hold of both of my hands and held them as if his very life depended on them. He pulled both my hands closer to him and kissed them repeatedly. It was at that point that I said, "This is adultery. In over 17 years I have never held anybody's hand like this, only David's. I have never cheated on him and I can't do this." He continued to hold on and so did I. I said, "I love my husband, and he does not deserve this." It is unexplainable, but somehow we were able to resurrect the same feelings and emotions that we had over 24 years ago. It was extremely powerful, and had an intoxicating effect on me. The phone rang. It was my cousin. I quickly told her I would call her back. She asked,

"What are you doing?"

"I'm gonna have to call you back." Then I hung up.

That was the first way of escape God provided. In **I Corinthians 10:13** Paul writes **"The temptations in your life are no different from what others experience. And God is faithful. He will not allow the temptation to be more than you can stand. When you are tempted, he will *show you a way out so that you can endure.*"(NLT)**

He recaptured my hands and we just sat there in silence for many moments. I was grieved because of this lost love. He still loved me after all these years and I was faced with resurrected emotions. I had no idea these emotions still existed in me. I did not understand how this was possible because I fully love my husband David. There was no doubt in my mind about that. The phone rang again. I looked down at the display box and this time it was my husband.

This was the second time that God made a way for me to escape. We both stared at the phone until it stopped ringing. My mind was in a whirlwind and I felt totally helpless, confused, and sad. With everything we shared with each other, we both felt cheated, deceived, and foolish because of our behavior all those years. Because of interference, deception and making assumptions we never allowed ourselves the opportunity to have a meaningful conversation until that night, but then it was too late.

I could tell by his body language that he was going to try and kiss me, and when he did I leaned in and kissed him back. I kissed him like I would have kissed him if I were allowed to go to Germany. The foreignness of the kiss registered in my mind, but I continued to kiss him because of who he was and what he represented in my life. He was my first love, the father of my firstborn, and the person I initially planned to spend my entire life with. The kiss was a blend of passion, sorrow, and pain. But, I still continued to kiss him. I held his face in my hands and touched his head and neck and then BOOM!!! I remembered David. The thought of him brought me back to reality. It took all my might to pull back. I had to pull back hard because I was falling rapidly into the emotion and love of the past. I said, "This is wrong, and I can't do this to David. He does not deserve this. He was the one who picked me up and help to fix me after I was broken, and has never done anything to hurt me."

The next few minutes we sat in silence. I broke the silence and said, "This is not who I am. I don't commit adultery. I just don't do this. I am a Christian first, then everything else. I know we were cheated out of our love, but there's nothing we can do about it. I'm with David and I love him." He shushed me and said, "I know, and that hurts. I would never hurt you, or your family. I'm proud of you and everything you have become, and I don't want any harm to come to any one, especially your kids. I am not envious of your husband no matter what you might think. I'm not even worth it. I'm no fool, I don't expect you to drop everything you have worked for and built all these years with him to be with me. My intent is not to uproot your life, I just needed you to know how much I love you, and that I will always love you, and as long as I live I will love you. It is good to know that you share the same feelings and I am not in this by myself."

As for me, all these feelings were new and very awkward. I had to flee for my life, because I was slipping fast. I said I had to go, and he replied, "Okay." He reached up and touched my face, stroked my cheek, and kissed it. I put my head down to avoid another kiss, reached to hug him, and we hugged tightly. He then said, "Let me let you go". He got out of the car, walked around to the driver side, leaned in, and kissed my forehead, nose, and lips and said goodbye. I said goodbye and drove home like a crazy person.

My heart was beating like crazy and breathing was difficult. I felt like an invisible weight had been clamped around my neck. It was terrible! I felt truly awful! I needed to beat David home, because I was supposed to already be there. When I turned onto my street I was pleased to see that he had not made it home yet. I rushed in the house, closed the garage door, and while I was going to get the mail my cell-phone rang. It was my ex-husband. He said, "I was just calling to make sure you were okay. You left so upset." I said, "I'm okay. Gotta go. Don't call me anymore, bye." As soon as I hung up the phone my Husband pulled in the driveway.

David walked into the house and said, "Look at you with your sexy self." And he kissed me. Oh my goodness! David's kiss was so incredible. His mouth was my home and I sunk into him. He responded as he always does to my kisses and we proceeded to make passionate love to each other. Afterwards, when we were talking I sat up in the bed and told him what happened. I told him the entire truth. I actually felt the weight drop off my neck. I confessed because I wanted to expose the truth for what it was. I did not want deception between us. I love David. I could not continue another moment without him knowing the truth. He responded differently than I had ever expected. He said, "Everyone makes mistakes." I apologized, and he replied, "I forgive you."

"Is he gone?"

"Yes."

"Good."

We then got up and went to dinner. While we were at dinner, I was sharing all the details of the experience with him and he asked what made me stop. I replied,

"The thought of you. Not the thought of God being angry with me (because in my mind God would forgive me), but I felt like you did not deserve that. I told him that you had never hurt me, only loved me, that you had never cheated on me, and that I'd never cheated on you and I could not break your heart. I told him the same way I was his first love, I was your first love, and I could not be responsible for hurting you like that."

While I was talking, my husband's face looked so odd. I said,

"You never cheated on me right?"

He shook his head no. Then I saw that he was lying. I asked the question again and said,

"You are lying!" Then he confessed.

"When?" I asked.

"Four and a half years go."

"With whom?"

"A girl at work."

"Have I ever met her?"

"Yes."

"The girl on the Metra train?"

"Yes."

"Oh my God!"

During this dialogue, I was not mad, but surprised. I had no idea this had happened and I would have bet my life and our children's lives on the fact that he never committed adultery. After he confessed, I actually saw the weight fall off his neck. For a moment, he looked truly relieved and then he started to cry and said that he was sorry. I continued to talk.

"Was it good?"

"No."

"Why? What was wrong?"

"It was not what I expected. It was weird."

"Oh!"

"Did she like it?"

"Yeah, I guess."

I reached my hand up to slap him a high five and said, "I'm glad you got that out of your system." He looked at me so bizarre and hesitantly gave me the most pitiful high five. We ordered our food and continued talking.

About five years ago David and I went through a particularly hard time when we moved to Applewood Lane. We went through a 'getting to know you' phase all over again. I had an unrealistic expectation of David to be something he was not ready to be. He resented my expectations of wanting him to be all 'lovey-dovey' now that

I was ready to be that. He felt like he had sat on the sidelines waiting on me for too many years and now that I was ready to give him my full attention and whole heart he did not want it.

At that time, David only made an effort to be with me when he wanted to have sex. I was completely lonely and felt used, but I loved my husband and tried to deal with it. I slept alone most of the time because he spent most of the late hours looking at porn. He picked this habit up while I was off doing what ever it was I was doing with my mother and extended family. I accepted porn as part of who he had become. Initially, I felt safe knowing that he was only looking at images, then after a while, it began to wear on me. I felt like he was having affairs with these images. I felt that if he kept poisoning his mind with these images he would eventually have to act on them plus, the perversion crept into our bedroom.

At first, I did not care because at least he was with me. But I could not keep up and compete with the perversion and the images that had been placed in his mind from Internet porn. After a while, I became progressively uninterested in sex and preferred to be alone. He made me feel inadequate and dirty, and he seemed completely miserable to continue to stay with me. At first, I was hurt to the bone and did not want him to be with me, if he did not want to. I was not trying to force him to stay and I was completely frustrated with my reality. I felt like I was living a lie and suffocating at the same time.

Out of this frustration, and some real sense of concern for him, I opened the door for him and planted a seed by suggesting that he should have sex with somebody else. He could not believe what I was saying and asked, "What are you going to be doing while I'm off doing that?" I said, "Well, let me know when you decide to do it and I'll do it too. I'm sure I can find someone to do it to me." He looked at me even more crazy and said, "You are being used by the devil." I replied, "No more than you."

I felt like it was inevitable anyway. In my mind, I was at a real disadvantage from the beginning of our relationship. I felt cursed because he had no prior experiences. I felt undervalued and unappreciated because he had nothing to compare me to. I did not know anyone who only had one sexual partner for his or her entire life. I on the other hand had the benefit of previous sexual experiences. I knew that David was the bomb. I appreciated him and desired no one else, but him. I desperately wanted him to get this out of his system, and in a crazy way, I felt a bit sorry for him. I was not really worried about him leaving me for another skirt; I was more concerned about having to live in this crazy space any longer. That was a hard place for me to live. I wanted out of that reality. Then he said,

"Wonder if we like it?"

"Then we were not meant to be together any way."

"What about the kids?"

"What about them?"

"This will hurt them."

"This is hurting me. We can't go on like this. I can't stand another moment of feeling like this. I need you to promise me two things. If you do decide to do this let me know, and wear a condom. I want you to get your roll out, but I don't want to die about it."

"We are not doing anything like that. I can't believe you are even saying this! The devil is making a fool out of you! This is not something you give permission for someone to do! That is crazy talk! We are not doing this!" He rebuked me so sharply I got embarrassed and said, "Okay." That was the last conversation we had about that, and because of his response I believed him and never thought he was capable of actually doing such a thing.

So hearing this was a trip, but at the same time I felt a great sense of relief that the inevitable was behind us by many years. Plus, he remained with me and had returned to loving me better than ever. I felt a very small sense of foolishness because of the fact that I told him about my indiscretion the same night that it happened, but he held his secret from me all those years. We talked some more, enjoyed our meal, and went home.

The next morning was odd to say the least. I had so much to do in one day. A real, dear friend was getting married and I was a hostess in her wedding. I had to get up early to get a manicure and pedicure. I also needed to pick up some things for David to wear to the wedding. I called my ex-husband when I got in the car to apologize for the kiss. The last thing I wanted to do was to hurt him any further. I did not want to give him a false sense of hope for something that could not be. I felt terrible about that.

He replied, “You can’t take that from me. That kiss was well over due. You did not give me false hope. That was just enough to hold me for another twenty years. I’m not a fool, and I don’t have any expectation of you to do anything. I’m a patient man. I feel like fate owes me. I’ll see ya at seventy-five.” We talked on the phone till my phone battery died.

After that, I went shopping for my husband. I rushed home, and David and I got ready to go to the wedding. On the way to the wedding, I remembered a dream I had the night before. In my dream, David said that the second time they had sex was different. After I remembered the dream, I asked David how many times he banged that girl. He hesitated, and then replied, “Twice.”

“Why didn’t you just tell me that last night?”

“I didn’t want to add fuel to the fire.”

He continued to say exactly what he said in my dream, “The second time was different because I did it in such a way that she wouldn't like me anymore." I was amazed at the accuracy of the dream.

Once we got to the church, I worked harder at hosting than I ever anticipated, and my feet hurt like they were being feet-capitated. While I was hosting, another hostess and friend said,

"A strange thing has been happening. It seems like I'm dreaming things before they actually occur."

"Me too, I dreamt my husband fooled around with a woman two times. I asked him about it, and he admitted it."

"What? When did this happen?"

"Today."

"What? And you're here?"

"He actually had the affair four and a half years ago, but I found out about it on Friday. He originally told me that it only happened once, but I had a dream last night that he said the second time was different because he did it in such a way that she wouldn't like him anymore."

"How are you doing?"

"Cool, it happened a long time ago.

"Are you sure you're okay?"

"Yeah, I'm good."

"I never would have thought that something like that happened to you. You seem so okay."

"I am really."

"Okay. If anybody's marriage can survive this, yours can. I know that David loves you. He must be really sorry for doing that."

"I think he's relieved too. That was a heavy weight to carry."

We got busy seating people and then it was time for us to take our seats to witness the beautiful ceremony, and that, it was! When they got to the marriage vows, something happened within me that I could not explain. I became overwhelmed with emotion, and I was trying my very best not to ruin my make-up. Some friends who were sitting across from me were laughing hysterically at me because they thought I was just a softy for weddings. They had no idea of the heavy, emotional distress I was experiencing. I managed to pull myself together, and was ready to go home, or somewhere to get my cry out.

A good friend, who was also serving as a hostess, asked me if I could help her decorate the ballroom. I wanted to say no a million times, but she looked desperate and I said okay. I told my husband the plan, and we drove to the reception. Once again, I had no idea of the work that was before me. While working, my dress split all the way down my back to the top of my butt. I was livid. I was having a hard time trying not to display my emotions. The friend I was helping thought I was angry with the bride for the lousy acknowledgment at the rehearsal dinner.

The bride was speaking from her heart, not mine. That was the truth of how she felt and my feelings were hurt. I was bruised, but I still had to do what was right. I still had to set up the ballroom for the wedding reception. So there I was, working like a Hebrew slave, and feeling completely under appreciated, which only infuriated me more due to my circumstances. While I was busy setting up, the full realization of what David had done hit me like a ton of bricks. It started at the church. During the wedding vows I had trouble breathing. Although, I didn't understand what I was feeling, my body was responding to the stress I was under. In retrospect, I understand why it happened at the church. It was the same church where David and I renewed our wedding vows. I became progressively irritated and had a terrible time trying to cover it up.

Once the decorations were complete, I met my husband in the hall and my heart broke into a gazillion pieces. I held back my tears as much as possible and went into a room, next to the ballroom, and cried my eyes out. I don't recall if my good friend was already in the room, or if she came in while I was crying, but she encouraged me. This is the same friend that I shared my situation with at the church. She repeated what she said at the church, and she said, "David loves you and everybody can see that. I know you are hurting and I'm sorry that this has happened to you. She went on and on about what a good husband I had. She said, "I know you're grieving, and that's expected, but know that David really loves you." I kept on saying that I could not believe that this was my life and because of how he loved me, he was in a league of his own. His love had made me forget about the trouble we had all those years ago, and hearing his confession of the truth was disconcerting. My reactions surprised me. It was like somebody pulled the rug out from under me. I don't know what I was feeling on Friday, but I never expected to feel like this on Saturday. Once the reality of what had happened settled, I could not believe how it was affecting me.

She hugged me and I tried to pull myself together. I went back to the reception long enough to locate David. I gestured for him to follow me. I went back into the same room I had just left, and broke down and cried for what seemed to be an eternity. David expressed genuine sorrow and he repented over and over. He also expressed relief that I finally broke down. He did not understand my initial reaction to his confession and it troubled him deeply. From the moment he confessed, he was in hell waiting for the proverbial shoe to drop. He said the anticipation of the inevitable was too much. He also said that he felt extra terrible because he fell and I didn't, and that I confessed and he didn't. The entire episode made him feel small.

He expressed in so many words he would have felt better if I had fallen too because it would have been easier to continue living without the thought of me possibly retaliating. We cried and cried. When I could talk again, I said, “I can’t believe you did that! You actually pressed yourself into another women!” I was annoyed with the fact that it was the thought of him, and only the thought of him, that made me refuse to commit the act of adultery. I loved him enough not to hurt him, but he went all the way. His love for me was not strong enough to keep him from committing adultery. I also did not understand why I ever had to find out about it. He had successfully kept his adultery secret all those years. I did not need to know this information. All it did for me was hurt me. I wanted to forget and for things to go back to the way they were. I wanted a lobotomy! I wanted to forget! I wanted things back to normal! I wanted David back where he belonged in my mind. MINE!!! ONLY MINE!!!!!! I don’t know how much time passed, but I finally took that last crying sigh, and the tears stopped.

My husband walked me to the bathroom so that I could pull myself together, but amazingly, I looked fine when I looked into the mirror. It did not look like I had cried at all. The bathroom attendant made a comment about how pretty I was. She also fixed my dress. I left her a tip and met my husband in the hall. We rejoined the reception and partied until our feet hurt. I had a great time. That was the best wedding reception I’d ever been to. It was off the hook! The DJ kept the party going and everyone was dancing the night away.

After the reception, we walked back to our hotel and talked about how much fun we had. Once we got to the room, I went to get changed for bed and David went on a quest to find a soda vending machine. I found the sexy clothes that my husband had packed and wondered for a minute if I was going to put them on. I decided to go ahead and make the best out of the night. I showered, dressed, and waited for David to return. When David came into the room, his arms were filled to capacity with ice and beverages.

He broke down a bit when he saw that I had put on the sexy outfit. He said that I was the best woman in the world and he loved me so deeply for loving him like that. After he gathered himself together, we started to kiss and he laid me down on the bed. Something happened in my mind when I looked at him over me. All I could think was, he actually pressed himself into that girl. Somebody got my stuff and my vagina closed shop. He recognized that I was messed up and he kissed me so tenderly that I was able to once again relax and continue to love him. The fact that I still loved the way he loved me also got on my nerve. I wanted not to like it anymore. I wanted to think about something else. So I decided to fantasize about my first love, but it was not successful.

Whenever I closed my eyes, all I could see was David, his image has been branded into my mind. I felt extra cheated and I could not wait for it to be over. Afterwards, we fell into complete silence and my heart was a mess. That was our first time making love since I recognized my heart had been broken. The next morning I had 1.25 million questions and he answered them all. He expressed his concern for me hearing the answers, but I thought it was good and necessary for the healing process.

We went to breakfast after leaving the hotel and talked some more. After breakfast, we went to pick up our kids and talked some more. Once, we got home I saw that our dog had ate my bible and my scripture index notebook. This was the icing on the cake. What kind of craziness was this? Who ever heard of a dog eating a bible? Out of all the things our dog could have chewed, why my bible? We were under serious attack from the enemy. That bible was my tool and instrument to locate the scriptures necessary to complete this book. I wanted to scream, but I just walked away. I cried again later that night.

Getting up Monday was especially hard. I felt heavy and different. My vagina was extremely irritated and I did not know why. I was just thanking God that I did not sleep with my ex-husband, because with the way I was feeling I would have sworn that he had given me a venereal disease.

I completely forgot that I had to be at work at 7:30 a.m. for a quarterly, managers meeting. I arrived at work at 9:00 a.m. Once I got there, I called a dear friend and told her what happened to me. She expressed her surprise, shock, and thoughts concerning my marriage's ability to survive this. She also asked me if I thought these events happened to me to complete the book. I replied no. I also had diarrhea all day Monday. How could I put this in the book when I was still living it out? It was too fresh and too painful. The idea of putting this in the book was ludicrous, and according to what I thought, the book was already complete. I had finished the book the week before.

The only thing that I had left to do was to add the addresses of the supporting scriptures to the chapters. I was done. Finally done! Just the thought of the possibility of having to write anymore got on my last nerve. I had been writing for a whole year straight. Writing during the good, the bad, the ugly, the tired, the uninterested, the kids, the school, the work, the unemployment, the midnight hours, the long hours over the weekend, the no TV, and through everything else! The book had taken over my life and I wanted it to be complete. I did not want to write anymore. At that point, all I wanted to do was sleep.

I received an email from my ex-husband that Monday as well. When I saw that he sent me an email my body responded in a way that was completely unnatural to me. I could not figure it out at first, but then I realized that my clitoris was excited. This really bothered me because I did not understand how his email affected me in this way. I am a Christian and my husband just broke my heart. My clitoris was also supposed to be connected with my heart and my heart was broken, but my clitoris was functioning just fine.

I responded to his email. I asked him some specific questions about when our son and I visited him in Washington. I got through the day at work, and when I walked through the door at home I told David that I forgave him. We embraced. Then I told him that he broke my heart and my vagina in the same day. He went to the store to get some Monistat-7. I had the worst yeast infection known to women.

On Tuesday, my ex-husband responded to my email and we talked on the phone. He explained that he waited for us, but was relieved when we did not show up. His reason was that he was not ready to face me, and a bit saddened because he recognized that we realized that he was not worth it. He also said the cab driver was full of it, and the location he asked us to meet him was not dangerous at all. My son's father said he did not come to the hotel because he thought we had left. His story was just that, his version of the story.

I told him about what David did and he responded oddly. It seemed to sadden him and we got off the phone soon after that. He text messaged several heart wrenching messages and each time I heard his voice, received a text, or email from him, my clitoris responded as a clitoris does when it is excited. These feelings conflicted me on every level. The enemy was trying to plant a seed that if my clitoris was responding to my ex-husband from a message, or a call, imagine what it would be like if we ever got together. The enemy was also stressing that my husband had already broken the marriage vows and I would be justified in tasting the forbidden fruit just once. This clitoral activity was down right painful and annoying, especially at work.

When I got home, David and I were talking and laughing, things were going really well. Once the kids went to bed, I asked him about something that was not adding up about the time line. I guess it was about 4 years ago on his birthday when we were invited to dinner at a church member's house. I could not say no, but we made it clear that we would only be able to stay for a little while because we had reservations for dinner at a steak house. While we were there I picked up my phone and saw I had some messages.

I put in my password and heard the oddest message. It was a lady singing happy birthday, 'Marilyn Monroe' style to my husband. I went to the bathroom and listened to it several times trying to determine if I knew the voice. I did not. I went out and got David from the festivities and asked him to follow me. When we were in the bathroom I slammed him against the wall, pressed the phone up to his head, and made him listen to the message. He held his composure. He said, "That's a lady I work with, she's just a friend." I went as crazy as you can go in the bathroom of someone else's house.

He swore up and down that there was nothing going on between them. I had inadvertently picked up his phone instead of mine. We had the same password. Therefore I was able access his voicemail. His birthday is in March. Based on the information he previously provided, the time line was not adding up. The affair started in December and the call came in March. What was up with that? He said they only did it twice and I wanted to know if he was lying about how many times they did it. He replied once again that they only did it the two times and he was just as shocked as I was about getting the message, because they had not gotten back together since the second time and the affair had ended already.

God was good to David that day. God only knows what I would have done if I had gotten that message at home. Ain't no telling what tragedy David would have faced from my wrath. When I heard the message, a rage went through me like fire, and his life was in instant jeopardy. The only reason he was given opportunity to address the question was because we were not home and he was graced with a chance to respond. I don't think he would have been allotted the same benefit if we were at home. I think I would have tapped his juggler with a butcher knife, made grits, or something like that. I was peeved! We still went to dinner and I threatened his very life that night. He never changed one word of his story and we never talked about it again.

So we are back at Tuesday night, and I asked him a question about something relative to the book that I could not remember. I said, "I think it was called this." And he replied, "Don't embellish." Then something went off in me so ugly I said, "I don't embellish and I'm not an adulteress @#!hole either!" He cried another river. He held me for hours and he would not leave me alone. He would not leave the room. When I asked him to leave he just cried and held me. He said he was sorry a billion times. I was awakened at 3:30 a.m. with pain in between my legs and more diarrhea. I was sick as a dog.

Wednesday, I was angry with God and frustrated with my new reality. I felt that God could have made things go differently so as to not allow me to experience such pain. Since He is in control of the entire universe, He could have done anything, but this, and spared me the pain. I could have lived my whole life without experiencing this type of heartbreak. I wanted to know the purpose to my pain. During my commute to work, I prayed for Him to hurry up and help me. I told Him that I really needed Him to show me where the main scripture was that I needed to complete His book.

I thought to call my cousin to help me locate the scripture. The Holy Spirit responded "No." "So, you're talking to me again? I can't call my cousin for help and you are not helping me. This is your book, not mine!" I was trying not to cry, but I was such an emotional wreck. I felt the weight of the world on me. My husband's unemployment, his affair, the clitoris activity, the diarrhea, I hated my job, school, and to top it all off, I had to complete this book. I wanted to go to sleep! I laid my bible on my lap and when I looked down at the bible it was opened to the scripture that I had been looking for, for months and Sundays. I could not hold back the tears any more.

> **And they have defeated him by the blood of the Lamb and by their testimony. And they did not love their lives so much that they were afraid to die. Revelation 12:11(NLT)**

I read the scripture several times because I never understood until that day, that it was related to testifying unto their death.

God began to reveal His word to me He lead me to, **Proverbs 28:13** where it reads, **"He that covereth his sins shall not prosper: but whoso confesseth and forsake them shall have mercy."(KJV)** This scripture explains why it was so important for David to confess. David was unable to prosper because he had not confessed his sin to anyone, and if David could not prosper, then I could not prosper either because we are one flesh. David had an interview schedule with the Sheriff's department the following week, and everything had been working out so well and quick for him. It was important for him to confess his sins before the interview to be qualified for God's best.

From that point on, things began to make sense. David and I suffered three floods. David had numerous car problems and some of them were extremely odd problems. He had experienced unemployment twice in four years, but before that he had been employed for ten years without interruption. Not to mention the squirrels in our attic and the many insect problems. I believe all of these consequences were associated with David's package deal of sin. My good friend who led us to the house we now live in, felt guilty because so many bad things happened there. My mother thought the house was cursed, but all I knew was that God was able to keep us.

I viewed all of the experiences as character builders, and down right annoyances. It seemed as though the devil had open range to attack us, but God being the God that He is, used those situations to develop me. Don't get me wrong; each and every situation caused me to cry, struggle, or question why so many bad things were allowed to happen. God used everything bad that happened for my spiritual development. Because of these experiences I'm better, faster, and stronger than I ever was before. No really, I am humble, grateful, wiser, and patient.

I thought all these events were only tests to see how we were going to behave in the midst of trouble. I had no idea these were actual repercussions to David's sin, but the amazing part is that God used those events to draw me closer to him. **(See Romans 8:28)**

I felt sorry for myself because I did not think it was fair that I had to suffer this pain because of David's sin. However, on the other hand, if he were being blessed I would want to be a part of that. David and I are one. My sin will have a negative effect on him and vice versa.

I wanted to know why it was necessary for him to confess to me? Why didn't he confess to somebody else and spare me the pain of knowing? I understood that it was necessary for David to confess his sins so that we could prosper. But just not to me. The pain was too great and I couldn't bear it.

The Lord reminded me that I initiated the conversation because of my own sin. My sin with my ex-husband set me up to be the recipient of David's confession. God also reminded me that it was I who planted the seed/idea of adultery into David's mind and heart many years ago.

Words kill, words give life; they're either poison or fruit—you choose. Proverbs 18:21(MSG)

Had I managed the situation according to God's word and instructions by praying and trusting in God for restoration, I would be in a very different position now. Instead, I acted out my frustrations and suggested that he step outside of our marriage to get relief. I basically spoke his adultery into existence. What I did was just as wrong as what Sarah did when she took matters into her own hands and suggested that Abraham sleep with her handmaiden to get her a baby. I suggested something completely out side of God's will and stepped right into sin, all to relieve my own frustration, instead of leaning and depending on Jesus and I reaped my harvest.

When you sow to the flesh, you reap to the flesh. No one is exempt from this biblical principle! Not you, not me, not anybody. This is key. Know that once you sow unto the flesh you will get (receive) the harvest from the flesh. You can repent and God will forgive you, but it does not kill or nullify the seed you sowed. You are still due your harvest. Whether to the flesh or to the spirit, the harvest is coming up based on what you planted. Let me give you an example. An unmarried woman can have sex, get pregnant, and really be sorry for her sin. She can repent and never do it again. She may even confess her sin to someone because of the extreme guilt she is feeling. God will forgive her, but His forgiveness does not take the baby away because the seed was planted and she has to receive her harvest from the seed she sowed. It is the same way with everything you do.

Words are very powerful. Learn from my mistake and watch what you say, especially when you are frustrated or angry. When we're frustrated and angry, we do the most damage to ourselves and to those we love. The enemy will hurt, harm, and kill you with your own mouth.

He revealed all of my mistakes one by one. The other part that was driving me extra crazy was the fact that David did not keep to our deal. He was selfish and snuck off and did his dirt. The Lord asked why was I expecting honor in an unholy alliance? Good question! I never really thought about it that way. Adultery is a selfish act altogether. Why would I believe that he would let me know when he was planning to do his dirt? He did not want anyone playing in his playground. He was much too selfish to even consider that. My anger concerning him not using any protection was unrealistic as well. The whole point of him having sex with another woman was to feel and experience the entire thing! Since David was in a selfish state of mind, the idea of using a condom went out the window, because it would have altered his feeling and experience. When people are being selfish and doing selfish, sinful things they do not have anyone's best interest in mind.

He was so caught up that he did not consider that this sin had the potential to destroy his marriage, lose his home and harm his children. It is important to note that he made a choice, not a mistake. A mistake is when you lock your keys in the car. You choose to commit adultery. It is just another choice. What you choose is important because choices impact your future. The simple act of adultery has altered and destroyed many marriages. In committing the act of adultery, no one considers the consequences and repercussions. It can lead to the destruction of their marriage, home, and children. They are not trying to put their loved ones in jeopardy; they are just trying to have a good time according to what the world had dictated to them as a good time. It is the enemy's job to deceive you. Deception is his area of expertise. Remember Eve and me.

On the way to school that night I shared what happened to me with a lady I chat with on the Metra train. After she heard my story she said, "Boy, my life is boring… That's a book or a movie on the lifetime channel!" I told her about the book and she asked if I was going to add this ordeal to the book. I replied no. I went to school as usual that evening, and when I got home I did not have an urge to cry.

Thursday went okay considering my state of mind and current affairs. I got through work without any incidents and I felt a little bit better in my body. On the way home I was talking to a dear friend about what God revealed to me about the situation on Wednesday and my confusing clitoral experiences. She felt strongly that the timing of the incident was not a coincidence and that this experience should be included in the book. We even stood outside in the cold discussing it after we got off the train. She continued to express why she believed this information would be helpful to others. I was annoyed because this friend is the most private of all my friends and she was suggesting that I should tell this awful chapter of my life, all in the spirit of helping others. What? I thought that was ludicrous!

I was dead set against this idea because my pain was too real and too fresh. This experience was unchartered territory and I did not know what was going to happen next. It was like all of my emotions had been separated and then mixed back up in a way that did not make any sense. I could be laughing one minute and then crying the next. I could be okay one minute and then get so angry the next; I felt like I wanted to punch something. I would be regular, and then suddenly fall into heavy sadness. I was a mess. I shared that it was unfair to even suggest that I should do this. No fair!

When I got into my car I heard a song that I've never heard before. The words of the song blew me away. I felt like it was God speaking directly to me through the song, letting me know that I was going to be okay and giving me further instructions. There is no doubt in my mind that there is ministry in music. I have been deeply moved by music before, but not to this extent. This time was different because of the timing and the words. These are the words to the song.

> "After while, after while, this too shall pass, after while.
> Scars will heal, you'll love again. It won't hurt you after
> while. It won't hurt after while. Stuck between, if and
> when you prayed and tried, but still no end. When will it

> end? God's purpose soon, you'll understand. It wont hurt you after while. It wont hurt you after while. After while, after while, this too shall pass, after while. Scars will heal, you'll love again. It won't hurt after while. So when the pain has come to end, and now your heart is whole again, help someone who needs to know, they need to know that it won't hurt them after while. Oh no, it won't them after while. It won't them after while."

As I listened to the words I could not believe my ears. The song was telling me that there was an end to my pain. It even addressed the issue of IF and WHEN. This was surreal because these were my plaguing questions. IF my ex-husband was making my body respond the way it was over the phone, then what would it be like to be in his arms, and WHEN would my marriage be restored? The song told me that I would understand God's purpose soon and that after my pain was over, He wanted me to tell someone who needs to know that it won't hurt them after while.

There are no coincidences in God. I believe with all my heart that God orchestrated the whole thing down to the overwhelming responses I received from my friends and the one Metra commuter. They all believed that my marriage was strong enough to survive and they thought this last experience should be the final chapter of the book. The conversation that I had with my dear friend on the train continued into the parking lot. Once I got into my car and started it, the song was on the radio. As much as I repelled it, all of these events were leading me to do God's will.

When the song ended, I cried a river and called a dear friend. I told her that I thought it was unfair for God to ask me to share this story with the world. I was still in pain! Didn't God see my pain? I just suffered the worst loss of security, comfort and trust. It seemed so unfair for God to ask me to do this while I was still hurting. I felt that He loved others more than me because no one protected me from having this experience, but He wants me to share my story to protect other people, all at my expense. God had done this repetitively in the past. It seemed to me that we had a pattern. Having a terrible experience and then Him leading me to share and guide others through whatever situation they were facing. I did not like this arrangement. Why did I have to be the fall guy?

In addition to that factor, if I conceded to His will I would have to tell the world the whole truth. I could not pretty it up. This is the type of story one would want to pretty up. It was ugly and the whole thing was initiated by my vanity. Who wants to admit to being so superficial? Starting this whole thing over my new look, because I thought I was cute. UHHHH!!!!! I kicked the whole thing off! Why would I want or agree to expose all the dirty deeds that had just happened to me. I was still in pain. No fair!!! Who tells these things? Nobody! So, why in the world would God want me to do this?

At some point during my drive home, I finally conceded, but only because I recognized that I could not win the fight. I did not want to be like Jonah. God is bigger than me and I know that when He tells you to do something, it is really not a request; it is a command. Once I pulled into the garage, it took me a while to get myself together enough to go in the house. My husband looked at me with concern and his own heaviness was apparent to me. He left for school and then God began to talk to me.

The Holy Spirit said, **(Romans 9:20) "Who are you, to talk back to me? Shall you who I created say to ME, Why did you make me like this? Why would you ask me to do this? (Romans 8:18) Your present suffering is not worth comparing with the glory that will be revealed. (Ecclesiastes 12:13) Here is the conclusion of the matter: Fear [revere and worship] me and keep my commandments, for this is the whole reason you were born. (I Corinthians 10:10) Do not grumble, as some of them did and were killed by the destroying angel. (Isaiah**

55:8) My thoughts are not your thoughts, neither are your ways my ways. (St. Luke 11:28) You are blessed if you hear the word of God and obey it. (Psalm 37:23) I order your steps and I delight in your way (Proverbs 31:30) Charm is deceptive, and your beauty is fleeting; but a woman who fears the LORD is to be praised. (Isaiah 43:18-20) But forget all that. It is nothing compared to what I am going to do, I am about to do something new. See, I have already begun! Can't you see it? I will make a pathway through the wilderness, so my chosen people can be refreshed. (Psalm 107:20) I am sending my word, to heal them, and delivered them from their destructions ***Emphasis Added***

God led me to each of these scriptures, one by one directing me to His Will. I wrote them all down and when my husband got home I shared them with him. During this impromptu bible study, something mystical happened. God manifested himself and rearranged our hearts. He took out all the hurt, anger, pain, embarrassment, guilt, shame, heaviness, and bitterness. We both felt a renewed deep, passionate love for each other, but we did not understand it. How could this be? I've never heard of anything like this. It confirmed for me the absolute necessity for Christian couples to pray and read their bibles together. In doing this, God becomes the nucleus and the subatomic glue that holds them together. God restored us! Thursday night we rested in the comfort God provided and in each other's arms.

Friday morning, on the train, I was thinking about how God communicated His word and will to me through each person with whom I shared my situation. In retrospect, I am awed at how all their responses were the same. They all believed that my marriage could survive and they all asked if I thought this should be the final chapter of my book.

I could not understand how they were even able to form this thought. It was weird because, to other people, I must have appeared different than I felt. I felt weak, but God must have made me strong. He made me strong enough to continue to do everything that was required of me. Work, conduct meetings, participate in meetings, talk to people, smile, laugh, take care of my kids, love my husband in spite of the situation, go to night school, do homework, you know, life.

My flesh, on the other hand, was tempted to boil grits with pennies in them, locate my husband's juggler vein and tap it one good time with a butcher knife, cry until there were no more tears, curse while throwing pots and pans, stay home in the bed, or flee to the arms of the forbidden love to satisfy my clitoral curiosity. None of this occurred. But don't forget I was angry, bitter, and experiencing feelings I had never experienced before. Until this experience, I could not relate to this type of pain or the reactions it would provoke. But despite my hurt feelings and broken heart, God kept me. He is a keeper, and He is able to keep your foot from slipping.

> **For the Lord shall be your confidence, firm and strong, and shall keep your foot from being caught [in a trap or some hidden danger]. Proverbs 3:26(AMP)**

To a watching world, my pain did not exist. Not because I was being phony, or wearing a mask, but because I was consciously applying the Word of God. I made an extreme effort not to give the devil any secret praise. All is bearable in God. God's grace is sufficient. He enabled me to bear it and to 'not lose my witness'.

> **I can do all things through Christ which strengtheneth me. Philippians 4:13(KJV)**

> **My grace is all you need. My power works best in weakness. So now I am glad to boast about my weaknesses, so that the power of Christ can work**

through me. That's why I take pleasure in my weaknesses, and in the insults, hardships, persecutions, and troubles that I suffer for Christ. For when I am weak, then I am strong. II Corinthians 12:9-10(NLT)

I do not know any situation quite like mine, but what I do know is that marriages fail daily because of selfishness, betrayal, deception, and adultery. Before this situation, I never understood why people felt like they had to move out of the house and could not stand to look at the person that had hurt them. I understand it now. I felt every painful emotion related to heartbreak, betrayal, deception and adultery. It was a daily choice not to act out the negativity of my emotions. I knew that if I did, the devil would get the victory. Sin is a slippery slope. Once you get on the ride it's hard to get off. There were moments when I wanted to go crazy, but I remembered His word, and it sustained me.

I learned from this experience that it is possible not to act on every thought or emotion. I have said and heard other people say I just couldn't help myself. That is a lie. You can do what you put your mind to. It is an applied discipline to choose right over wrong, and good over evil.

I do not want to paint a false impression as if I did everything perfect after my husband's confession. I did not! I badly failed a few times, but not to the extent my flesh and mind wanted too. I was warring daily against the enemy in my mind, which was taunting me almost every moment.

But don't just listen to God's word. You must do what it says. Otherwise, you are only fooling yourselves. James 1:22(NLT)

I am being transformed daily by the Word of God into His image. Over time, I've picked up on some of His character traits. This experience has shown me how much I've been transformed. I remember a time in my marriage, when every other week, I was talking about divorce. I'm sure my friends remember that time as well. This situation would have been a no-brainer. It would have been goodbye and good riddance.

What David did was wrong, but it did not justify me to do anything. It did not validate me to act out in sin, or vindicate myself in any way. I could have chosen to do so, but I recognized that it would have been to my own demise. I did not want my selfish reaction, or behavior to be the reason, or cause for altering my children's lives.

Christian's actions should be dictated only by the Word of God, and not by outside influences, situations, or people. For me, it boiled down to, "Am I for real, or am I for play in my relationship with God?"

> **Do not be conformed to this world (this age), [fashioned after and adapted to its external, superficial customs], but be transformed (changed) by the [entire] renewal of your mind [by its new ideals and its new attitude], so that you may prove [for yourselves] what is the good and acceptable and perfect will of God, even the thing which is good and acceptable and perfect [in his sight for you]. Romans 12:2(AMP)**

God formed us. The devil deformed us. Christ transformed us. The bible even encourages self-examination

> **Examine yourselves to see whether you are in the faith; test yourselves. Do you not realize that Christ Jesus is in you—unless, of course, you fail the test? II Corinthians 13:5(NIV)**

How you respond to stressful situations displays to you and a watching world, exactly where you are in your relationship with God. It is easy to say what you would do if you were in a situation, but it is a very different thing what you actually do when placed in that situation. It is easy to criticize others for what they have done while you speak with arrogance and pride of how you would have handled the situation differently. Anybody can claim to be a Christian and act like a Christian when everything is going fine, but what are the actions and responses when things get uncomfortable. Forget uncomfortable. What about when they get down right unbearable? Christians need to remember that Christ lives in them. Therefore, they are able to bear any situation that comes along. Christians need to be confident that God will bring them out victoriously.

> **A righteous man may have many troubles, but the LORD delivers him from them all. Psalm 34:19(NIV)**

I vowed, "Till death do us part" when I married David and not "Till you break my heart". The value and sanctity of my marriage vows increased when I became in relationship with Christ. My husband removed himself from that special place in my mind. It was that place that stopped me from falling deeper into my ex-husbands love. What he did affected how I viewed him in everyway. What he did saddened my soul, but he was still my husband, and I still loved him. David and I have been together 17 years of good, bad, beautiful, and ugly. David is my home. I believed, that in time, along with therapy, would eventually make us better. Then God showed up and showed out Thursday night and made us instantly WHOLE.

It was extremely hard for me to accept that God made us whole in an instant. Then the Spirit of God asked, "Why was it so hard to believe that I restored your marriage? Do you believe Satan is stronger than I?"

"No."

"Surely, if he can break you in a day, I can restore you in a day."

Even after that conversation with God, I still did not tell anyone what He had done for us. Now keep in mind that I shared my heartbreak, but I was hard pressed to share God's goodness, and His healing, restorative power because it seemed to good to be true. I didn't want people to think I was trippin'. God instructed me to tell everyone that I shared my situation with that He healed my marriage. So I did.

> **Let the redeemed of the Lord say so, whom He has delivered from the hand of the adversary. Psalm 107:2(AMP)**

This is another reason it was necessary to include this chapter. Mainly because people need to know that God can restore, and make whole in a moments time, even better than they were before.

Friday morning, David said that he was going to send me some pictures of the kids to my cell phone. I received the messages, but I was unable to view the pictures. When I got home that night he asked me if I saw the pictures and I told him I was unable to view them.

He took my phone to see what the problem was. He assumed I did not know what I was doing. He located the pictures and showed me. We took our children to my mother's house that night, and then we went to dinner. While driving to the restaurant David said, "I saw the text messages in your phone." I think my heart skipped a beat. I forgot they were there, and once again, God orchestrated David sending the pictures so that the text messages could be revealed. I initially saved the messages because I could not bring my self to delete them. My intent was to look back at them later, but the funny thing was that after God restored us and made us whole, I forgot they were there. However, God did not, and He wanted them exposed and deleted, and so they were.

At dinner we discussed the miracle God performed in our hearts the night before. We were both amazed at how quick and powerful He moved on our behalf. We enjoyed each other's company to the fullest. Our marriage is better than it was before. During dinner, I had a sharp pain in my side and my husband immediately began to pray for me. After he prayed I felt so blessed. We finished up dinner, and laughed and talked all the way home. When we got home, the passion between us was unexplainable; there are no words to express the extent of the restoration. The kisses alone were phenomenal. I was trying to resist David's advances because of my yeast infection, but to both of our surprise it was gone. He said, "I thought you had a yeast infection." I said, "I did, but not any more." Everything was beyond all right! It was beautifully amazing! God is good!!

One of the benefits of being married, and the purpose of how God created our bodies is to enjoy making love. Making love was first birthed in the mind of God. It is His crafty handy work that created all the intricate parts of the body. The genital areas are essential for their own unique purposes. This is when I thank God for my clitoris. Without it I would not be able to enjoy the sensations and stimuli that are necessary for me to reach sexual fulfillment. Reaching sexual fulfillment with my husband is God's will for me. God made my clitoris to do exactly what it does, and it is good. I used to have a hard time relaxing in my sexuality because the world portrays sex as nasty and dirty. But actually, it is wonderful and beautiful when it is in the context of marriage.

> **You made all the delicate, inner parts of my body and knit me together in my mother's womb. Thank you for making me so wonderfully complex! Your workmanship is marvelous how well I know it. Psalm 139:13-14(NLT)**

Sex in marriage pleases God. **Proverbs 5:18-19** reads **"Let your wife be a fountain of blessing for you. Rejoice in the wife of your youth. She is a loving deer, a**

graceful doe. Let her breasts satisfy you always. May you always be captivated by her love."(NLT)

Friday night, right before I went to bed, the Holy Spirit said, "You have to start the chapter from the beginning." I thought about what that meant. It meant that I would have to write the love story of my very first love. I was concerned about the effect this would have on David, especially because we were just made whole. I did not want to hurt him. It also held a sense of irony for me because when I was about sixteen or seventeen years old, I told my mother that I wanted to write a book about my first love. My mother responded, "Don't nobody want to hear about that...." My dream of writing that story died that day, and I never mentioned it again.

The key person God used, to direct me to the publishing company also wrote and published a book about her first love. This was an amazing thing for me because we both shared the same dream. The only difference was that she lived hers out. I had forgotten about that dream, until the day that I met her. As for my mother, I can only speculate why she responded the way she did to my interest in writing that story. I don't believe she intended to destroy anything in me. I believe she was probably responding to her own life's pressure and frustration.

Saturday morning David and I were talking about writing this chapter when he said, "You know you're going to have to give your audience a point of reference about your relationship with your ex-husband so they can understand how and why things came to this conclusion." I could not believe my ears. God was using my own husband in this special way to prompt me to write my first love story. I replied, "Where should I start?" He said, "From the beginning." WOW!!!

Once I got to the computer to write this chapter and finish the book, the first thing revealed to me was I did not have a title for this chapter. All the other chapter's titles, the

Holy Spirit gave me in advance. The next thing revealed to me was that I was not writing from a position of pain, like I thought I would be, when I agreed to write this chapter. It happened just like the song said it would. {When the pain has come to an end and now your heart is whole again help someone, they need to know that it won't hurt them after while.} God is awesome!! I was blessed to be able to write this chapter from a restored, complete, whole perspective.

Truthfully, I was not satisfied with the way the book ended prior to adding this chapter, but I had not shared that fact with anybody. I had said everything I had to say and God was silent as well. So I thought that it was a done deal. Complete! The only thing I thought was left to do was to insert the supporting scriptures and to send it to editing. However, the scriptures I needed eluded me for the entire week and The Lord was silent. Then this entire chapter happened which enables me to compete the assignment. God gave me the title of the chapter the following Monday night at 3:30 a.m. and I was pleased.

In all **truth,** I cannot deny what I felt in the moments of being in my first love's embrace and the emotional connection I still have for him today. To do so would be a gross violation of the purpose and truth that this book is to represent. To acknowledge the truth of what I feel is one thing, but to act on these feelings would be a very different thing. And if I did **choose** to act on these emotions (feelings), it would be just that, a **choice**. It would be willful sin and in direct conflict with the covenant promise I made to God and David.

Our enemy Satan is deceptive and he knows what to present to you to make you fall from grace. Satan would not present something to you that you would not find tempting or appealing. He knows exactly what cake to bake you. He knows everyone's favorite flavor, including mine. To get me to trip up he reached way back and resurrected a deep emotional connection. This was an incredibly low blow, but our enemy stoops low daily. My grandmother would say that he played his trump card. Some would say he pulled out the big guns. I call it baking my cake.

As a Christian and David's wife, I have to bring these feelings, thoughts, and emotions into the obedience of God's word. It might be a daily fight, but I'm victorious because Christ lives in me. A trap has been set and I see it, you see it and my husband sees it. The enemy is sneaky and sly, but he has been exposed as the lying enemy of my faith.

In a subsequent conversation with my first love/ex husband, he stated that he did not see us getting together as sinful because I was his wife first. For a second he had me twisted because he was speaking from his heart and it sounded so romantic, but it was a lie. God's wisdom responded. I said, "Once you divorced me you forfeited your rights to me. You pushed me into the world and I eventually landed in David's arms. So, therefore, you have no rights to me in any way. I fully belong to David and David only, and if we got together let's call it what it would be, sin. I ain't goin' out like no punk." He did not rebut. God's wisdom corrected him.

As for me I am disciplining my body like an athlete, training it to do what it should. Otherwise, I fear that after preaching to others I myself might be disqualified. ***I Corinthians 9:27NLT***

The conclusion of the whole matter is that my heart belongs to David. Hands down, he does it for me and I feel honored to be in his love. I believe God created David with me in mind and that makes me smile. David is my home, my comfort, my intimacy, and my glow. In him, I'm loved, satisfied, and content. I recognize him as a blessing. In his sweet love I choose to remain. Some might find my saying this a bit mushy or odd, but it is not. It is an excellent thing to know and appreciate what you have. It is a beautiful thing when you are content and satisfied. It is an admirable thing to be honorable. So many people don't even realize what they have. They are much too busy looking around at what other people have. Love, romance, and intimacy do not only happen on special occasions, weddings nights, and anniversaries. It's a daily thing, if you are aware of what you have. The beauty of our marriage is that we recognize what we have. In doing so, makes us special. It liberates us to be free to express our love for one another without limitation, embarrassment, or any concern of being hurt.

I could not have come to any of these truths, choices, or conclusions without God's word living in my heart. Getting the Word of God into your heart to the point of overflow is essential to your ability to correctly respond to the difficulties that you will face in this life. Without God's Word to lead, guide, and direct you, you will lose. You will make bad choices based on emotions, fears and pride, which are typically the tools the enemy uses once you wander into that territory. Don't forget that Satan knows the word too therefore he knows how to manipulate it for his purpose.

The Word of God is a living thing and essential to the Christian walk. **Hebrews 4:12** reads **"For the word of God is quick, and powerful, and sharper than any twoedged sword, piercing even to the dividing asunder of soul and spirit, and of the joints and marrow, and is a discerner of the thoughts and intents of the heart."(KJV)**

> **Every promise of God proves true; he protects everyone who runs to him for help. Proverbs 30:5 (MSG)**

People are failing and falling daily because they are spiritually malnourished. **Hosea 4:6** reads, **"My people are destroyed from lack of knowledge."(KJV)** Whose fault is this? Ignorance is no longer an acceptable excuse. There are too many available resources with the knowledge pertaining to life and godliness to prevent any one from being spiritually emaciated.

By his divine power, God has given us everything we need for living a godly life. We have received all of this by coming to know him, the one who called us to himself by means of his marvelous glory and excellence. And because of his glory and excellence, he has given us great and precious promises. These are the promises that enable you to share his divine nature and escape the world's corruption caused by human desires. II Peter 1:3-4(NLT)

Another reason this chapter was necessary was because people are not utilizing the tools available to build them up in the word of God. The word is the only thing that can transform us into the image of God there by making us His ambassadors.

So we are Christ's ambassadors; God is making his appeal through us. We speak for Christ when we plead, "Come back to God! II Corinthians 5:20(NLT)

Christians are the only representation of Jesus some people will see. So be mindful to represent Him well. **Matthew 5:16** reads, **"In the same way, let your light shine before men, that they may see your good deeds and praise your Father in heaven."(NIV)** The lack of good representation leads to a negative image of Christians, which translates into a negative image of Christ.

Yet another reason this last chapter was essential was because Christians need to know that God can restore your marriages and heal your broken hearts. There is nothing too hard for Him. Since God lives in both David and I, divorce was never an option. God being in me was enough to continue to represent Him as best I could and strong enough to enable me to forgive my husband. I'm positive that if God were not living in me, things would have turned out terribly different. We would have never gotten to the good part. God is key and He is a keeper of your heart and mind. Even though I was angry with God, He still took the most excellent care of me, held me, blessed me, and kept me.

Divorce should not be an option among Christians because there is no situation harder than God's ability to solve. This is written in **Jeremiah 32:17** it reads, "**Ah Lord GOD! behold, thou hast made the heaven and the earth by thy great power and stretched out arm, and there is nothing too hard for thee"(KJV)** He can fix all. The number one reason for divorce is selfishness. When we began to put our personal feelings and priorities above our mates and children we are acting out of our own selfish will. The cause for most people to resort to this level of selfishness, or self-preservation is due to frustration and disappointment in the marriage partner. The enemy loves divorce, he loves to break hearts, and alter peoples live forever. Ain't nothing pretty about divorce. It is awful and it has a long-term residual effect on all parties.

Divorce was not a part of God's original plan. He allowed it because of the hardness of people's hearts Marriage is about a covenant promise made to God between a women and a man. It is not about happiness. It is about a commitment Marriage is not the formula for happiness.

> **Jesus said, "Moses wrote this command only as a concession to your hardhearted ways. In the original creation, God made male and female to be together. Because of this, a man leaves father and mother, and in marriage he becomes one flesh with a woman—no longer two individuals, but forming a new unity. Because God created this organic union of the two sexes, no one should desecrate his art by cutting them apart." Mark 10:5-9(MSG)**

Society places so much pressure on women to get married, buy a house, and have children. Biological clocks are ticking away, and women make many bad choices because of this invisible pressure. Many people believe in the institution of marriage and desire the security of being loved by someone for the rest of their lives. But most people don't fully recognize the ongoing hard work, commitment, and personal sacrifice that marriage entails.

The way society packages marriage and everything else is very deceiving. Our enemy Satan plants seeds of self-centeredness with the deception that it is all about our comfort. It is not. In marriage, there will plenty of uncomfortable moments and situations. It is part of the package. Society validates and confirms divorce. The world accepts walking away if you are uncomfortable. Satan plants these little seeds (lies) throughout our lives that have taken root and grew into a harvest in our hearts. Over time, this process of deception makes it easier to believe these lies as absolute truths. So, we are deceived by Satan's words because he is subtle, manipulative, and out to destroy us. Once we take the time to filter our thoughts and words through the word of God, we recognize they are in direct conflict with God's word. Therefore, they are sin. Marriage is about a covenant promise to love, and to love is a choice.

While Jesus was on earth, He left two commandments, the first was to love God with all your heart, and the second was to love our neighbor, as are selves. The second one sounds unreasonable. How does God expect us to love our neighbor as ourselves? To love our neighbor automatically causes us to be vulnerable and open to potential hurt. So the heart of the matter is TRUST. In order for us to effectively do what God wants us to do, we have to trust Him. He will do exactly what He said He would do. Our job is to obey God and God's job is to take care of us. When we don't do what He says, (disobedience) it is due to rebellion, selfishness, hard-heartedness, and lack of patience. We don't want to wait on God to keep His promises because it seems as though He takes too long and it requires us to be patient and trust. If we really examine our hearts a lot of times we are not certain if God will show up. We believe and accept the enemy's words over God's words.

The enemy is a master at persuading us into thinking that God doesn't know what is best for us. Therefore, we decide to make our own decisions (deceived) without considering God's will for us. In doing any of the above, God's will is being ignored and our enemy deceives us into taking matters into our own hands. This causes us to separate ourselves from God because we have been enticed, then sin manifests itself. At the time of divorce, I don't believe anyone can fully know, or comprehend the impact this will have on their life, because whether or not the person committing the sin knows, SIN BRINGS FORTH DEATH! During the deception, the options available seem appropriate and reasonable. Your heart is not to be trusted in these matters.

> **He who leans on, trusts in, *and is confident of his own mind and heart is* a [self-confident] fool, but he who walks in skillful and godly Wisdom shall be delivered. Proverbs 28:26(AMP)**

God made us free will agents. We either, decide and choose to do what we want or, listen to the direction of God through His Word and the Holy Spirit. God created us that way. Remember Adam and Eve. God told them both not to eat of the fruit of the tree of knowledge. The enemy told Eve something different than what God told her. She listened, pondered, believed, and then finally acted on what the enemy said, and not what God instructed. Eve had a free will just like us. None of us can really blame Eve for the fall of man. We are Eve daily. We as humans, override God's will with our own will. Eve did exactly what we would have done. She decided to listen to something other than God and ate the fruit. She did this because the enemy presented her with options that were not a part of God's will. After giving it some thought, she did not like the one restriction God had placed on her.

The forbidden fruit looked good to eat and it was desirable because it would make her wise. Not being able to eat the forbidden fruit made her unhappy. Eve thought eating the fruit would make her happy. She had two reasons why she should disobey God. She wanted to be happy and she wanted to be wise. She felt justified in her decision to disobey God and ate the fruit. She chose to disobey because of her own desires. Sound familiar? In doing this, she stepped into sin. Soon after, she received her payment for disobedience, which was spiritual death, separation from God, and natural death.

> **But now that you've found you don't have to listen to sin tell you what to do, and have discovered the delight of listening to God telling you, what a surprise! A whole, healed, put-together life right now, with more and more of life on the way! *Work hard for sin your whole life and your pension is death. But God's gift is real life, eternal life, delivered by Jesus, our Master.* Romans 6:22-23(MSG)**

God didn't come down from heaven and slap the fruit out of Eve's hand. He allowed it because he had already given the authority of the earth to Adam and Eve. He could not violate His own law even though He knew she would have to endure much suffering for her choice.

> **And God blessed them, and God said unto them, Be fruitful, and multiply, and replenish the earth, and subdue it: and have <u>dominion</u> over the fish of the sea, and over the fowl of the air, and over every living thing that moveth upon the earth. Genesis 1:28(KJV)**

Eve's first wrong choice was listening to, and conversing with the enemy. Her second wrong choice was putting her will over God's will. Eve did not bank on the extremity of the consequences of her actions. The devil did not disclose the price she would pay for her disobedience. God had already made clear what would happen, but the enemy deceived Eve. She chose to believe the enemy instead of God.

Eve was deceived like we all have been. Satan is the father of all lies, a deceiver. That is what he does. It's funny, because when you are outside of a situation you can see the deception, but when you are in the situation you cannot see that you are being deceived. Deceived people are the last ones to know it. To avoid deception, every situation should be held up and measured against God's word. Eve did not know that her disobedience would cause her to be separated from God, evicted from paradise, and responsible for the fall of humanity. She just wanted to be happy. You cannot rely solely on your heart because it is flesh, and it can be deceived.

> **There is a way, which seems right to a man, but its end is the way of death. Proverbs 14:12(NASB)**

Just like Eve, we all have the ability to control our own actions and make our own choices, but we have no control over the consequences of our actions. Any decision outside of God's will (which is the written word of God) is to our demise. Your enemy is a deceiver. Satan's focus and main job is to kill, steal, and destroy you. Satan is after Christians, and everything associated with them. Satan deceives you, condemns you, places you in bondage, and hinders your prosperity. Sin is birthed in the pursuit of a false sense of happiness that is driven by selfishness.

> **But every man is tempted, when he is drawn away of his own lust, and enticed. Then when lust hath conceived, it bringeth forth sin: and sin, when it is finished, bringeth forth death. James 1:14-15(KJV)**

Once the enemy convinces you to sin, he then uses that sin to condemn you. Satan places a heavy weight of guilt, shame, and fear over the sinner. This causes the sinner to cover up the sin, because Satan knows that hidden or un confessed sin holds the sinner at a stand still. Therefore, the sinner cannot prosper.

> **He that covereth his sins shall not prosper: but whoso confesseth and forsaketh them shall have mercy. Proverbs 28:13(KJV)**

Satan is after you because of who you are. You are a Christian and therefore targeted for irritation, frustration, confusion, and destruction. But the bible says, many are the afflictions of the righteous, but the Lord delivers them from them all. Christian marriages are big, red targets because the enemy knows the importance, and symbolic role they play in the spiritual world. (Christ being the Groom and the Church being the Bride). Satan rejoices when he causes Christian marriages to fail. Satan wants to abolish all covenant relationships because he is jealous of the relationship mankind has with God. Satan wants us to stay in a state of un-forgiveness, but God desires us to forgive one another just as Christ forgives us daily. Forgiveness is just a choice, like everything else. Love is required and it is the most important of all the commandments.

Disobedience births consequences. It is part of Satan's deception for us to believe we are able to bear the consequences of our actions. As you may have already experienced, sometimes the consequences are worse than what was expected. That's where the saying "If I knew then what I know now, I would have ..."comes from. We don't have to live every experience to know something is bad. The word of God was given to us as an example and instruction in righteousness.

All scripture is given by inspiration of God, and is profitable for doctrine, for reproof, for correction, for instruction in righteousness: II Timothy 3:16(KJV)

By his divine power, God has given us everything we need for living a godly life. We have received all of this by coming to know Him, the one who called us to Himself by means of his marvelous glory and excellence. And because of his glory and excellence, He has given us great and precious promises. These are the promises that enable you to share his divine nature and escape the world's corruption caused by human desires.

In view of all this, make every effort to respond to God's promises. Supplement your faith with a generous provision of moral excellence, and moral excellence with knowledge, and knowledge with self-control, and self-control with patient endurance, and patient endurance with godliness, and godliness with brotherly affection, and brotherly affection with love for everyone.

The more you grow like this, the more productive and useful you will be in your knowledge of our Lord Jesus Christ. But those who fail to develop in this way are shortsighted or blind, forgetting that they have been cleansed from their old sins.

So, dear brothers and sisters, work hard to prove that you really are among those God has called and chosen. Do these things, and you will never fall away. Then God will give you a grand entrance into the eternal Kingdom of our Lord and Savior Jesus Christ. II Peter 1:3-11(NLT)

As we learn better, we should do better. It is important to be able to appropriately apply knowledge and wisdom as we gain it.

Divorce hurts everyone involved including our children. It also affects how Christians perceive marriage. Divorce typically has negative affects on the children. I'm not saying that there is never a reason to get a divorce. I am saying that God is able to keep and restore. When we are consumed by our situation, we are not as watchful of what we say and the messages we are sending to our audience (our children). Kids watch what we do, not what we say. We teach our children, by default of our own actions, that once something gets hard, uncomfortable, or makes them unhappy, it is okay to quit, give up, and walk away. How we respond to life's hardships is how we teach our children to have good, strong morals and quality character.

I'm not suggesting that anyone stay in an unhealthy marriage for just the children's sake alone. What I'm hoping for is that maybe some of what I shared will enable the Christian who is contemplating divorce to take a moment and consider the power that is in the God we serve. God is able to do exceeding abundantly above all we can ask or think.

> **Now unto him that is able to do exceeding abundantly above all that we ask or think, according to the power that worketh *in* us. Ephesians 3:20(KJV)**

God's best for everyone is located in His will, which is in the word of God (Bible). Being in our own will is not experiencing God's best for our lives. When we are in our own will, He still loves us and takes care of us, but it is still not what He had in mind for us. There are three wills. God's perfect will, His allowable will, and your will. Know with surety that His will is the best of all three.

40. The Power of the Clitoris, the Booty, and Beauty

Do not underestimate the influence and power of the clitoris, beauty and booty. **I John 2:16** reads, **"For all that is in the world--the lust of the flesh [craving for sensual gratification] and the lust of the eyes [greedy longings of the mind] and the pride of life [assurance in one's own resources or in the stability of earthly things] these do not come from the Father but are from the world [itself]."(AMP)** Many men have fallen into sin because of a beautiful woman. In this day and age, it is more so because of booty, than beauty, but all the same.

> **Lust not after her beauty in your heart, neither let her capture you with her eyelids. For on account of a harlot a man is brought to a piece of bread, and the adulteress stalks and snares [as with a hook] the precious life [of a man]. Proverbs 6:25-26(AMP)**

Many women are responding to the tingling sensations of their clitoris' to their own demise. Your flesh will trick you. The enemy loves to use this trick because it has such a high success rate and no one talks about it. Satan knows how to arouse your flesh to the degree where you feel you don't have a choice, but to yield. That is a lie. You have a choice! You can choose to recognize that Jesus is living inside of you, and that He is stronger than the devil.

> **But you belong to God, my dear children. You have already won a victory over those people, because the Spirit who lives in you is *greater than the spirit who lives in the world* I John 4:4(NLT)**

As Christians we must control our sexual urges and careful not to surrender our bodies to evil. We have to place them under the subjection of God's word. Our inability to keep ourselves holy is really a heart issue. Our hearts are evil and uncommitted to the things of God and we cave into the demands of the desires of our hearts. It is possible to resist these temptations and be victorious.

> **Submit yourselves therefore to God. Resist the devil, and he will flee from you. James 4:7(KJV)**

The first step to victory is submitting your will to God. The second step is to resist the devil. Can you say that you have accomplished **Hebrews 12:4** which reads, **"Ye have not yet resisted unto blood striving against sin."(KJV)** This formula makes the devil flee. Are you able to see the clear direction and instructions in righteousness that God has given you?

Do not trust your heart because your heart is tied to your emotion, your emotion is tied to your flesh, and your flesh responds to its own desires. Your heart and emotion can be deceptive and can lead you to believe that you have to yield to its desires.

> **Every man is tempted when he is drawn away of his own lust and enticed. Then when lust has conceived, it brings forth sin: and sin, when it is finished it brings forth death. James 1:14-15(KJV)**

If you follow the direction of your flesh, recognize that it is a choice not a mistake, and in doing so you will displease God. **Romans 8:8** reads, **"Those controlled by the sinful nature cannot please God."(NIV)**

> **A person without self-control is like a house with its doors and windows knocked out. Proverbs 25:28(MSG)**

And know that the devil is not really interested in you having an excellent sexual experience. The pleasure that you may or may not experience from sinful, sexual encounters is only a by-product of the enemy's ultimate purpose and goal. He desires to destroy you and everything associated with you.

> **Simon, stay on your toes. Satan has tried his best to separate all of you from me, like chaff from wheat. Simon, I've prayed for you in particular that you not give in or give out. When you have come through the time of testing, turn to your companions and give them a fresh start. Luke 22:31-32(MSG)**

Satan is a deceiver, and attempts to deceive women into believing, and ultimately responding, to the tingling clitoris in pursuit of the ultimate sexual experience. Satan is a deceiver, and attempts to deceive men into believing, and ultimately responding, to a women's booty or beauty. Since the enemy's primary purpose is to deceive you, please consider that there is a strong possibility that the actual experience may leave you disappointed, empty, and convicted. The enemy's standard mode of operation is to magnify fantasies and problems. Don't fall for the tricky trap! No matter how desirable, delicious, or delectable it may appear, because what it really is is **DECEPTION**!!!

You can choose to apply and follow the instruction given in **II Corinthians 10:4-5** which states, **"For the weapons of our warfare are not physical [weapons of flesh and blood], but they are mighty before God for the overthrow and destruction of strongholds, [Inasmuch as we] refute arguments and theories and reasoning's and every proud and lofty thing that sets itself up against the [true] knowledge of God; and we lead every thought and purpose away captive into the obedience of Christ (the Messiah, the Anointed One)"(AMP)**

If your clitoris is tingling and you are not married you should not respond to it. You should call that feeling into the subjection of God's word. Sex before marriage is sin and so is masturbation. Both are choices, not mistakes, and a holy God is watching you. You are going to have to account for every evil deed done in your body. **(See II Corinthians 5:10)** If you are married and your clitoris is tingling in response to someone other than your husband, you are not to respond to act on that feeling. You are instructed to call that feeling into subjection of God's Word.

The same rules apply for men as it relates to women's booty and beauty. Practical application of God's word is your only hope. It doesn't matter how mentally strong you think you are, your will is not enough to keep you from falling. If flattery and lust are not strong enough components to get you to fall, other factors will. The only thing that guarantees your success is the applied word of God to your situation. It is a spiritual battle and you can only fight it with the word of God.

Just imagine if everyone responded to every feeling and desire that they felt. It would be a mess! Every limitation God placed on man through His word was done for our own good. He did this to protect us from our natural born, evil selves. Sin is not something you have to be taught; we sin automatically. However, you have to be taught to do what is right. God already knows what is good and bad for us because He made us. Remember God formed us, Satan deformed us, and Christ transforms us. God gave us instructions concerning these things so that we have the ability to make good choices based on His guidance through His word.

If you choose to sin please keep your harvest in mind. Later, when all is finished and done, and you are suffering or being tormented, don't think for one second that you are being attacked by the devil, you are just reaping the corruption you have sowed.

Be not deceived; God is not mocked: for whatsoever a man soweth, that shall he also reap. Galatians 6:7(KJV)

If you sow to the flesh, you will reap to the flesh. You can only receive a harvest of the seeds you've planted. It is the same thing in the natural. You would not look for watermelons if you planted corn. You get what you plant. In addition to reaping a corruptible harvest, you halt the production of your actual desired dreams. God is not going to give you your heart's desires until you stop sinning and begin to delight yourself in Him. Then, and only then, will you be able to get God's best for your life. So in all actuality, you have the power to bless your life or curse it by your own actions.

Today I have given you the choice between life and death, between blessings and curses. Now I call on heaven and earth to witness the choice you make. Oh, that you would choose life, so that you and your descendants might live! Deuteronomy 30:19 (NLT)

Some people try to justify their actions by saying they are not hurting anybody because they are consenting adults. That is a lie from Satan! If you have children they are at risk because they did not consent to the sin, or the consequences that will affect them as a result of your choices.

The LORD is slow to anger, abounding in love and forgiving sin and rebellion. Yet He does not leave the guilty unpunished; He punishes the children for the sin of the fathers to the *third and fourth generation*. Numbers 14:18(NIV)

Your body is the temple of the Holy Ghost and you have been bought with a price; your body is not your own

Do you not know that your body is the temple (the very sanctuary) of the Holy Spirit Who lives within you, whom you have received (as a Gift) from God? You are not your own, I Corinthians 6:19(AMP)

But that's no life for you. You learned Christ! My assumption is that you have paid careful attention to him, been well instructed in the truth precisely as we have it in Jesus. Since, then, we do not have the excuse of ignorance, everything—and I do mean everything—connected with that old way of life has to go. It's rotten through and through. Get rid of it! And then take on an entirely new way of life—a God-fashioned life, a life renewed from the inside and working itself into your conduct as God accurately reproduces his character in you. Ephesians 4:22-23(MSG)

If you have already given your life to Christ and you are in relationship with God, be sincere, feed your spiritual man daily by reading your word, and take a pulse check often to make sure that you are living in a way that pleases God.

And we pray this in order that you may live a life worthy of the Lord and may please him in every way: bearing fruit in every good work, growing in the knowledge of God, Colossians 1:10(NIV)

If you have not surrendered your life to Christ and accepted Him as your personal Lord and Savior, (born again) and you desire to do this, you can pray right now and ask God to come into your heart to receive the new birth. Simply talk to Him as you would talk to another person. You might pray a prayer similar to this:

Sinners Prayer

"God, I come to you in the name of Jesus, I do not know you personally, but I want to know you. I believe that Your Word, the Bible is true. I repent for hardening my heart toward you, and for indulging in things you hate. I don't want to go to hell; I really want to be free of my sin. Dear God, I ask Jesus to come into my heart and cleanse me of the guilt of my sins and give me the power to overcome those sins. I want to be Your child and learn of Your ways. Keep me from evil and save my soul. I am asking to receive Jesus Christ as Savior and Lord so that I can experience God's love and plan for my life. Amen."

If you said this prayer and meant it from your heart, you are now a child of God. Welcome to the body of Christ!!!! Angels are rejoicing over you today.

> **In the same way, I tell you, there is rejoicing in the presence of the angels of God over one sinner who repents. Luke 15:10(NIV)**

The End